What Schools
Can Do

Joseph Featherstone

What Schools Can Do

Liveright New York

FIRST EDITION

Library of Congress Cataloging in Publication Data
Featherstone, Joseph.
    What schools can do.

    1. Education—United States.   2. School environment.
I. Title.
LA217.F42   1976   370'.973   76–23382
ISBN 0 87140 619 5

1 2 3 4 5 6 7 8 9 0

To Rosemary Featherstone

Contents

Acknowledgments

"Open Schools: Tempering a Fad" is adapted from an excerpted version of *Informal Schools in Britain Today: An Introduction*, © Schools Council Publications, 1971, and reproduced by permission of Schools Council Publications, Macmillian Education and Citation Press, a division of Scholastic Magazines Inc.

"The Fourth 'R" is based on material originally published in 1972 in *The Fourth 'R: A Commentary on Youth, Education and the Arts*, reprinted by permission of Associated Councils of the Arts, 1564 Broadway, New York, N.Y. 10036.

"John Dewey Revisited," "A Failure of Political Imagination," "Youth Deferred," "Measuring What Schools Achieve," "Children Out of School," and "Boston Desegregation: Thoughts on a Bicentennial City" are adapted from articles appearing in *The New Republic* and reprinted by permission of *The New Republic*.

"Children and Youth in the Past" is adapted from "Children and Youth in America" and reprinted by permission of the Harvard Educational Review.

"Notes on Practice" adapted from "Notes on Educational Practice," originally published in the *HGSEA Bulletin*, Vol. XIX, Number 3, is reprinted by permission of the Harvard Graduate School of Education.

"Among Schoolteachers" is based on an essay reprinted from "The Review of Education," Volume 2, Number 1, February 1976, and reprinted by permission of the Redgrave Publishing Company, division of Docent Corporation, Pleasantville, N.Y.

"Participation Revisited" is adapted from an introduction to *Schools Where Parents Make a Difference,* and reprinted by permission of Citation Press and the Institute for Responsive Education.

Preface

Inevitably pieces written at different times overlap. I've tried to cut out some repetitions, but most of the essays are substantially as they appeared.

It is again a pleasure to acknowledge many debts to Gilbert Harrison, friend and former editor-in-chief of *The New Republic*. I want to thank my colleagues and students at the Harvard Graduate School of Education. I'm grateful for help on the open school pieces to Marjorie Martus, the Ford Foundation, the Schools Council, and Maurice Kogan. Marty Peretz, Ron Edmonds, and David Riesman gave help and criticism on the Boston desegregation essay. My general thinking these days is especially influenced by my fellow teachers, David Cohen and Sara Lawrence Lightfoot, who may recognize stolen ideas here and there. My usual debt to my wife Helen is compounded in this case, because she is coauthor of the essay "Among Schoolteachers."

What Schools
Can Do

Introduction

The essays collected here have appeared in *The New Republic* and other journals over the past five years. They range over such topics as the pitfalls and opportunities of classroom reform, good models for learning, fads, the nature of practice, John Dewey, children's art, measuring (school) achievement, the social contexts of schooling, the lot of children and the young today and in the past, parent participation, children out of school, schoolteaching as a profession, the pathologies of professionalism, and desegregation in Boston. Whatever else they do and are, schools remain our national mirror and kaleidoscope, and I hope the pieces assembled here can serve as a kind of chronicle of our recent past.

Educational reform stands in a curious but quite real relationship to the political and cultural climate. These essays move from a time of waning political optimism to a period of pessimism. Schools never really stand apart from politics, and in many schools, budget cuts, swelling class sizes, layoffs, and the tensions arising from desegregation make change unpromising, to say the least. Nor are the difficulties made any easier by a climate of educational reaction—prompted in some cases by reform excesses—in which slogans about skills and basics temporarily enjoy more of a hearing than slogans about children's creativity. The pendulum of educational opinion swings back and forth, in part, at least, because the truths about schools and children's learning are in fact very complex, and in part because we are a very faddish culture. Some of these essays try to put our faddishness in perspective, arguing the case for a point of view that I would rather not characterize—slogans being one of our troubles—but which, when pressed, I would term a sober progressivism. Some of these pieces are critical of the simplicities of much neo-Romantic thinking about children and schools. I don't at all, however, want to conceal my continuing belief that we need to build on the psychological and pedagogical work of the best child-centered progressives like Dewey. In education, as in other cultural realms, Americans face a complicated fate. We inherit a good many profoundly Romantic ideas, hopes, and attitudes about children and the schools, and we fight a battle to preserve the deepest insights of romanticism without succumbing to its sentimentality, craziness, and anti-intellectual disregard for standards. Dewey struggled with this; so do we, whether or not we are conscious of the struggle. The best recent work I've seen in our classrooms, like the best work in developmental psychology, is trying to demonstrate in modest and empirical terms that children's minds are active, not passive; there is a core of clinical truth in the old Romantic assertion of human autonomy and the power of the imagination, even though the protests of new and old Romantics against all boundaries and restraints are clearly doomed.

One theme in these essays is the strengths and weaknesses of the second round of the New Education in the past eighty years. In a gloomy time, we are apt to forget how much solid hard work has been done in classrooms; the recent wave of informal, open classroom reform has not always been a success, but it has made more parents and teachers conscious of the importance of the realm of educational practice. I think, too, that a good many people have emerged with a belief that variety in education is a good thing. This was never an idea much honored in our educational past—which is a long, futile search for the one best method of teaching all children. Many of us now are aware that getting decent schools is a very hard day-by-day business, and that no body of educational theory has a monopoly on decency. We've learned as well that there is no single lever to pull.

Educational fads come and go, but certain issues raised by the newest round of the New Education may very well endure. Many thoughtful people have come to question the traditional tendency of schools to treat children as passive objects of education, and teachers as passive conduits of curriculum and policy. It may well be, as I argue in several of these essays, that our growing appreciation of the diversity and variety of childhood depends less on short-term trends in education, and more on long-term shifts in the culture. Families have evolved from units of production to units of leisure, consumption, and childrearing. The bonds between parents and children are now emotional, not economic; these changes underlie the shift in the status of children from marginal, exploited figures to something close to culture heroes; a position not without its own drawbacks. Although we are very far from being a child-centered culture, we are more of one than we were in the past we sentimentalize so shamelessly. Part of our current malaise in education stems from the fact that the recognition of the importance of childhood has not yet moved us collectively any farther than making children spend more and more time in impersonal bureaucratic schools—environments that are often not good for either children or teachers.

All of these essays are attempts to set such matters as the New Education in perspective. They argue that education is a complex affair, and that schools are complex institutions. Directly or indirectly, these essays point out that we need to appreciate this complexity without being overwhelmed by it. Two aspects of schooling are stressed throughout—the micro world of teachers and children in classrooms, and the macro world of social forces, institutions, and politics. The pieces on open schools, art, classroom reform, and schoolteachers discuss pedagogy. Other pieces are clearly in the macro realm. The long essay on Daniel Bell's thinking is an attempt to suggest the general contexts in which we discuss such "postmodern" issues as the quality of schools. "Measuring What Schools Achieve" touches on distinctly macro issues and debates, and "Youth Deferred" attempts to place debates over deschooling and the changing estate of the young in a general social and historical framework. The final piece on desegregation in Boston offers a historical perspective on the serious problems there, and expresses my own frustration at the way politics continues to hem us in. "Participation Revisited" deals with the broad and (to me, at least) unresolved problem of squaring professionalism and mass bureaucracy with democratic tradition, a dilemma by no means confined to schools alone.

Frequently in these essays, I've tried to place these issues within a historical dimension. This reflects my conviction that America suffers from a bad case of amnesia that keeps forcing us to start over again from scratch. This disease affects education and a host of other realms, and accounts for the sense we have that our troubles with cities, poverty, and institutions like schools are unprecedented. In fact, the history of our cities, of education, and of institutional reform in general reveals many familiar features, and we need to see how old and enduring some of our most basic social dilemmas are. The contrast between our egalitarian visions of schooling and the realities of inequality and privilege go back a long way. Struggles between outsiders and elites over the definition of schooling are not new. There are both recurring problems and enduring strengths that we need to know about. "Children and Youth in the Past," "Notes on Practice," the Boston piece, and parts of other essays touch on these ideas.

An essay on John Dewey, part of a work in progress, suggests the outline of my slowly emerging interpretation of Dewey. Other essays bear indirectly on this interpretation, for they too involve challenges that Dewey embodied in a magnificently complicated fashion—making elite educational and cultural traditions serve democratic and egalitarian ends, squaring democracy and participation with science and professionalism, putting science in the service of human values, forging what I call the high Romantic synthesis of emotion and knowledge that underlies some of our best educational theory and practice. Dewey was trying to force a Romantic cultural tradition to make room for scientific standards; and he was trying to make the quest for scientific, intellectual, and cultural standards serve populist and egalitarian ends, instead of elite interests. The commitment to cultural standards and to democracy has never been easy in American life—at times they have clearly been in opposition—and I'm all too conscious of the inadequacy of some of the splices in the pages that follow. Nonetheless, although the tradition embodies a set of hopes, rather than settled achievements, it's the side of the street I want to work on.

My thinking about education now and in the past has been profoundly influenced by Richard Titmuss's notion that the central issue of social policy is what we are willing to do for strangers. In America, the question of the kind of schools people were willing to provide for the stranger's children has been very much complicated by the fact that America's strangers came not only from different social classes but different peoples and races. Schools for the stranger's children have never been adequate. The troubles facing a city like Boston today go back a long way, and they reflect historic dilemmas of all social services in a profoundly unequal society.

In a period of social reform, people made too many promises in the name of schools. Now, in a period of reaction, they expect too little. Schools can change; they can temper the degree in which they participate in the systematic inequalities of American life. They can become decent enviroments for children and teachers. Education should not ever, perhaps, be the main instrument on which we pin our hopes of change. But education is clearly one of many realms in which we are struggling—desperately in some places—to establish intrinsic ends and values to hold up against the mainly economic values that prevail throughout American life.

Over the last decade, we've learned something about the macro issues. More of us understand what should have been obvious all along—that schools are only part of children's lives, and not a major part at that. Now we have to learn some micro lessons as well, one being that the day-to-day quality of children's lives in school—the neglected realm—is important too. We need to understand both the constraints on schools and their possibilities.

One last word about the title of this collection. I thought of calling it "Schools, Strangers, and Romantics," but that seemed willfully obscure. I like the simpler title *What Schools Can Do* but understand that there is something ironic in the phrase. Some of these pieces, after all, are about the things schools can't do. Enough said. The title is not meant as irony, even though it can be taken that way. It reflects an aspiration that many of us still hope for. The old theologians were right to teach us that hope is a necessary virtue, although they forgot to add that living with hope is also painful.

1

Open Schools: Tempering a Fad

American interest in British primary schools is one distinct and powerful stream in the turbulent, movement for something called, variously "open" or informal schools—a movement that includes such diverse figures as John Holt and the head of New York City's teachers' union, Albert Shanker. Certain features of the English reforms are familiar. They have been pointed out by me in *Schools Where Children Learn*, by Charles Silberman in his massive Carnegie study, *Crisis in the Classroom*, by Liza and Casey Murrow in their useful and neglected book, *Children Come First*, and by Lillian Weber's excellent *The English Infant School and Informal Education*. Let me run through the familiar features quickly and then discuss some less familiar points.

Although there are many prophets rising in our land, there is no educational Gospel. What good British practitioners have to offer is the fairly widespread and promising beginnings of an alternative approach to teaching, an approach that for all its drawbacks—and there are many—seems closer than conventional formal methods to what we know about children and the nature of the learning process. The most impressive aspect of the British experience is the way ordinary teachers in different kinds of schools are coming to share a common approach and vision of what they should be aiming at, even though the quality of teaching and children's work may vary greatly. No one, I hope, imagines that it is either possible or desirable to transplant British practices whole to America. Our traditions and institutions are different; good American practice along these lines will spread slowly and in ways unique to American classrooms.

American enthusiasts need to remember that only something like a third of British schools are working along informal lines, that these tend to cluster in a handful of local authorities where informal methods are a reigning orthodoxy, and that the approach has spread farthest in the infant schools. Schools working with older children are doing excellent and significant work in a few places and we have much to learn from them, but too often education in the upper grades of British primary schools resembles the standard dreary fare of the upper grades in our elementary schools. Partly this lag is a chronological matter: reforms started with young children and are working slowly upward. Partly, too, it reflects real difficulties in organizing active learning for older children. In *Experience and Education,* written in the wake of some of the excesses of progressive neo-Romanticism, John Dewey pointed to recurring difficulties with older children: "It is harder to find out the background of the experiences of individuals and harder to find out just how the subject-matters already contained in that experience shall be directed so as to lead out to larger and better-organized fields." Selecting and organizing good, open-minded curriculum problems are challenging the better British junior schools, and there are other problems as well—for instance, the appropriate use of specialist teachers in informal settings.

The slow progress of the junior schools can also be partially accounted for by pressure from tests and an inflexible secondary school system. Those promoting informal education in both England and America should be frank to admit that in neither country is there emerging a body of new work on the secondary level to compare with the emerging vision of what a good primary school should look like. In both countries there are deep and often contradictory criticisms of the secondary schools, but there is no clear sense of a proper direction for reform. (It is curious that the recent "Black Paper" educational debates in England—over whether secondary schools should be comprehensive, and whether "progressive" methods have been watering down the traditional curriculum in secondary schools —have continued to focus public attention on secondary schools; the profound changes taking place in the primary schools continue to be largely ignored.)

American admirers of informal education should also remember that England remains, like America, a caste-ridden capitalist social order. A morbid visitor to England can track down many schools, particularly in slum and immigrant areas, that are failing in exactly the way our slum schools fail. Nonetheless, many British schools working informally are doing a good job teaching poor children; such schools exist, they are possible. Within the sharp limits of an unequal social order, many British primary schools are creating decent environments for a broad range of young children—not the children of the extremely wealthy or the extremely poor, but the children of the lower-middle and working class. That is not the social millenium— schools rarely bring millenia—but it is impressive.

A number of observers have noted that the characteristic innovations in British primary schools were first worked out over the years in a handful of progressive nursery schools run by followers of Montessori, the MacMillans, the Isaacs, and Dewey and Piaget. Thus for some time it has seemed natural for good English teachers to relate teaching practice to basic theories of young children's development. The ideas of developmental psychology have been in the air, matching classroom practice. Yet while a body of intertwined theory and pedagogical practice is appearing, teachers and principals successful in practice are sometimes unable to clearly formulate their aims. The best educational practice far outstrips the best current theory. The lesson of good British schools is not that theory is unimportant, but that it can be of practical use only when it has a living relationship with teachers and children; without an intimate link to the realm of practice, theory grows abstract and sterile, academic in the bad sense of the word.

Emerging slowly from work in good British schools is the initial, tentative outline of what may one day be articulated as a unified approach to children's learning throughout the curriculum. It has been developed by teachers in classrooms, not handed down full blown by curriculum planners and outside experts. The practitioners emphasize different things, but they would probably agree that good teachers start with the lives of children here and now, and proceed from their experiences toward more disciplined inquiry. Teaching is more effective if teachers can find out where learners are by watching them in action and talking with them; learning is more effective if it grows out of the interests of the learner. (And of course interests are not just there, like flowers waiting to bud: they are formed and cultivated by good teaching.) Experience and theory suggest that active learning is better than passive. Giving children choices within a planned environment helps them develop initiative, competence, and an ability to think for themselves. A good curriculum offers children knowledge worth acquiring. It is essential that children learn reading skills, for example, but they must also see the point of being literate, taking an interest in books and knowing how to use them. Teaching practice ought to reflect the enormous diversities among children, treating them as individuals, and proceeding, when possible, from their strengths, rather than from their weaknesses. For this reason and not for any intrinsic merits in openness or informality, teachers ought to be able, as much as possible, to set informal schedules, physical arrangements, and patterns of grouping and instruction. No technique of teaching or organizational change is as important as the normal social and emotional context of learning, for the ordinary relationships among children and between adults and children are of supreme importance. Much learning in a good educational setting receives direction and takes shape in the course of ordinary conversation.

The aim of the enterprise is to influence students to become thinking, autonomous, sensitive people. Good teachers work with a mental picture of the qualities of a good thinker: confidence, concentration, and an ability to make informed, rather than haphazard guesses and estimates; mental habits of synthesizing ideas and making analogies; the capacity to communicate thoughts and feelings in various ways.

Put in such terms all this is familiar, perhaps too familiar. This is still the theory preached in many of our schools of education. To American practitioners it must seem a counsel of perfection and therefore of despair. Administrators and teachers often understand these principles, but seldom feel able to put them into practice. A host of what are seen as necessary evils—tests, tracks, discipline, the imperatives of administration—overwhelms the schools.

The question is the extent to which the evils are necessary. As a practical matter, the framework in which these principles are slowly being turned into practice is curriculum reform. The hypothesis is that in the right sort of setting ordinary teachers and children can do without many of the formal structures of schools. But the hypothesis will stand or fall by whether teachers and children have important, useful things to do with their freedom. This is why the most significant part of the British reforms may be the working out of a new conception of the school curriculum. The pamphlet series "Informal Schools in Britain Today" consists of practitioners' accounts of work in areas such as art, music, mathematics, and children's writing. Such detailed description is vital for understanding. Here I can only draw together a few important points.

In music, for example, we have scattered hints of young children's ability to understand and work with basic musical structures. In movement, math, and writing, common threads in good practice are becoming more distinct. Whatever the subject, there is an emphasis on active learning and engagement with materials. Teaching starts with children's experiences and moves them toward more disciplined effort. There is a stress on expressiveness and a variety of ways of communicating different sorts of knowledge, including the kind of knowledge of the inner and outer worlds we associate with art. Work in one area spills over into other areas.

Too many accounts—including my own—have not sufficiently stressed the aims and objectives of informal teaching. If we are concerned with creating a school atmosphere in which children can flourish, then we are talking about all parts of school life—a whole approach to children and their learning. This means considering everything from subjects and patterns of administration and discipline to school lunches, playgrounds, and the use of space: the whole intellectual and human environment. This need for a whole approach is one reason experienced informal practitioners are often suspicious of piecemeal descriptions of good practice. They worry about the natural human tendency to seize upon a bit of apparatus or a technique developed in one classroom and apply it to a new situation without any consideration of the ends it was supposed to serve. Being as concrete as possible is helpful, for concreteness makes descriptions vivid, without turning them into a formula.

In thinking about the school as a whole physical environment, Americans may want to look at developments in British school architecture, where the design of new buildings reflects how informal practitioners actually use space, not the way architects hope space will be used in the future. Generally those in America who decide on school plans are architects, administrators, and school-board officials —never practicing teachers. In recent years many American school boards have been building "open plan" schools without dividing walls, often designed by architects who are trying to force traditional teachers' hands and dictate informality and freedom. This is an obvious reversal of sound practice. Open school designs ought to serve practitioners, not dictate to them. (Similarly, organizational patterns such as "team teaching" ought to evolve out of working relationships among congenial practitioners in a school, not be imposed on them by outside authority.) Architectural openness is not at all the same thing as informal teaching. Witness what happens in most of our new open-plan buildings, where teachers and children huddle together in the great, cavernous structures, trying to build imaginary walls around themselves, and where teaching methods remain as formal as ever. American champions of open-plan architecture should also note that there are disagreements among English teachers and principals on the desirability of the newer, more radically open-plan buildings. Some practitioners insist on the merits of individual classrooms or at least defined home spaces for the younger children, and they argue for what might be called "openable" plan buildings: flexible space with plenty of opportunities to build in privacy, as well as for cooperation.

It is in such practical areas as curriculum and the use of space that the possibilities of extending informal approaches are being worked out. Yet there is no reason to think that a trend that is good is all the better if taken to its logical conclusion. A sympathetic British critic of the reforms, Mr. Richard Palmer, rightly warns: "This fallacy of the logical conclusion bedevils a good deal of progressive educational thinking, as teachers, being human, seize on a currently fashionable practice and decide to go one better, often against their teaching judgment."

Good informal practitioners might reply to Mr. Palmer and other

critics that they do not consider their classrooms "unstructured"—
insisting that good environments are "structured" in space and in
many other ways, if not always in time. But his point is well taken.
He is right in thinking that slow, careful progress is better than the
exhausting and often pointless pendulum swing to radical educational
reform, then back to angry reaction.

We could all proceed more wisely if we had better notions of how
to evaluate learning in informal settings, but we don't. Many British
practitioners are now at a point where they feel they should be
developing better ways of keeping track of children. Again, Mr.
Palmer makes a sensible observation:

> Where measurable outcomes only are assessed, it often seems to turn
> out that schools using modern methods of organization in the teaching
> of reading or mathematics do no better than schools working on more
> traditional lines. Such findings leave us a little less confident that we
> know all the answers. Could it be, however, that some of these findings
> have in principle a single explanation, namely, that in the progressive
> schools in these samples, the unstructuring has been pushed beyond a
> point where keeping track is possible?

A common complaint of Americans confronted with the example
of the British reforms is the absence of measurable objectives. Our
critics can perform a useful service if they nudge British practitioners
out of what often seems a complacent romanticism. On the other
hand, if the British lack rigor, we lack many examples of good practice; far too many of our school systems have emphasized conventional measurement and ignored children's learning: forgetting the
principle that children and teachers do not get any heavier for being
weighed.

On measurable achievement in conventional tests, children in
formal British schools do slightly better than children in informal
schools, though uniformly the differences are very slight. This is not
surprising: formal schools teach children to take tests. The surprising
thing to me is that the test results are so similar. Charles Silberman's
Crisis in the Classroom summarizes several decades of research on
informal as opposed to formal schools, drawing on studies of American "progressive" schools in the past, as well as contemporary British
schools. All the studies make similar conclusions: there is generally

no important difference between formal and informal schooling in terms of mastery of conventional subjects. "Progressive" students show up better than formally taught students in those characteristics that "progressive" schools value: initiative, critical thinking, ability to express oneself in writing, capacity to pursue a task on one's own, and so on. This research is a morass, but from it we know that there is no evidence that reducing the amount of formal control over students impairs conventional academic skills. On the other hand, it is plainly impossible to make inflated claims for informal teaching in terms of conventional test scores.

We do need new kinds of diagnostic tests in many areas, but tests are a side issue. We need different values, too. In evaluating a reading program, we certainly want to test children's skills, but we also have to push past that narrow kind of measurement to broader questions: Do the children like reading? Do they pursue particular interests in books? Can they read for a purpose? Has the reading program strengthened their mastery of language and built on it, or has it weakened it? And, most important, is reading part of a whole environment that encourages children to become thinking, sensitive, autonomous people?

One important set of preconditions for the English reforms that American observers have neglected is the particular institutional ethos in British primary schools, a subtle blend of independence for principals and teachers, along with a great deal of active support and the encouragement of a healthy professionalism. This blend of independence and support should interest the growing number of Americans concerned with reforming the pathological professionalism of our educators. Some have suggested that this institutional ethos is a reflection of English national character and tradition and therefore not for export, and this is partly true. No one is suggesting that British administrative patterns can be stamped on American school systems. But since the ways they administer education contribute to healthy environments for teachers and children, we should understand them. The argument that these practices are not simply an emanation from the English landscape is strengthened somewhat by the fact that there remain in England many rigidly administered schools, facing the same problems as ours. And, as Maurice Kogan has pointed out, other social services in England tend to be administered in an authoritarian, top-down fashion, quite unlike the practice in good schools. Thus even within the English context, there is something extraordinary about the good primary schools.

In a world increasingly organized into large bureaucracies, an entire nation's primary school system is attempting with some success to give teachers and principals a mixture of support and autonomy. Within a generation, a decent and humane atmosphere has begun to prevail in a powerful cohort of primary schools. These schools set the pace, so that a majority of primary schools are touched by the mood, even if they don't completely share it. These developments run counter to the way schools are organized in most countries. In most, a school is an outpost of a public administration system; it is not thought of primarily as an environment for children and teachers. Controls are external, the assumption being that the normal pattern of learning is something close to rote. Procedures are laid down from the top. The opposite assumption is that teachers working with children ought to be the prime agents making decisions, and that the proper locus of such decisions is the classroom; that procedures should flow out of relationships between teachers and children.

The traditional autonomy of British principals was important in bringing about some of these changes, but by itself was not sufficient: British principals enjoyed freedom for many years, and for many years schools remained the same. There had to be support, and a sense of professional movement. A class of people emerged whose exact role is hard to describe: "advisers" is perhaps the best general term. They are experienced teachers and specialists, agents for spreading change: people skilled at helping without bossing. Variants of the advisory role are being tried out now in America, but we are apt to forget that the British advisories spring from a professional context. In America simply appointing advisers—and we do not yet have many good teachers experienced at informal work—may mean adding another layer of nonteaching bureaucracy on the administrative coral reef. Indeed the most important "advisory" figure in most good English schools is the principal—whose title, significantly, is "head teacher."

It would be easy to idealize the role of an English principal, and easy to forget that autonomy granted to incompetents and petty tyrants can be a mixed blessing. But the sense of what a principal's job ought to be comes through clearly from conversations with good

English heads. They see themselves first and foremost as supporters and catalysts for the continued growth of their teaching staff. Many teach classes; those who can't spend much of their day working in classrooms with teachers and children. They were chosen, among other things, for their ability to provide good examples of ways of working with children, for their talent in leading a teaching staff, not administering a plant.

There is a general misapprehension in America that all kids and teachers need is for administrators to get off their backs. That is certainly a first step, but it will not necessarily promote the kind of careful growth over time that ordinary teachers are capable of when they can get support. I'm not saying the help always has to come from a principal—I'm not much of an admirer of "great man" theories of institutional reform—and clearly it can come from other teachers or advisers. But it has been an immense gain for English teachers that the role of the principal has evolved in the directions I've described. The relative absence of this kind of leadership by principals in our schools is one important reason why, although you see a growing number of informal American classrooms, you rarely encounter an entire American school environment working successfully in an informal fashion. Of course you find able American principals. But our systems do nothing to encourage them, as good principals are the first to say. The priorities of our system are on administration, at the expense of teachers, children, and parents.

American readers must wonder what British parents make of all these reforms. There is no doubt that British schools feel rather smugly insulated from parental pressures or public opinion. No doubt, too, this has had a bearing on their readiness to work out new approaches. My impression is that freedom for principals and teachers within the walls of a school is more important than insulation from parents altogether, which of course is neither desirable nor possible in America.

Parents in both countries frequently approve of informal approaches if they understand them, and if they have confidence in the people implementing them. That assertion may have a naïve ring to some embattled American administrators; it is nonetheless true. I'm aware of the excesses of the Right, of the anger and suspicion between professionals and parents in our ghettos. But in every case I know of where sound education is going on in America, including the best of the community-controlled schools, it is recognized that all parties to the educational process—children, parents, professionals, and the general community—have rights and obligations. Where the pendulum has swung too far in one direction; where professionals are hiding behind administrative structures to keep parents out, as in so many of our big-city systems; the balance has to be restored. Where parents seek to dictate teaching practices, even in the name of "open education," another balance has to be evened.

As ideological battle lines sharpen we may forget the obvious point once made to me by a principal in a ghetto school: "If you aren't serving parents in a way that makes sense to them, you'd better close down." This holds for England as well as America. Some critics in England are beginning to argue that the remoteness of the schools from parents is bad, particularly in schools dealing with poor and immigrant children. Participation may be an issue of the seventies for England, as well as America.

This discussion of parents has, I hope, indicated some of the distance between ourselves and the English, suggesting the need for very different paths to the creation of good schools. America is not England (we keep forgetting how big and various this country is, how different the educational climate from place to place). In some areas, our professionals are encouraged to act. In others, they need to forge alliances with parents and other community groups in order to move in any direction at all. In still others, parents and outside institutions —new forms of teachers' colleges, for example—are attempting to link up with willing teachers, bypassing sluggish school bureaucracies. In still others—the most tragically desperate situations—parent and community groups confront immovable school systems all alone. Tactics will vary, and the English example will be of no direct help.

It should, however, be an indirect reminder that our schools characteristically emphasize administration at the expense of teaching. Physically, our schools are too big, and need to be broken down into humanly manageable units. Institutionally, their priorities are badly twisted. Why are there separate training programs for school administrators in our education schools? Why is it an exception, rather than the rule, for people who have distinguished themselves as teachers to enter the administrative ranks? This separation of administration from practice is, like the separation of theory from practice, sterile.

For many reasons, some of them buried deep in our history, there are too many people in our overadministered school systems not directly involved with principals, teachers, and children. American teachers thus have the worst of two worlds: they are constantly being harassed by the administration and they are lonely in their work. A good school—be it in a suburb or a community-controlled ghetto district—would give them a mixture of autonomy and support so they might grow as professionals.

Amid the grinding factionalism and rising cries for vengeance, this may seem a remote and utopian ideal. But it is worth keeping in long-run perspective, as desperation prompts us to consider more extreme alternatives. Demolishing our great, useless administrative superstructure is a necessary first step toward reconstructing our schools; but demolition itself will do nothing to promote a common vision of good teaching. It has to be accompanied by what I am sure will be misunderstood if I call it a humane bureaucracy; people to help. Otherwise it is unlikely that a renewed professionalism, truly serving clients, can ever come forth. I'm in deep sympathy with attempts to decentralize schools and other institutions, to restore varieties of control and participation where participation can mean something—particularly at the level of individual schools. At the same time, whatever our short-run tactics, the long-term issue is clear: in many areas of our national life the issue is not whether to have administration, bureaucracies and professionals, but whether it is possible to create bureaucracies and professions that are humane and democratically responsible to clients.

Schools are always part of a much wider scene. We have emerged from a period when professionalization of a certain kind grew apace, with little consideration of ends to be served. Our vast and complicated educational apparatus, with its machinery for credentialing teachers and administrators, is, as Charles Silberman puts it, mindless in its workings. Education is, however, only an extreme instance of a social order that characteristically drifts from accident to accident. The debate on the purposes of education that Silberman and others have opened up is part of a broader discussion of the ends and purposes of professionalism and the social order itself—a debate made all the more bitter and unpromising by the confrontations of black, minority, and poor groups with professionals. Attempts to remake the schools to serve the public are paralleled by attempts to reorder other unresponsive institutions: university and corporate reform, the growth of public service law, and, in the field of medicine, developments such as community health care, a new focus on social and environmental issues, and the demand for new priorities in dispensing services. Where these new demands will take us, nobody knows. A continuing problem will be squaring legitimate new demands with legitimate older values: academic freedom and the pursuit of disinterested scholarship in the universities, traditional professional autonomy in medicine and professional and union rights in education. In the process, traditions worth preserving will be threatened, at the same time that indefensible vested interests will be unmasked.

For those fighting the battles for the schools, it will be helpful to keep in mind that one of the several failures of that ambiguous movement known as progressive education was that it became, in the end, so exclusively a professional affair. From today's perspective, one of the most striking features of the public school wing of the movement was its coincidence with the extension of the bureaucratic and professional structures that now make our schools intolerably unresponsive. The rhetoric was for individual growth; the main concern, in too many places, was management and administration. One lesson from the recent past is that no American educational reform movement can survive without vigorous lay support; it is vital both politically and intellectually.

We've learned about British reforms in a time of cultural and political ferment, and our interest in these reforms must be seen as one element in a complex and many-sided cultural movement. Within our own schools, there is nearly a pedagogical vacuum. Few reformers have come forward with practical alternatives; even fewer have deigned to address themselves to working teachers. The grass-roots nature of the English reforms has a great appeal for people who are victims of the general staff mentality of our school reformers and managers. Blacks and other minorities are interested in new approaches simply because they reject all the workings of the schools as they stand; some of the best of the community-control ventures, such as the East Harlem Block Schools, have promoted informal methods, as did some of the parent-controlled Headstart programs in the past. And numbers of middle- and upper-middle-class parents favor "open" and "informal," not to mention "free," schooling, even though they are vague on the pedagogical implications of these terms.

The most cogent chapters in Charles Silberman's *Crisis in the Classroom* are a plea for American educators to consider the English example. Silberman's book is interesting as a cultural document, as well as a statement in its own right, for it registers an important shift in opinion. Silberman is arguing that too many American schools are grim and joyless for both children and teachers. What was once said by a handful of radical critics is now very close to being official wisdom. Silberman, it should be added, distinguishes himself from many critics of the schools in that he is deeply sympathetic to ordinary classroom teachers and has a clear sense of the crucial importance of the teacher's role in creating a decent setting for learning.

By now I've visited a fair number of American classrooms working along informal lines. The best are as good as anything I've seen in England; the worst are a shambles. In the efforts that look most promising, people are proceeding slowly, understanding that preparing the way for further improvements and long-term growth is more important than any single "innovation." (As I've noted, there are too few entire school environments run along informal lines.)

Understanding the need for slow growth and hard work with teachers and children, many of the informal American practitioners I've talked to are alarmed at the dimensions of the current fad for "open" schools. There are reasons for skepticism. From today's perspective, which is no doubt morbid and too disheartened, it seems that our successive waves of educational reform have been, at best, intellectual and ideological justifications for institutions whose actual workings never changed all that much. At the worst, the suspicion is that past reform movements, whatever their rhetoric, have only reinforced the role schools play in promoting social inequality. The realization that schools alone cannot save the social order—which should have been obvious all along—has prompted some to despair over ever getting decent education.

Added to these sobering reflections is a fresh sense of dismay over the outcomes of the past ten years of "innovation." For we have finished a decade of busy reform with little to show for it. Classrooms are the same. Teachers conduct monologues or more or less forced class discussions; too much learning is still rote; textbooks, timetables, clocks set the pace; discipline is an obsession. The curriculum reform efforts of the sixties brought forth excellent materials in some cases —materials still essential for good informal classrooms—but they took the existing environment of the schools for granted. Perhaps because so many were outsiders, the reformers failed to engage teachers in continuous thought and creation, with the result that the teachers ended up teaching the new materials in the old ways. Being for the most part university people, specialists, the reformers were ignorant of classrooms and children: of pedagogy. They concentrated on content—organized in the form of the standard graduate school disciplines—and ignored the nature of children and their ways of learning. The reformers lacked a coherent vision of the school environment as a whole. It was characteristic of the movement that it ignored the arts and children's expressiveness.

In the philosophical chaos of the curriculum projects, the proponents of precision had a debater's advantage. They were able to state their goals in precise, measurable, often behavioral terms. For a time this false precision encouraged a false sense of security. And for a while the behaviorists and the education technology businessmen were allies: they imagined that a new era of educational hardware was dawning, promising profits commensurate with those in the advanced defense and aerospace industries. Now that the bubble has burst, it seems evident to more and more people that this curious alliance had all along been talking about training, not education. Training means imparting skills. It is an aspect of education, but not all of it. I suggest a reading example: if I teach you phonic skills, that is a kind of training. Unless you go on to use them, to develop interests in books, you are not educated. This ought to be the common sense of the matter, but it isn't. Our technicians conceive of reading as a training problem on the order of training spotters to recognize airplane silhouettes. If a sixth grader in a ghetto school is reading two years below grade level, as so many are, the problem may not be reading skills at all. A fourth-grade reading level often represents a grasp of the necessary skills: part of the problem is surely that the sixth grader isn't reading books and isn't interested.

Another reason some practitioners are dubious about "open" education reflects a further skepticism about the evangelical American mode of reform, with its hunger for absolutes and its weakness for rhetoric. Our "progressive" education movement often neglected pedagogy and the realities of life in classrooms and instead concentrated on lofty abstractions. It will be essential in promoting good practice today to abandon many old ideological debates. Yet the English example is now part of a whole diverse American cultural mood, which means that it is already ranged on one side of an ideological debate. The American milieu is polarized culturally and politically; this polarization conditions American responses to accounts of informal teaching. The responses tend to fall into the stereotyped categories of a cultural cold war raging between the hip, emancipated upper middle class and the straight, middle and working classes. It is a class and cultural conflict, and it takes the form of battles between those who see life as essentially a matter of scarcity —and defend the virtues of a scarce order, such as thrift, discipline, hard work—and those who see life as essentially abundant—and preach newer virtues, such as openness, feelings, spontaneity. The latter group likes the idea of open classrooms because they seem to give children freedom; straight people fear the supposed absence of order, discipline, and adult authority.

If I portray this conflict in highly abstract terms, it is because it seems to me remote from the concerns of good American and British practitioners actually teaching in informal settings. Take the issue of freedom, for example. Letting children talk and move about is helpful in establishing a setting in which a teacher can find out about students; it helps children learn actively, to get the habit of framing purposes independently, using their own judgment. But this freedom is a means to an end, not a goal in itself. As a goal, freedom is empty and meaningless—"a breakfast food," as e. e. cummings once put it.

There are always those who argue that freedom is something negative—freedom from—and those who argue that freedom is positive. From authoritarians like Plato to libertarians like Kant and Dewey, the second line of argument has linked freedom with knowledge— the free use of reason or intelligence and, sometimes, action with knowledge. Whatever the merits of the positions in this fascinating perpetual debate, it is surely more appropriate for educators of the young to conceive of freedom in the second sense, not a momentary thing at all, but the result of a process of discipline and learning. Informality is pointless unless it leads to intellectual stimulation. Many children in our "free" schools are not happy, and one suspects that part of the reason is that they are bored with their own lack of intellectual progress. As William Hull remarks in a trenchant critique of the current fad for "open" eduction: "Children are not going to be happy for very long in schools in which they realize they are not accomplishing very much."

Or take the issue of authority. That it *is* an issue is a mark of deep cultural confusion, as well as a reflection of the frequent misuse of legitimate authority in America. Whatever their politics, good practitioners assume as a matter of course that teachers have a responsibility to create an environment hospitable to learning, that there is what might be called a natural, legitimate basis for the authority of an adult working with children. In his superb little book *The Lives of Children*, George Dennison outlines some aspects of this legitimate authority:

> Its attributes are obvious: adults are larger, more experienced, possess more words, have entered into prior agreements with themselves. When all this takes on a positive instead of a merely negative character, the children see the adults as protectors and as sources of certitude, approval, novelty, skills. In the fact that adults have entered into prior agreements, children intuit a seriousness and a web of relations in the life that surrounds them. If it is a bit mysterious, it is also impressive and somewhat attractive; they see it quite correctly as the way of the world, and they are not indifferent to its benefits and demands. . . . [For a child] the adult is his ally, his model—and his obstacle [for there are natural conflicts, too, and they must be given their due].

Disciplinary matters and the rest of the structure of authority in American schools work against the exercise of legitimate authority. And thus, in reaction to the schools, the education opposition movement foolishly assumes that all adult guidance is an invasion of children's freedom. Actually, in a proper informal setting, as John Dewey pointed out, adults ought to become more important: "Basing education upon personal experience may mean more multiplied and more intimate contacts between the mature and the immature than ever existed in the traditional schools, and consequently more rather than less guidance."

If you remove adult authority from a given group of children, you are not necessarily freeing them. Instead, as David Riesman and his colleagues noted in *The Lonely Crowd*'s critique of "progressive" education, you are often sentencing them to the tyranny of their peers. And unacknowledged adult authority has a way of creeping back in subtle and manipulative ways that can be more arbitrary than its formal exercise.

Another fake issue in the debate on open education is the distinction between education as something developed from within and education as something formed from without, the old, boring question of whether to have, as they say, a child-centered or an adult-directed classroom. There are, to be sure, certain respects in which the best informal practice is childcentered. The basic conception of learning, after all, reflects the image of Piaget's child-inventor, fashioning an orderly model of the universe from his varied encounters with experience. The child's experience *is* the starting point of all good informal teaching. But passive teaching has no place in a good informal setting, any more than passive children do. Active teaching is essential, and one of the appeals of this approach to experienced teachers is that it transforms the teacher's role. From enacting somebody else's text or curriculum, the teacher moves toward working out his or her own responses to children's learning. The teacher is responsible for creating the learning environment.

Still another confusion on the American scene lies in the notion that liberalizing the repressive atmosphere of our schools—which is worth doing for its own sake—will automatically promote intellectual development. It won't. We need more humane schools, but we also need a steady concern for intellectual progress and workmanship. Without this, it is unlikely that we will get any sort of cumulative development, and we will never establish practical standards by which to judge good and bad work.

Some American practitioners question the utility of slogans such as the "open school," or "informal education." The terms are suspect because they become clichés, because they don't convey the necessary values underlying this kind of teaching, because they suggest a hucksterized package, and because they divide teaching staffs into the "we" doing the open approach and the "they" who are not. Some imitate the philosopher Charles Saunders Pierce, who changed his "pragmatism" to the much uglier-sounding "pragmaticism"—in order, he said, to keep his ideas safe from kidnapers. They prefer an awkward and reasonably neutral term like "less formal." A brave few are modestly willing to march under a banner inscribed "decent schools."

This suspicion of slogans can be carried to ludicrous extremes. But at the heart of the evasiveness is an important point: Educating children or working with teachers is an entire process. A good informal setting should not be thought of as a "model" or as an "experiment," but as an environment in which to support educational growth in directions that have already proved sound.

Some observers fear the manner in which our schools implement reforms in a way that destroys the possibility for further development of teachers. (There are already instances where principals have dictated "open education" to their staffs.) There is a deep—and I think altogether justified—mistrust of the conventional channels of reform from the top down: pronunciamentos by educational statesmen, the roll of ceremonial drums, the swishing sound of entrepreneurs shaking the money tree. Most of the serious American informal practitioners are self-consciously local in their orientation. They are interested in planting themselves in Vermont, Philadelphia, North Carolina, New York City, North Dakota, or wherever, and working at the grass roots. They imagine that it will take a very long time to get good schools, and they do not believe that big-wig oratory or White House conferences on education are any substitute for direct engagement with teachers and children in classrooms.

The changes they are starting are small but they have large implications. All teachers, no matter how they teach, suffer from the climate of our schools, and every serious attempt at reform will soon find itself talking about lunchrooms, toilet passes, the whole internal control structure of the schools, relationships to parents, relationships to supervisory staff, the ways in which supplies are ordered, the links between an individual school and the central bureaucracies; ultimately issues of politics, power, and money.

As schools move in informal directions, there will be an increasing criticism of our system of training and credentialing teachers and administrators. The training of administrators will come under attack, and in some places separate training programs for administrators will be abolished. The inadequacy of teacher training will also become more evident, although it is far from clear how to improve it. What we do know is that theory has to be reunited with practice. Without a solid grounding in child development, much of our informal teaching will be gimmickry; and without a sound base in actual practice in classrooms, theory will remain useless.

The enormous variety of the American educational landscape makes it difficult to speak in general terms. In certain areas, education schools willing to restore an emphasis on classroom practice may unite with school systems ready to move in informal directions. In other areas, where the education schools are unable to change their mandarin ways, school systems will have to assume more and more of the responsibility for training and credentialing teachers. Whichever the pattern, a central feature of successful programs will be periods of work in good informal settings. Thus a prerequisite to any scheme of training will be the existence of good schools and classrooms to work in. The single most important task is the reform of schools and classrooms, for good informal classrooms provide the best teacher training sites.

Whether the current interest in informal teaching leads to cumulative change will depend on many things. Two are worth repeating: whether enough people can understand the essentially different outlook on children's intellectual development that good informal work must be based on, and whether our schools can be reorganized to give teachers sustained on-the-job support. I'm somewhat optimistic about the first: the ideas are in the air, and many teachers, on their own, are already questioning the assumptions behind the traditional classroom. The second question will be much harder to answer satisfactorily. In some places, the schools are ripe for change; in others change will come slowly and painfully, if at all; and in others the chances for growth are almost zero. Those promoting informal teaching ought to be wary of suggesting good practices to teachers working in institutional settings where real professional growth is out of the question. In such a setting, all obstacles mesh together to form what people rightly call the System. Right now it seems unlikely that the System in our worst school systems will ever permit teachers to teach and children to learn. But things may have looked that way to some British educational authorities in the thirties, too.

A final word on the faddishness of our educational concerns. The appearance of new ideas such as the clamor for open, informal schools does not cancel out old ideas. "Open education" will be a sham unless those supporting it also address themselves to recurring fundamental problems, such as the basic inequality and racism of our society. The most pressing American educational dilemma is not the lack of informality in classrooms: it is whether we can build a more equal multiracial society. Issues like school integration and community control have not disappeared, to be replaced by issues like open education. The agenda simply gets more crowded. It will be all the more essential, however, to keep alive in bad times a vision of the kind of education that—in a famous phrase—all wise parents want for their children.

2

The Fourth R

Schools ought to be everybody's business. So should issues like war and peace, or the state of the environment. Yet in practice we all wind up cultivating our own gardens. That artists, businessmen, and figures in official cultural institutions met in St. Louis at an ACA (Associated Council of the Arts) conference to talk about the arts with people from the schools represented an exploration of possible connections, rather than any sort of full commitment to school reform. It wasn't clear in everybody's mind that improving schools should be a central priority of groups promoting the arts. It wasn't clear that schools—as distinct from museums, parks, storefronts, or streets—are necessarily the best places to introduce young people to the arts. And it was far from clear, in the end, what outsiders can contribute to reforming the lot of teachers and children in classrooms.

Nonetheless, everybody had left their gardens for a while. The ACA St. Louis conference reflected a growing awareness that there is a crisis in our schools, and that a part of the crisis concerns the place of art, of feelings and values in children's lives. The conference was an attempt to mesh the world of cultural affairs—not only museums, symphonies, and art galleries, but the quality of public life in all its aspects—with the very different world of schools. What various people brought away from these meetings, I can't say. The following reflections are presented as an attempt to draw out of it some particular ideas that may shed light on the schools, the arts, and what the rest of us might perceive as the right sort of education for our children.

The conference itself is a symptom of the general wave of interest in education reaching many different kinds of communities all over the country. This interest is reflected in traditional forms of school politics: PTA meetings, elections, hassles within school boards, disputes over school bond issues, fights over community control. There are other manifestations, however. One of the interesting points in Charles Silberman's *Crisis in the Classroom* is the observation that all professions are currently redefining their obligations; and that in many instances the new, emerging definitions are somehow bound up with education, taking the word in its broadest sense. Consumerism and new doctrines of corporate responsibility and accountability are percolating upward into business circles. Journalists, who have always been educators, although not always responsible ones, are coming to be more serious about their obligations to educate. Lawyers have often been told, usually in graduating ceremonies, that the law is the school of citizenship; that its great lesson is the way that means shape ends, substance never being separable from procedure. This has remained a somewhat dusty ideal, remote from daily practice. Yet the growth of public service law has linked practice with this lofty preaching. Lawyers concerned with extending legal services to the poor, for example, discover that it is not enough simply to offer services to their new clients in the same old ways that served the interests of corporate clients so admirably. Lawyers for the poor find themselves questioning the goals of legal service, and they often wind up pushing for institutional change within the profession to achieve new goals. In this new role, a lawyer is apt to discover that much of his job is educating the profession, as well as the public. In medicine, community health care, preventive medicine, and social and environmental health issues are urgent new concerns. Many doctors are beginning to see their role as educative and, in a sense, political: helping people understand what steps they have to take to save their health and their environment. Even very staid public services are touched by these changes: a new crop of social workers, for example, is likely to be interested in working with the poor to understand and change the conditions of their poverty, instead of merely helping them adjust to their lot.

Along with this broad insistence that we must all in some sense re-educate ourselves is a growing conviction that many of the settled institutions of American life—professions, unions, universities, hierarchies and bureaucracies of all sorts—have ceased to be responsive to the needs of the people they are supposed to serve. Thoughtful medical men, for example, are aware that their profession is becoming more accountable to the public for its priorities: the problem, which is real, is to reconcile such new demands with older traditions of professional autonomy. Similarly, to take an even more complex and troubling instance, universities are being forced to pay attention to the needs of students and problems of the social order. Greater participation is inevitable, and universities—particularly those in urban settings—will have to serve their surrounding communities in new ways. Again, these demands have to be squared with traditions of scholarship, disinterested research, and professional autonomy. But they are being made.

Schools are only the first and most conspicuous area of American life in which all these general forces—the push for an enlarged conception of education, for a new professionalism, and for more participation and accountability—have emerged. It is, of course, no secret that a vast, various, disgruntled constituency is massing today to make the educational profession more responsive to its clients. As in other realms, valuable traditions, often worth cherishing, are threatened at the same time that indefensible vested interests are being unmasked.

And, to add another layer of complexity to these matters, something of a cultural revolution is under way transforming many people's expectations of the schools. Middle-class parents are beginning to voice dissatisfactions with the schools that sound much like those articulated by the embattled urban minorities. For apart from fundamental social inequalities and institutional racism—central features of the educational system—the things wrong with the education of poor children are also wrong with the education of the children of the affluent. All children (and all teachers, too) suffer from the cold-ness and impersonality of our schools, from their rigid groupings, their compulsive scheduling, and their emphasis on rote learning. No child benefits from schools whose main lesson is that life is to be lived passively, fenced in by massive constraints on self-expression and self-fulfillment. All children need to learn actively, with their minds, hearts, bodies, and senses.

Thus critics of the schools are sounding a relatively new note, at least for our time. Parents are demanding that the schools teach the basic subjects better, of course; but they are also insisting that they be more humane and open, too. There is a revival of interest in formulating what might be called a philosophy of education. Most of us have lived through a period when discussions of the aims of education were peculiarly boring and pointless; they always sounded as though they took place in pockets of what scientists call dead air. Yet now the questions raised in debates on the schools are giving life to what once seemed tedious and scholastic issues: What kind of men and women should our children become? What should they know? How should they live? What can they hope for?

These have never been easy questions, and we are far from answers to them. For one thing, the words we use are encrusted with old and obsolete moral, religious, and philosophical traditions. And for an-other, the present cultural climate makes it hard for us to discuss them sensibly. Think of the way, for example, that educational issues tend to be couched in terms of conflict between generations, as though the rightness of one's views were simply a matter of the timing of one's birth. An eloquent spokesman for this cultural trans-formation at the ACA conference was Harold Taylor, who presented what might be called the brief for the Party of Hope. He stressed the generosity and vision of young people today:

> When the students protest against the lack of relevance in the cur-riculum in which they are imprisoned, they are saying a great many things, only one of which is that the studies they are forced to carry out are unrelated to the problems of their own lives and their own society. What they're also saying is that there is no spiritual, intellectual, or esthetic nourishment in the teaching and learning, whether it be in the arts or the sciences. They are therefore turning to their own culture and its resources for the enjoyment of art

forms and modes of experience which are simply unavailable inside
the education system. As a result, the schools and colleges have lost
touch with their own students, and have fallen behind the culture,
while the new youth culture, with its own style, its own pace, and
its own heroes, is thriving, inside and outside the academy. . . .
[Students] form a generation whose medium of art is the film, the
tape, the multi-media, the skies, the mountains, and an entire world
in which everything is art and art can be anything. . . . What must
be done is, in fact, very simple. It is simply to transform the
schools and colleges into centers for life. To make them into places
where the imagination can run free and children and older ones can
enjoy the art of learning together. The path toward that transformation is the path the young have already taken, through their experimental colleges, their underground newspapers, their communes,
their films, their songs, their dancing, their theatre, their demonstrations, their graffiti, and their revolt against the culture.

This was said with Mr. Taylor's characteristic *élan,* and it probably
still needs saying.

Somewhat more descriptively and a little less enthusiastically, another speaker at St. Louis, Robert Lifton, outlined the emergence of
what he called the "Protean" style of psychological behavior in the
culture. With the collapse of traditional symbols and forms, the
development of the mass media, and the creation of ultimately de-
structive weapons, Lifton sees an accompanying new social character,
"Protean Man," whom he named for Proteus, the mythical figure
who could assume any shape. "Protean Man" is characterized by
continuous exploration, experimentation, and fluctuating identities,
beliefs, and cultural pursuits. He has a deep sense of absurdity, and
cultivates a spirit of mockery. He is profoundly ambivalent toward the
technology and science that create his affluence and at the same time
threaten the existence of his world. He distrusts systems of ideas, as
well as the culture he has inherited.

This seems a reasonably accurate portrait of a contemporary state
of mind. It is reflected in our arts, with their spirit of the absurd, the
prevalence of the put-on, the restless search for new forms, the sense
of permanent and perpetual flux, the mixed modes and media. And
it is plain that this is the mood of masses of people, not just colonies
of artists, Bohemians, and hippies. Anyone concerned about the
culture, and certainly anyone interested in schools and universities,

ought to try to understand the degree to which we—no less than our children—share this Protean style, simply by virtue of our involvement with the times.

The question is, however, whether Taylor and Lifton—and they are far from alone—are right to applaud the new sensibility without reservation. Lifton says that, at its best, the Protean character is "in the service of the creation, rather than the destruction, of form, even though it must move in flux and in constantly shifting fashion." I agree, but what about at its worst? If some aspects of the Protean culture enhance life, others do not. If we praise some, there are plainly others we must condemn—nihilism, a shallow lack of historical consciousness, a penchant for violence, and a readiness to be exploited as mass commercialized vulgarity.

This lack of critical thinking has some bearing on any discussion of the arts and education. So many critics today are celebrating cultural phenomena that seem mixed blessings, at best. They are taking ambiguous trends in the culture, pointing to healthy directions they may or may not take, and then insisting that what is new is healthy, which doesn't follow. An interesting question is why such intelligent, concerned men should accept the contemporary scene as a source of new values without much criticism, without a conscious attempt to sort out the creative from the sterile. Part of the reason, I imagine, is that they, like the rest of us, are speaking within a highly polarized cultural setting, in which taking sides on one issue is seen as taking sides on a host of others as well. After the killings at Kent State and Jackson State, after listening to the vindictive voices of the nation's leadership, it seemed necessary to side with the beleaguered young. The truth is that our society is nearly as culturally polarized as it is politically divided, and the results have not been good for politics or for art. Certainly they have been bad for thought and criticism. The art world is often a swirl of contending, equally smelly orthodoxies, the cult of the hip and the new vying with gloomy cultural bigotry and reactionary Old Guardism. And so, like politics, art gets reduced to a series of polemical gestures. Similarly, the visions of a new education presented to us as alternatives to the existing tedium of the schools are often little more than polemical gestures relying for justification on the continued existence of a discredited establishment. They, too, count on an atmosphere heavy with contending dogmatisms. And they, too, with the exception of a few profoundly humane works like Herbert Kohl's *36 Children,* or George Dennison's *The Lives of Children,* have been almost entirely negative.

The American cult of a book like A.S. Neill's *Summerhill* is a case in point. It is, in the strict sense of the word, a reactionary book, a statement of rebellion against a vanished Victorian sexual and cultural world. Neill is a grand, even an heroic figure, but he freely admits he has no interest whatsoever in developing children's talents or their minds. Many visitors to Summerhill, including myself, have felt that the children there are bored stiff. If one is to judge Summerhill, however, it has to be on Neill's own terms: for him, the main thing is living together. Summerhill's merit must be assessed in terms of its value as a children's commune, rather than a school. (A commune, it should be added, where a benevolent Scotch patriarch lays down the rules and kicks you out for smoking.) I hope my point here won't be mistaken. I'm not attacking Summerhill, which is, after all, a courageous experiment in a world where simply living together does seem an accomplishment. I'm only noting the minimal and negative character of this vision of schooling that so many American readers have embraced. It seems to me that a school where there is almost no art, music, literature, crafts, or science, where no importance is attached to good teaching and where adults are thought to have little to give to the children—that such a school is not ideal. It asks too little from the children, and from life. And yet to many in this country Summerhill is an idyll.

Such is the intellectual climate in which we discuss reforming the schools. This polarized political and cultural milieu conditions our responses to what we hear. I've been talking to groups of people over the last few years about open, informal classrooms. Inevitably, audiences range themselves on opposite sides of what immediately turns into an issue: hip people like the idea because it seems to involve giving kids freedom, whereas straight people deplore the supposed absence of discipline and structure. Often the debate turns into another episode in this society's curious, depressing cold war between the emancipated upper-middle class and the middle and lower-middle classes. As a debate, I must say I find it wholly unreal. American and British teachers who are successfully teaching informally are not concerned about Freedom versus Order. Their concerns run on less ideological tracks. They tend to be worried about how to reach a boy who isn't getting anything out of school, how to scrounge for materials (there is never enough *stuff* in a good informal classroom), how to keep the momentum of an activity going, how to talk to a very shy child, how to find time to work with a child who needs lots of help in reading, how to set challenges that insecure children can meet in order to gain confidence in themselves. To me, such concerns suggest the real, legitimate authority of a teacher as an adult responsible for developing a nurturing environment for children and their talents. Freeing children is part of the point; encouraging them to make significant choices is certainly desirable, because the choices often reflect their needs, and in any case that is how children learn to develop initiative and think for themselves. But by itself freedom is an empty and cold educational ideal, which tells us nothing about the human encounters involved in learning and teaching. As an ideal it bears the mark of the vacuum from which it emerges.

So one difficulty in finding our way out of the mazes we are in is a climate of thought that encourages abstractions. There can be no question that we must find our way out. The fact that debates on schools are heavily ideological and abstract does not mean that the critics of the schools are wrong. A largely negative, reactionary criticism is by no means automatically invalid, and because the litany of complaint grows monotonous and shrill is no reason for us to deny that it is generally right. Our schools are, by and large, dispiriting, repressive places for children and for teachers. They do ignore the connection between feeling and thinking; they are bad environments for people. And one of the several ways in which they are bad environments is surely their systematic neglect of the arts.

A strong-minded minority at the ACA Youth, Education, and the Arts conference plainly thought that sentiments like those in the preceding sentence were irrelevant. A number of them were people with long experience in the schools. Their conviction was that art, cultural change, the quality of school environments, and all the rest were beside the point: to them the main thing was that schools aren't teaching children the fundamentals—like reading and math—necessary for survival in this society. Why discuss frills and fringes, the argument ran, when the basic fabric is so tattered?

Like so many questions about the schools, this one throws us back
to purposes and human nature: philosophy. One reason to talk about
the arts in the schools is that everything we know about human
nature—and in particular the nature of children—points to the centrality of expressiveness. The arts are the language of human experience. John Blackie, an Englishman who has taken a hand in the
reform of his country's primary schools, points out that, although
there are always some children who seem to have trouble learning to
read, few young children have any difficulty learning to paint. (The
power of the children's art in any good school for the "handicapped"
is food for thought.) Adults are a different story, of course; many
confess they can't express themselves with color and form, just as
many have been trained by the schools to believe that they have no
head for mathematics. And Blackie notes that there are grounds for
thinking that the arts are more important than the three R's as
conventionally conceived; after all, people have done without the
three R's throughout most of the existence of the human race, but
never at any point have they done without art.

The case for the importance of the arts in schools is usually boxed
into conventional school categories: subjects, timetables, the curriculum, and so on. This is difficult to avoid: few people at the ACA
conference were able to get around this mode of speaking and thinking. Yet the concern of a school ought to be not subjects, not specific
aspects of the curriculum, art or whatever, but the lives of the children. This assumption runs counter to the assumptions of most of our
schools, even most of the schools that had good things to display at
the conference meetings. What children mostly learn about art in our
schools is that it is a frill; sometimes art instruction is heavily influenced by the academy, the model in teachers' minds being all too
often art history, a subject that is easily perverted. But while there
are many aspects of art education to criticize, the main problem with
art in schools is the problem of the entire curriculum—the whole
approach to children and their learning.

In short, adding art courses, even good ones, onto what exists is not
going to change much. It is, indeed, impossible to talk sensibly about
the art curriculum for very long without also discussing aspects of the
school environment that are seldom even touched on in educational
discussions. A simple example will demonstrate this: if we were really

serious about developing esthetic values in our children, we would demand decent school lunches. Beyond simple nutrition—and we must remember, as citizens of this opulent social order, that there are hungry American children—we would care about the quality of the meals and the atmosphere in which children eat. A concern for food is one good index of the extent to which a school is a nurturing environment. Schools that take no interest in whether their children have eaten breakfast, for instance, are not caring for their basic welfare. But food is also an index of whether a school is a civilized place. Just to hear that statement will make experienced teachers smile; they know that the food is wretched in our schools, that it might, for all the decorum that reigns, be served in troughs. Lunchrooms are chaotic places where frightened children get more upset, or else they are rigidly policed settings where human speech is unwelcome. Most of the trouble in racially mixed schools breaks out in the cafeterias. Most teachers dread cafeteria duty, with good reason. What is needed, as Harold Taylor might say, is very simple; good food, a pleasant setting, and an atmosphere in which meals become social occasions. Every sensible parent knows this. Why don't the schools?

Nor will any single course in music or art alter the fact that school buildings are generally ugly, dull places, where there is little space for conversation. The Ontario Provincial Committee on Aims and Objectives in Education wrote in its eloquent report, *Living and Learning:*

> The school environment sends messages to all children. The space that invites, the color that warms, the parkland that lures, the human accents of the planning of the school and its surroundings are intuitively grasped by every child. Children thrive when they can touch, see, hear, and feel beauty. Early sensory awareness can mark significant steps in the never-ending joy of discovery and appreciation of the esthetic. Works of visual art, sculpture, gardens, fountains, and trees should be an integral part of the planning of every school, for the bricks and mortar of the schools are themselves the 'silent teachers.'

This is written from the planners' point of view, of course. It should be borne in mind not only in planning new buildings, however, for it applies to the use people make of old buildings, as well. Many old buildings, however difficult to work in, have been turned into warm environments for children. An increasing number of our educational institutions are making use of "found" space in converted buildings, instead of constructing massive, expensive school buildings. Like food, the basic environment reflects the assumptions of the school, its human climate, and the quality of the relationships within it. The assumption of schools where learning flourishes—not only in the arts, but in every aspect—is that childhood is something to be cherished, to be valued for itself, for what can emerge in the lives of the children here and now.

If there are dangers in confining ourselves to the arts as part of the curriculum, there are dangers, too, in talking as outsiders about how to change the schools, as though schools were machines to be moved by levers instead of tangled relationships among people. During the 1960s, as Charles Silberman has reminded us, there was intense educational reform in nearly every part of the country. But ten years of determined effort produced almost no significant change. Classes still largely consist of monologues by teachers, broken by more or less forced group discussions. Most learning is still rote memorization. There is very little individual learning. Textbooks predominate. Discipline continues to be harsh. And timetables and clocks set the pace for everyone. Those interested in the fate of the arts in the schools should take a hard look at the teaching of English, which is, after all, supposed to be a humane subject concerned with values and esthetics. Most high-school students still choke down *Silas Marner* and then take multiple-choice tests requiring specific ridiculously detailed factual answers. There is very little student expression of any sort: when students are made to write, which is rarely, it is easy to understand why the writing comes out in the horrible passives, abstract nouns, and academese that only a handful of students will ever get a chance to employ writing PhD theses.

Appeals to a rosy vision of the whole environment of school are—like appeals for the centrality of the arts in the curriculum—apt to sound merely pious without examples of schools in which the approach to learning is integrated and whole. My convictions about the place of the arts in education is derived, in large part, from observation of British primary schools. I would like to explain a few aspects of the British experience that may be useful to us as we struggle toward a sense of what our schools ought to be aiming at. My use of the British example is purely illustrative; they have no "model" to offer us, and Britain is far from being an educational utopia, but some British schools can help us gain some practical notion of what a unified approach to learning would be like, at least on the primary-school level.

In 1967 an official government body in England published the Plowden Report, *Children and Their Primary Schools*. This report called attention to the changes in British schools, and the gradual establishment of certain conditions for good learning on a fairly large, national scale. How these changes have come about is a long chapter in social and cultural history. What is important to grasp is that schools for children within a publicly supported educational system in a mass industrial society not unlike our own have taken strides toward the kind of humane education that reformers and philosophers have urged over the centuries. The Plowden Report and various other accounts of the British reform—including large portions of Silberman's study—suggest a new way of looking at schools, involving new conceptions of the role of the teacher, the organization of the classroom, the nature of children's learning, how the school day should proceed, and what constitutes a proper curriculum for children. The fact is that many British principals and teachers are coming to think of a good school as one in which children are trained to work independently in an environment thoughtfully planned to permit choices from an array of materials—water, sand, clay and pottery kilns, musical instruments, pets, practical math apparatus and science equipment, all kinds of reference books and books for individual reading, private word books and free writing notebooks, powder paint, easels, puppet theatres, playhouses.

In such informal classes the emphasis is on active learning. Teachers and children are given choices to an extent that there is no longer a fixed curriculum or a set timetable. Children move around at their tasks, and they are encouraged to talk to each other, for *that* is how they learn. The teacher is not considered the sole generating force of learning, as is the case in most of our schools. The teacher is organizer, catalyst, and consultant for the activities of children. It is important for Americans to understand that the teacher's role in these new settings is no less important than in formal classes; in some ways it is more important. The teacher sets the pace, listens, diagnoses, gives advice, introduces new words and materials.

There is nothing strikingly new in the kinds of teaching and learning promoted in these schools. There are no special techniques or methods involved. They incorporate sound practices used by good teachers everywhere over the ages. What is striking is the extent to which teachers in different kinds of communities all over England are coming to share a common vision of what they should be aiming at, even though the quality of work in their schools and classrooms may differ greatly.

Along with this vision is a definite philosophy of teaching. As the Plowden Report says, "It lays special stress on individual discovery, on first-hand experience, and on opportunities for creative work. It insists that knowledge does not fall in neatly separate compartments, and that work and play are not opposite, but complementary." Developmental psychology has given some underpinning to work in good classrooms. The fusion of developmental theory and classroom practice is perhaps easiest to see in mathematics, where certain assumptions, such as Piaget's idea that young children need to build up layers of experience before they master abstractions, are beginning to pervade classrooms and shape the direction of further innovation. Yet while theory plays a role, it is important to note what the Plowden Report also suggests: that principals and teachers most successful in practice are often unable to formulate their aims clearly.

As for the curriculum, much of what goes on arises from mutual interests and activities of children and teachers, not some fixed notion of what must be taught, or what has to be, as we say, "covered." Often patterns of individual learning develop in one subject and then spread to others. For some schools art was the first subject in which children were encouraged to choose the content of their work, in others, "movement," mime, and interpretative dancing took the place of calisthenics in physical education classes. Some introduced German composer Carl Orff's musical instruments. Two parts of the curriculum have flourished in recent years: children's writing and mathematics. An emphasis on children's writing—autobiographical sketches, poetry, precise writing on math and science projects—is now being established as fundamental to a proper education. And mathematics has become an important catalyst for schools making the transition from formal teaching to informal, active learning. New curriculum materials and practical math apparatus have helped here. In contrast to most of our curriculum projects, which are in the hands of university people and specialists remote from classroom teaching, the British projects have taken pains to enlist working teachers in the process of creating and spreading new ideas. The best materials are handbooks and practical guides for teachers, not potted lessons, and they are filled with samples of actual children's work.

Reports of these reforms are likely to emphasize the surface aspects: classroom organization, the altered nature of the curriculum, the quality of children's writing and art work. In some ways it is good for us to pay attention to these matters. Too much of our talk about education is divorced from specific concrete classroom realities. But there are certain underlying features of the British reform that we should keep in mind in developing our own ideas about schools. First, there is general agreement that young children have distinct needs and distinct patterns of learning—that they learn best in what David Hawkins calls the concrete mode, messing around with stuff. Second, there has been a growing skepticism as to whether crude quantitative standards such as IQ and conventional test scores should determine individual decisions about the education of young children. Third, there has been an emergence both nationally and locally of a class of people whose precise function is hard to describe: advisers—people experienced at teaching in informal settings—whose job is solely to spot good schools and willing principals and teachers and give them help without bossing them around.

The British example suggests that it is a mistake to attempt to know and control everything that goes on in a learning situation. This is not said in any anti-intellectual or romantically mystic sense. It is said, I hope, in a truly scientific and experimental spirit. We do not have precise information about children's learning—the best way to read for a particular child, for example. There is no one best system of learning for everyone, nor is there one best system of teaching. This, among other things, is an argument for having classroom environments where teachers can talk to children freely and watch them trying their hand at different activities. Such an approach puts a good deal of faith in teachers. In this country we lack that sort of faith.

Our schools assume the worst of teachers, as well as of children. One of the great problems with our cult of research is that in all its workings it discounts the value of a teacher's own experience, to say nothing of a child's.

An essential aspect of the British reform has been the existence of good work. That may be a truism, but it is nonetheless true for all that. Good writing, good art work, a good atmosphere for teaching and learning—these are the kinds of things that make teachers and parents confident of accepting other standards besides conventional test scores. The existence of good classrooms gives people an idea of what they should be aiming at. And it gives everybody a criterion by which to judge botched classrooms that might otherwise be passed off as examples of open teaching. In other words, good work, besides offering standards, also acts to protect an educational reform movement from being judged by its silliest excesses.

These reforms spread at the grass roots, not from the top down, and they spread slowly. We are talking about a span of perhaps thirty years, although the pace of change has quickened in England in the last decade. That, too, is something for Americans to keep in mind as we rush to discuss this year's newest educational fashion. In art, in particular, the reforms go back at least as far as the 1930s when children in a few places were encouraged to use real paints, not pencils or water colors—which, although schools prefer them, are extremely difficult media. Teachers encouraged the children to soak their brushes in cheap powder paints and work with masses of textured colors on large surfaces, newspaper, for example. Instead of set, traditional subjects—the British equivalents to the inevitable Thanksgiving Pilgrims and turkeys our children still dutifully draw—children were encouraged to paint what they liked, and the results were interesting. Once the idea of accurate drawing disappeared, it turned out that young children think symbolically and abstractly and can paint in what looks like a very modern idiom.

Handicrafts also developed, particularly in schools lucky enough to get some woodworking tools or a pottery kiln. Crafts in most of our schools seldom go beyond plasticene and pipe cleaners; even when schools do have good equipment, crafts are likely to be separate subjects, cut off from the intellectual life of the school and taught by teachers who, for all their technical proficiency, take little interest in developing children's expressiveness. Particularly with young children, a different approach can get more interesting results. If, in the early years, children learn to handle tools and are accustomed to working with pieces of junk, wood, and scraps of material, they can fashion constructions that are true works of the imagination. They also love working with fabrics. Tie-dyeing has caught on in this country, but significantly not in the schools. Erling Heistad told a conference session on rural schools how the Haystack-Hinckley School of Crafts' summer program helps teachers scrounge for materials—getting short ends off woolen mills' bobbins, for example —but this sort of thing is still rare in our schools. Throwing pots on a wheel is hard for young kids, and electric kilns are expensive, but building up pots with coils of clay is something small children can tackle and a simple kiln can be constructed with bricks and sawdust. Elwyn Richardson's classic account of a rural New Zealand school, *In the Early World,* takes the children's explorations with clay as a paradigm of the process of experimentation, learning, and self-criticism that go on in other areas of the curriculum, particularly children's writing. Under Richardson's guidance, children learned to make judgments on the quality of work. Crafts can be taught so they are not frills, but alternate approaches to expression and communication, the central concern of the school.

A dimension of the British curriculum almost totally absent from our schools is what is loosely called movement. This may start with physical education: along with organized team sports and calisthenics, a number of schools have introduced various kinds of climbing frames and apparatus that promote individual work. Teachers noticed the scope of children's inventiveness at this kind of activity and began developing a range of expressive movement. Influenced by such figures as Laban, other teachers encouraged children to explore the body's capacities for motion—heavy, light, large, small, fast, slow movements, all contributing to a sense of the body as a whole. A teacher in a movement class might suggest that the children make big strong movements, using the space around them, developing the lesson from there. This gives all children experience in moving and controlling the body. In some schools, movement fuses with dance, mime, and drama, accompanied by simple musical instruments. The drama emerging from this sort of work is put on by the children for their own benefit, and it is not confined to the somewhat artificial conventions of the stage. Children use whatever space exists and work with few props.

Again, expression and communication are of the essence: these short sketches of different "subjects" in the area called "the arts" could easily be repeated for more conventional schools subjects, like writing and mathematics. The point is the common approach. The various arts can be viewed as alternative ways of communicating— in painting, rendering a conception through line, color, texture, and form. Using the materials of a specific medium imposes a particular discipline on the effort, and a rich variety of art materials encourages children's experimentation analogous in most ways with experimentation with practical mathematical and scientific materials. If you use a roller to ink linoleum blocks, why not use the rollers for painting, too? If you can apply colors with a roller, what else comes to mind? Fingers, sponges, pieces of paper, a paint pallette; a hundred ideas emerge.

Recently a British principal discussed art in his school in a pamphlet written for a joint project of the Schools Council and the Ford Foundation. Talking of the discipline inherent in working with particular art materials, Henry Pluckrose suggested:

> The teacher has an especially significant role to play. One does not want to destroy the child's innate curiosity with technique lessons unrelated to his particular needs and accomplishments. At the same time, some materials have to be understood before they can be used fully, and to leave expensive materials out to be played with until their properties are discovered is both unrealistic and foolhardy. How the balance is achieved between the two contrasting aims of child discovery and adult direction is virtually impossible to describe. It happens if the climate of the classroom is such that the teacher is one who inspires rather than dictates, where the discoveries about the nature of materials are discussed so that children learn through each other's experience as well as from the teacher. A group of ten-year-olds, for example, might discover that wax crayons resist water-based ink. From this starting point (simple wax resists) the gifted teacher will try to create situations in which the process of using wax to repel water is examined in as many contrasting ways as possible.

Again, this could be said of good work in every subject, not simply art. In every subject, you want to create a situation where the teacher isn't setting the particular methods children choose in order to make a statement; but where the teacher provides experiences and then introduces the children to a variety of means of expression. The teacher has to be able to allow plenty of time for children to assimilate the experiences, and then extend and develop them. Creative work in art, like creative work in other subjects, requires a schedule flexible enough so children can see a piece of work through to their satisfaction. It requires a classroom stocked with materials to use, things to see and touch. And all this implies a style of teaching in which the classroom is organized to permit children to work individually, a space in which the essential enterprise is the cultivation of varieties of communication, talk. A working premise of such a classroom is the necessity for as many varied experiences and activities as teachers and children can handle, to stimulate different tastes and temperaments and cultivate different skills—to give every child a chance to develop personal confidence and competence. Confident work in one part of the curriculum will affect work in another: if the approach is common.

Music is one part of the curriculum in British schools that is still far from developed, but there are enormously significant stirrings. As in some of our schools, there have been new influences in Britain. To John Curwen's work in developing class singing have been added Kodály methods, solfège, and the work of Carl Orff. Recorders are popular, and there are now varieties of classroom instruments on which children can play tunes: glockenspiels, chime bars, xylophones.

These instruments and the new methods involved in their use are raising interesting questions about the arts in general, not just music. Music has always been in many respects the toughest case for proponents of a new art education, for music is the citadel of old orthodoxies. Traditionally, the work of schools in the arts everywhere has emphasized historical study, analysis, some amount of imitation, and, in subjects like drama and music, performance according to a playwright's or composer's design. Movement, drama, and the visual arts, as I've noted, were the first to break away from this pattern to introduce expressive elements. The question is whether this can happen in music, too, or whether the difficulties inherent in the language of music mean that the creativity of the composer will always be the restricted pleasure of a gifted minority.

The returns on this question are far from in, and it would be misleading to make exaggerated claims for music in British schools.

In a few places, however, there are developments that may become significant, not just for music and the arts, but for all efforts to improve children's learning. Carl Orff's instruments for example, are easy for children to play; they quickly learn to experiment with them the same way they experiment with art materials, math apparatus, or varieties of writing. The instruments are tuned on the diatonic scale, but they can be converted to a pentatonic scale. (A musically illiterate reader like myself may recall that the diatonic scale is the white keys on the piano, beginning with C, whereas the pentatonic scale conforms to the black keys.) Folk songs in many countries are on the pentatonic scale, which is lovely, but it has another advantage for small children as they mess around: there are no semitones, so no discords are possible. Two children improvising on Orff instruments can produce nice harmonic effects without knowing a good deal about music. The chime bar, which is a simple glockenspiel note detached and mounted so that it can be used separately, is an example of musical materials analogous to some of the new practical apparatus in mathematics. Children can collect chime bars note by note to build up various kinds of musical scales, and sets of these bars can be used in many ways: playing melodies, improvisation, making chords. Besides introducing new scales and liberating musical instruction from certain conventions, such as major and minor, the Orff methods have brought a new sense of the possibilities of experiment with rhythm, using physical movement and speech, as well as a new interest in exploring the properties of sounds for their own sake. Above all, the work in a few schools eclectically inspired by Orff and other new influences has raised the possibility of an approach to musical education that would include expression and creation, as well as performance.

What might such an approach look like? We wouldn't know except for an admirable pamphlet by John Horton. It would begin, very early on, with instruments like chime bars and a general introduction to sounds, pitches, and tones of all sorts of different materials, such as wood, partly filled bottles, and so on. Then, as Horton (in another Schools Council-Ford Foundation pamphlet) describes it:

Improvisation can range from the imitation of verbal rhythms or a single note repeated as an ostinato to the elaboration of chord series and the building of larger musical structures by the introduction of contrasting ideas. Pre-existing melodic material, such as folk-song, may be taken as a basis, and some find it helpful to follow both Orff and Kodály in restricting the range of sounds to the pentatonic scales. . . . Others encourage the freer exploration of sounds of every kind, whether 'musical' in the older sense or otherwise.

Teachers make use of poetry, pictures, and evocative themes to stir children's imaginations. Horton describes one group of children's efforts to find a "Chinese" scale, different from their accustomed pentatonic scale, for a particular Oriental project. After experimenting some, they substituted B-flat bars for B naturals giving them a scale which they called "spooky," and which, unlike the normal pentatonic scale, contained a semitone. As Horton points out, "Experienced adult musicians would be unlikely to arrive at such a scale except, like Bartòk, by way of folk-music study, like Busoni, by theoretical formulation, or by imitation of non-European melodic patterns such as the Indian *ragas.*" In another school, Horton pointed out:

All of the expressive and creative arts are closely interrelated, a favourite pattern of expression being the mosaic or sequence in which passages of the children's own verse or prose are interspersed with movement and improvised music. In this school also improvisation is carried on without the aid of notation (though notation is taught in connection with other musical activities), and as many as 30 children are able to reproduce an elaborate, improvised piece lasting up to two minutes, without a conductor. . . . This result is achieved through the growth of an instinctive sense of form which owes nothing to a knowledge of note-durations, rests, phrase-marks, staves, and other supposed essentials of accurate ensemble performance, nor to the kind of analytical approach to musical form that is normally considered to belong to comparatively advanced stages of executant musicianship. To an adult observer, both the appearance and sound of one of these improvising groups is strongly reminiscent of the Indonesian *gamelan.*

Horton cannot point to many schools where such work goes on, but he doesn't need to in order to make his basic argument. That such work exists suggests what many people have begun to suspect about music after watching children's efforts in other areas of the curriculum: that children have innate capacities for understanding rhythms, and they possess the ability to invent, remember, and reproduce complex musical structures without necessarily knowing the conventions of notation. (The tape recorder, of course, can preserve a child-composer's work.)

The teacher's role in promoting this kind of musical expression is the same as the teacher's role in the rest of informal teaching: to provide the environment and materials for such work to be possible, and then to build on the children's expression. Among other things, a teacher has to decide how much time to spend on this sort of free work, and how much to devote to more traditional, formal kinds of musical instruction, such as notation, performing, and listening, which no one in his right mind would want to abandon.

I've gone into music at some length, not because so much good musical work exists—it is in fact very rare—but because the kind of thing that is emerging is beginning to confirm many discoveries about learning processes and children's potential in general. Active learning, engagement with materials, playing from children's talents and interests, the encouragement of expressiveness—these are, of course, not features distinctive to the handful of English and American schools experimenting with the music curriculum. They fit an emerging vision of what all the activities in schools ought to be aiming at. In the schools Mr. Horton describes, music is not a diversion. It is, like the rest of the arts, central, involved with many levels of expression: dance, drama, words. This is surely what we should want in all the arts, and, indeed, in all subjects.

The work of good English primary schools is mainly useful to give us concrete ideas of how we might begin thinking about reforming our schools. It is important to be able to discuss the aims of education in specific terms, to have a graphic sense of what a new approach might mean in a subject like music, for example. This is a way of avoiding abstract and ideological debates. For in abstract terms, the qualities necessary for promoting creative work in schools have often been spelled out—with very little effect on schools. Many thinkers and observers of children over the years have contributed to a vision of what a good school should do. There has been substantial agreement that it should treat students as individuals, giving them an opportunity to make significant choices; it should build on the interests, experiences, and expressiveness of teachers and children, stressing the active involvement of people in their own education. And it should concern itself with students' and teachers' feelings, the normal, inescapable emotional context of communication; acting on the premise that relations among children and adults, and among children and other children, are of supreme educational importance, inside or outside of school.

All this has been said, perhaps too often. In the absence of a grounding in specific pedagogical realities, however, this ideal vision has often promoted foolishness, quackery, and an abdication of adult authority. We can expect to see more of all this. The British example can start us thinking, but it cannot, of course, do the necessary work: pinning down theory to the day-to-day lives of real teachers and real children in real classrooms. That, as the old hymn says, is a road we will have to walk alone.

If the way seems unclear at present, it is because, while we sense the ailing parts, we have yet to grab onto a vision of the whole. Many of the projects at the ACA conference went beyond specific parts of the curriculum being developed by British schools. Thus, when it comes to involving schools in the life of the surrounding community, a program like Urban Gateways in Chicago has nothing to learn from the British. Similarly, there is little in England to compare with the excellent work in film and videotape by people in this country, or the unusual efforts in schools of the theatre groups like Project Discovery in Providence, or the witty improvisational talent of the Academy Theater of Atlanta. In general, there is more interesting arts education at the secondary school level in America than in Great Britain.

The point, however, is not to compare England and America, which is like comparing apples and oranges. The point is to use the good work that exists as a basis for rethinking the total life of our schools. This sense of the whole was missing at the St. Louis conference. Herbert Kohl's Other Ways School was the only entire school to be represented at the conference, and certainly the Other Ways people were not able to articulate a clear vision of what the learning environment as a whole ought to be like.

Nor am I, but I want to draw out some points from two of the presentations at the conference, hoping that I can keep my argument specific enough. From what I've said about English schools, it follows that a central aim of a good school is the cultivation of children's powers of expression. We are used to thinking about creativity with artistic materials—at least those of us interested in arts education are

—but we seldom think about creativity with words. One reason for this is the nearly universal neglect of writing in our schools. This is why a program like the Teachers and Writers Collaborative in New York is so intriguing. Although limited in scope, it demonstrates children's powers of expression, and it suggests some of the ways in which a conventional part of the curriculum—the mastery and use of language—can be taught as the arts ought to be taught. Its virtues then, are applicable to all of the arts and all aspects of the curriculum; its weaknesses as a project also point to some lessons.

The Collaborative places professional writers in classrooms where they work with teachers and children on an extended basis, as colleagues, not just visiting firemen or performers. (Most of the people at the ACA conference working with artists in schools agreed that they must become part of the school's staff in some fashion. Anthony Keller, of the Connecticut Commission on the Arts Project Create, insisted that, above all, "The thing to avoid is the one-shot deal, 'See me, I'm an artist.' ") The Collaborative also runs teacher workshops, develops materials, and puts out a newsletter in the form of a magazine. The newsletter indicates the possible range of expression of children's writing: fables, poems, blues, haiku, comic strips, a parody of a Dick and Jane reader, bestiaries, word collages, printograms (words run together to form a drawing), straight interviews, and set prose pieces.

If you read this newsletter or talk to the Collaborative people, you won't discover any special techniques for developing children's writing. There aren't any. (Nor are there any in the other arts.) No fixed methods exist to be abstracted from a particular teacher's classroom and transferred to another setting. What the Collaborative's work does offer is a set of good suggestions for starting children on their way, along with persuasive evidence that encouraging different varieties of expression is a good idea. Some Collaborative teachers have played around with "found" poems, for example—poems formed by picking sentences and words at random from books and street signs and putting them all together. Students can be intrigued by the discovery that they all know poetry—street poetry, like skip rope chants, "Charlie Chaplin went to France," and other perennial bits of children's lore. And there are old formulas that teachers keep rediscovering in their efforts to give uncertain children a framework on which to hang a first piece of writing, like the theme, "I used to be a _____ but now I'm a _____."

One of the Collaborative's poets in St. Louis was Kenneth Koch, who regularly taught classes at PS 61 on the Lower East Side of New York.* Koch explained how he started with poems that were created collectively by the whole class, and then slowly got some kids to branch out on their own. They did poems in which every line states a wish—a device whose repetition automatically gives a poem a certain sing-song structure. Koch made a few suggestions helpful to the children: avoid rhyme, make the poem fantastic, crazy, or silly, put a comparison, or a noise, or a color in every line. Here is a nice set of comparisons and colors one child worked together in the fantastic vein:

> Snow is as white as the sun shines.
> The sky is as blue as a waterfall.
> A rose is as red as a beating of drums.
> The clouds are as white as the busting of a firecracker.
> A tree is as green as a roaring lion.

Koch discovered what other teachers have also noted, that the process of writing (and any other kind of expression) becomes cumulative, with the children building on each other's efforts. From poems about wishes, comparisons, colors, and noises, the class moved on to poems about dreams, and, sure enough, these incorporated lots of wishes, comparisons, colors, and noises. Mistakes and flukes proved to be a source of inspiration for a few children. Metaphorical poems developed after a child mistakenly wrote about a "swan" of bees, instead of a "swarm." Students played with words: "I had a dream of my banana pillow/And of my pyjamas of oranges." Children constantly influenced each other. If one wrote: "I used to be a fish/But now I'm a nurse," another listened and played variations:

> I used to be a nurse
> But now I am a dead person.
> I always was Mr. Coke.
> But now I am Mrs. Seven-Up.

---

*Many of the poems he read and some of those quoted in the following text appear in Mr. Koch's anthology of children's writing, Wishes, Lies, Dreams, published by Chelsea House, distributed by Random House. 1970 © by Kenneth Koch.

Through similar exercises, many of them fairly mechanical, Koch and his class built up their own literary tradition, so to speak, based on all the different sorts of poems they achieved or at least heard others in the class achieve. Until there was this common tradition, based on practical work in the classroom, Koch noted that children were mainly stimulated by each other's example. But with the increasing sophistication of range of expression the children were exposed to, some began to make use of adult poetry. Koch read Wallace Stevens, and echoes of the "Harmonium" poems emerged: "Owl go like who and who. Who and who and who . . ." Or, "The sun had the glare of glass in it."

The children played with Spanish words and poetic forms like the sestina. They wrote poems in which every line had to be a lie. Out of this last assignment, strangely enough, came a haunting poem by Jeff Morley, a fifth grader. Marvin Hoffman, the Collaborative's director, read "The Dawn of Me" to a hushed audience at St. Louis:

> *I was born nowhere*
> *And I live in a tree*
> *I never leave my tree*
> *It is very crowded*
> *I am stacked up right against a bird*
> *But I won't leave my tree*
> *Everything is dark*
> *No light!*
> *I hear the bird sing*
> *I wish I could sing*
> *My eyes, they open*
> *And all around my house*
> *The Sea*
> *Slowly I get down in the water*
> *The cool blue water*
> *Oh and the space*
> *I laugh swim and cry for joy*
> *This is my home*
> > *For Ever*

Koch's students preferred working in the classroom rather than taking work home, which was too much like homework. The noise and talk didn't bother them, and they seemed to like the idea of writing together. His job, he said, was to help them with hard words and give them ideas, applause, and encouragement: "So I was useful in the classroom for getting the children in a good mood to write and then for keeping them going. And they were useful to each other in creating a humming and buzzing creative ambience."

The Collaborative effort represents some tentative steps in the right direction; it is by no means a blueprint for changing the schools. Marvin Hoffman was modest about what had been accomplished. It hasn't had to face an issue that many educational enterprises in the arts will have to face: getting teaching credentials for its artists. And it certainly hasn't solved the problems of dealing with a pathological big-city school system like New York's. A small but significant indication of the state of the city's high schools is the fact that a project like the Collaborative can't work in them, even though it has found plenty of elementary and junior high schools to work in. Another ailment the Collaborative suffers from is shared by many projects in the arts: it is dependent on charity and what funds exist are given out on the questionable assumption that a good project will soon find its own base of support.

Another general problem the Collaborative meets daily is recruiting writers who can teach and are willing to work with teachers. It stands to reason that some writers, like some sculptors or any other adults, are not suited to teaching; and it also makes sense that some who can work well with children are not good at dealing with other adults. One of the many difficulties in the way of reforming our schools also crops up: American teachers are constantly victimized by outside experts of one sort or another who sweep into their classrooms, tell them how it should be done, and then depart, pocketing their fat consultant fees. The Collaborative writers clearly have something to offer interested teachers—this distinguishes them sharply from many of the people plaguing the schools—but they need immense tact and diplomacy to make any sort of lasting impact.

There are also difficulties in the narrowness of the Collaborative's approach. The contents of the newsletter plainly reflect the concerns of professional writers, and, in particular, of New York City's poets. The kind of children's writing that is encouraged is "literary" in the sense that it takes place in a separate realm—consciously poetic at its best, as in Jeff Morley's poem, and cute, contrived, and artificial at its worst. It is probably not the Collaborative people's fault there is no decent writing on science or math projects—they are working with schools as they exist, after all—but the newsletter lacks good examples of straightforward children's prose on real experiences, in or out of school. Not all of us are poets. And, anyway, most of us would not write consistently well if we were called upon to make poems daily for a special period in an ordinary, bare classroom—even if the encouragement came from such an engaging figure as Kenneth Koch. Some would do well, and for a while most of us might be learning something about poetic forms and poets. We would certainly profit from participating in the ongoing literary endeavor that seems to me to have been Koch's main achievement at PS 61. After a while, however, I suspect that we would lack things to write about: more stimulation, experiences to feed on. We would be like those people in "creative writing" classes, all dressed up with no place to go. Many of us would tire of the specialty called poetry and the class period called writing.

The limits of the Collaborative's excellent endeavor suggest some general problems of all specializations in the schools, and they speak with particular relevance to attempts to get the arts to flourish in school settings. Obviously having crack writers—like having professional artists and sculptors—regularly coming into any school is a blessing. Even apart from the specific skills and the technical training they have to offer, such people ought to be in schools. It is, after all, rare for children to come across an adult who really knows one of the conventional academic subjects. It is even more rare for them to meet grownups who are good at their respective craft, who have something to teach they live for. (This, of course, applies to lawyers and carpenters, as well as artists, writers, and musicians.) But the schools have a way of closing around the specialists they do get, isolating them from the rest of school life. (In poor schools, this isolation protects the specialists and often leaves their classrooms little oases of good work.) A project like the Collaborative should begin cooperating with teachers to remake the school curriculum entirely. Reaching the teachers is at the heart of the current movement to reform the schools, and, like efforts elsewhere in our society, the movement is sure to fail to the extent that it fails to reach teachers. Baiting people trapped within the system—like calling the police "pigs"—is pointless, as well as immoral, for they are the people in our children's classrooms. In the meantime, the Collaborative's work is proof of something that has to be trumpeted at the schools until their walls come tumbling down: children can write, lyrically, playfully, and seriously. A school where the children aren't writing is not doing its job.

Writing is not an isolated "innovation," to be stuck, like the "art period," on top of the standard curriculum. Those who plead for more children's writing in our schools are not asking for crash programs to drill children in written expression. This would be a victory comparable in its hollowness to succeeding in replacing geography with conventional art appreciation sterilities. Expressive writing on a variety of subjects is a symptom of a healthy school environment that encourages expression in all forms. It suggests an emphasis on working from children's strengths in the language that they possess, for example, instead of destroying their confidence in language, which is what our formal reading programs often do. By its nature, writing is a matter that each child will approach differently, with different interests and skills: therefore, it requires a classroom where people are treated as distinct individuals. Good writing is also apt to reflect relationships within the school: children won't write for people they mistrust, and they are not apt to develop their writing unless they are sometimes free to talk. An emphasis on writing says a good deal about the school's general standards, too: whether its teachers are in the shadow of standard test scores, for instance. Also, since people generally write best about what they have experienced directly, good writing is apt to be the product of a classroom environment in which there is a great variety of materials and books appealing to a wide range of interests and talents. Further, the role of a teacher in developing children's writing must differ from that of a teacher in an ordinary formal classroom: the role, which is no less central, involves shifting from being in some sense the source of whatever learning is going on in the classroom to becoming the organizer of children's activities. Finally, helping children with their writing—something any literate adult can do—is a way to offer a real service, for there are genuine skills and workmanship to be learned and whole worlds of literature to explore and imitate. Much of what goes on in schools is no real service to anybody, and this colors everyone's responses to school.

B. Eliot Wigginton, the faculty adviser to *Foxfire*, attended the ACA conference and spoke eloquently on his students' work at the session on rural schools. *Foxfire* is a quarterly put out by the students at the Rabun Gap-Nacoochee High School in Rabun Gap, Georgia. Its staff is seriously concerned with accurately recording Appalachian folkways, arts, crafts, and traditions. It includes some regional writing —book reviews, poetry, and art work by adult contributors—but the heart of the enterprise is an extensive series of taped interviews done by students with mountain people, discussing aspects of the region's traditional life. One entire issue was about log cabins; another had pieces of quilting, making chairs and soap, and other crafts. One issue had extremely detailed anecdotes, notes, and photographs of hunting and training dogs; and directions for dressing and cooking raccoon, possum, and groundhog, as well as more familiar game animals like deer. A long section explains all about slaughtering, curing, and cooking hogs. There is a splendid interview with a vividly outspoken old lady named Aunt Arie, who lives alone in a log cabin. As the students help her cook a pig's head, she describes her terror when a freezing spell swelled the door to her food cellar and she couldn't get in for supplies. An angry editorial attacks antique dealers who exploit and swindle people of the region. One victim of a dealer describes a scoundrelly freeloader who might have stepped out of the pages of Mark Twain:

> But he can pray a good prayer. He come one evenin' an' it come up a storm an' he got down on his knees on one side a'th'well, an' see, I can't get down on my knees, an'—got down on his knees; an' you never heared such a prayer come out'a nobody in yore life as come out'a that man. An' I's standin' there about t'faint a'standin' there s'long. I'd been run all day and starved t'death anyhow; an' I 'uz just glad when he got done. He prayed a good prayer though. He just prayed a real good'n. He comes in about time I got dinner ready, an' he comes in and eats.

Faced with something as interesting as *Foxfire*, or as good as Jeff Morley's poem, or a superb piece of art done by a child, we are tempted to praise the work itself, and to forget the kinds of experiences over time that usually precede good work. Most children, like most adults, are not great artists, and it is worth keeping in mind in all discussions of art in schools that the finished works, the poems, the paintings or whatever, are not the main point: the main point, always, is how the experience helps the student to grow and develop. After all, the aim of children's art is their own development, not the products they make, certainly not "masterpieces." This holds true for collective ventures like *Foxfire*, which relies so heavily on the tape recorder and the camera: it is not the artifact, it is the experience of putting it all together that counts. It's easy to believe that some students in Rabun Gap are really learning something.

Apart from its value as testimony to the kind of work students in high schools ought to be doing, *Foxfire* suggests two important things. It is significant as an attempt to quicken the interests of students from a minority culture in their culture—to develop their enthusiasms in a disciplined way, involving many different kinds of skills, writing, research, photography, interviewing, editing, thinking up projects,assessing the significance of certain strands of tradition to the region, and so on. In this case the minority happens to be people in Appalachia, whose rural ways appeal to a vein of nostalgia in all Americans. But surely the significance of the example extends to all cultural minorities, and one can imagine counterparts to *Foxfire* in schools all over the country—on Indian reservations, among ethnic and racial ghettos in the cities, and indeed, wherever there is any distinctive cultural or geographical turf. The second point about *Foxfire* is more prosaic. Eliot Wigginton said that he had conceived of English—meaning all forms of expression—as the basis for a sensible high-school curriculum, replacing *Silas Marner* and *A Tale of Two Cities*. *Foxfire* thus represents a step toward a different kind of high school curriculum, stressing active learning, instead of the taxidermy so prevalent in our schools.

Throughout these notes, my aim has been to sharpen our picture of what a good job looks like. Clarity of thought can be deceptive, however, when it comes to direct action, and I must confess that when I turn to the question of what institutions such as arts councils can contribute to humane education, I have no easy answers to offer. Plainly the general climate of public expectation affects the schools; a book like Silberman's *Crisis in the Classroom* is a welcome sign that the conventional wisdom of the social order is becoming reflective about the schools. The clamor of parents' and citizens' groups does eventually reach the ears of school administrators, and it stands to reason that groups like arts councils have a role to play in articulating new concerns. As we press for open, informal, humane—or whatever —schools, we must be permanently wary of the faddism of the culture; the appearance of new issues—the cry for humane schools, for instance—cannot cancel out old issues such as integration.

Reformers of our schools will have to reckon with all the diverse, turbulent, ominous elements of the picture. This is what critics ought to mean when they talk about the existence of a System: one problem links to another. A group that embarks on one aspect of school reform should, if it is serious about what it's doing, undertake responsibility for following up each new implication of each succeeding obstacle they encounter. There will have to be the right mix of pressures for reform from inside and outside the system. It will take—besides the money—time and a commitment to working inside the schools.

In all these matters we have to think in terms of the entire curriculum, and more than that, of the whole approach to children and their learning. Of course people will always find it necessary to mount isolated programs in the arts—because that's how it is in the real world of limited budgets, time, energy, and all the other oppressive practicalities. Of course such programs can be worthwhile—the schools need all the money, materials, and talent they can get. But from the broader perspective I've been trying to sketch in these notes, it seems obvious that too many of our specialized programs are conceived in narrow, pinched terms. Too many reach too few teachers and children; too many are promotional for adults, rather than educational for children, by which I mean that the programs are designed primarily to enhance the prestige and position of institutions like museums and symphony orchestras. (One of the consequences of our general niggardliness in providing money for the arts is that necessity makes promoters and exploiters of us all.) As a rule of thumb, we should insist that programs in the arts focus on working with teachers to develop an entire approach to teaching and learning, that they try to make an impact on the life of the school as a whole. In turn, the artists and specialists offering programs should alter them as they respond to particular schools, teachers, and children. An arts program not distinctively part of a school, or a program that looks the same in execution as it did on paper, is suspect.

Of course good programs will take thousands of shapes. As I said, I have a bias against art appreciation courses with a historical bent, not because I disapprove of art history, but because I think that usually it's more profitable to engage children actively with practical materials in a real medium. This doesn't mean that art history or theoretical analysis might not be the next step.

Nor is this an argument against planning and direction on the part of teachers; it is a criticism of the kind of courses, planning, and direction that now exist in the schools. Teachers have to plan; they must have in their heads a constantly shifting set of aims and purposes. Of course they also need good materials. But the plans, aims, and materials have to be open-ended. So much of what is going on now in classrooms does not correspond to any natural intellectual development; the sequences set forth on paper seldom match the way people actually learn. Hence so much of school work in all subjects —including, curiously, mathematics and the arts—is devoted to memorizing strings of words, concepts devoid of real experience and meaning. As I've said, the curriculum reforms of the sixties are sober reminders. You can get similarly discouraging results by isolating specialist teachers from other teachers, instead of letting them use their expertise to help teachers in an advisory capacity. The point is to help teachers to think about their work, to try out new ideas.

Unless outside groups are deeply involved with the schools on a day-to-day basis, they are not likely to be of much help. They may be a nuisance. Within the schools, a recurring pattern in the history of reform has been simply adding on new administrative layers to the existing bureaucracy. Programs requiring a great deal of administration, that don't directly involve teachers and children in classrooms, are probably a waste of money. This is not an argument against the proper sort of administration that actually works to support individual teachers in their classrooms and individual principals in schools. It is an argument against any form of administration that cannot provide support at these two important levels.

There are two further aspects to what might be called the bureaucracy question. The first is getting to be a commonplace: by and large our school systems are horribly overadministered. This is glaringly true of the mammoth big-city systems, but is even true of a city like New Haven, where there is a school administrative official for every nine teachers. The reasons for bureaucracy are complex and historical. Partly the administrative tiers represent a historic desire of school systems to monitor and control precisely what goes on in classrooms, a desire no less powerful for being delusory. Traditions of accountability to the public—and, paradoxically, traditions of building up barriers against public and political interference with the schools—also play an important part. But whatever the historical reasons, there are too many people in our school systems not directly involved with principals, teachers, or children. The central priority is on administration at the expense of teaching and learning. For example, the basic job of a principal should be staff development: he or she should see himself or herself and others should see the principal as a head teacher, able to work in classrooms setting an example of good ways of working with children. Good principals are doing this in some of our schools, but the good principals are the first to complain that the priorities of the system are on managing the plant.

A corollary of the fact that our schools are overadministered is the fact that they are also too big, particularly the elementary schools. We need smaller units; and we need to break down our huge castle-factories into more humanly manageable subunits. But as we dismantle the pathological administrative coral reefs of our schools, we will have to build up other structures. At the moment our teachers have the worst of two worlds: they are harassed by a school administration whose priorities are not supportive of good teaching, and at the same time they are lonely in their work. What they need is the sort of mixture of autonomy and professional support that is emerging in the best British primary schools.

At the very least, then, proposals for school reform should conform to the aims of giving teachers more autonomy and support. It may or may not be desirable to staff state education bureaucracies with more people in the arts, for instance. If they function as bureaucrats, politicking for an "arts" constituency, they are an added hindrance. If they are composed of people who can function in classrooms in a true advisory fashion, spotting schools and teachers eager for help, then they could be of tremendous value. Rural schools are starved for support; so are schools and teachers everywhere, even those most cynical about the game of bigwigs and consultants, the big-city schoolteachers.

If a school is ready to move, that's where the help should go. Too many of the programs of the federal government and the foundations have been predicated on a kind of false egalitarianism, spreading money to people regardless of the quality of their work and thought. It will be important to get working examples of good schools, for then educational reformers and the rest of us can begin developing a feeling for quality, practical standards by which to appraise the work of the schools. It should go without saying, but needs saying, that if no willing people exist in a school system—if there is no possibility for professional growth—the money for the arts should go to other institutions, museums, libraries.

Thus the necessary job of demolishing the administrative coral reef, will not be sufficient; there will also have to be support for principals and classroom teachers, people to help. I'm in deep sympathy with the attempts to decentralize schools and other institutions, to restore varieties of participation where participation can mean something. At the same time, I think we are sufficiently far into the twentieth century to see that the issue in many areas of our national life is not whether to have bureaucracies, professions, and administration, but whether it is possible to create professions that serve the interests of clients in a humane way. A vein of escapism and nostalgia makes us reluctant to concede this point. We hunger for simple answers. We are tempted to imagine that by simply dismantling existing social services we can restore an era of liberated human energy, as though something could come of nothing.

But it is the complicated and difficult mixture that the rest of us —like the teachers—need: autonomy, yes, but support, too. I suppose everybody in the end argues social policy from a particular angle of perspective, a private vision of what the social order is like, as well as a utopian picture of what it ought to be like. I hope a partial vision of my own educational Utopia has become sketchily apparent in this essay. My vision of what things are actually like resembles the vision of Frederick Wiseman's extraordinary documentary film, *Hospital.* *Hospital* shows the consequences for a big-city hospital of a social order starved for human structures of support, love, and care. It is the hospital's impossible task to face the dilemma of a father whose children have no day care; doctors futilely advise people that their job, which requires standing all day, is killing them. Many problems are not medical at all. The buck gets passed to the hospital because —in the appalling vacuum of social services in what we sometimes think of as a welfare state—people have noplace else to go. In the last scene, the camera draws back from the huge hospital building. It stands cut off from the rest of a city by a superhighway, the cars whooshing by, looking like an ungainly ark in a flood, bearing survivors from some incomprehensible catastrophe.

That is part of my vision of life in America today. It informs what I have to say about the organization of our social services, including our schools. And ultimately it informs my sense of what is needed in the realm of art education. It is a dark vision, but not devoid of hope. We have a long way to go, but a sensible first step along the way is to see what the possibilities are, and what we should aim for over the very long period of time it will take to get decent schools in this country. That is what I've tried to do in these notes.

3

John Dewey Reconsidered

John Dewey lived a long time, from 1859 to 1952; some of his best work was written at an age when most men have retired. The single most persistent thread in his far-ranging career was a determination to establish the unity of all experience, to reunite separate realms and distinct modes of thought in a culture splintered by its philosophical dualisms. The search for a continuity between literature and life, thought and action, mind and body, self and society, carried him through three phases.

In the first, which lasted up to the early 1890s, Dewey was a philosophical idealist. He followed the British Hegelians in defining knowledge as a kind of participation, seeking to connect the mind to the objects it knows. Hegel was important to him because Hegel promised a resolution of dualisms and contradictions, a vision of life that was whole and of a piece. Even after he abandoned Hegelianism, Dewey was permanently indebted to Hegel for a social conception of the human mind, for the idea that freedom was rational self-realization, and for the view that logic and morals were evolutionary phenomena, changing over time.

From the 1890s to the early 1920s there was a second phase in

Dewey's thought. This was when he put together his basic philosophical outlook, instrumentalism, and elaborated a pragmatic approach to logic, ethics, psychology, education, and social thought. Now Dewey followed Darwin in attempting to integrate human knowledge and human action into a framework of nature and natural processes: the mind was an instrument of evolutionary adaptation, and the terms of Hegel's dialectic became those of a biological creature interacting with its environment in a never-ending spiral of mastery and adjustment. Indirectly, Darwin gave Dewey the idea that philosophy itself was a sort of evolutionary criticism, an ongoing critique of old ideas in the light of new circumstances. Like Veblen and Marx, Dewey had a particularly vivid sense of the oppressive weight of dead ideas on the minds of the living.

Dewey fused certain traditional aspects of Protestantism, its reverence for experience and its belief in the application of intelligence to morals, with ideals of science and democracy. Like other disciples of Hegel on the left, he emphasized the realm of action as a vital concern of philosophy—developing his own concept of what the Marxists call *praxis*. The function of thought was to guide action; to believe a proposition was in some sense to act on it; the test of meaning and truth was experiential. Dewey warned genteel America of the folly of idle abstractions, cut off from real experience—what William James termed "vicious intellectualism"—and, equally, he reminded Teddy Roosevelt's admirers of the danger of all action not informed by intelligence. He contended that ethics was a branch of knowledge, and he developed a logic that tried to end what he saw as the "scandal" involved in the culture's divorce of science from morals. Along with William James he laid the foundations for a new psychology, and he worked out the outlines of a new philosophy of education.

This Dewey was an extraordinary, Protean figure, who immeasurably enriched American thought, putting his decisive stamp on a vast range of issues in a dozen fields. Certain flaws kept surfacing in his social thought, however, and they are worth pondering because they suggest general weaknesses in the outlook of many members of Dewey's generation, the Progressives who came of intellectual age in the years between 1880 and 1920.

William James and Dewey were the two opposite poles of American social thought—James with his supremely romantic emphasis on individual experience, and Dewey with his characteristic emphasis on the social context of all experience. Both were inclined to talk a good deal about "adjustment," a term that derived from pragmatism's central metaphor, the Darwinian adjustment or adaptation of the creature to its environment. Applied to social life, the biological metaphor was misleading in one respect and ambiguous in another. It was misleading because it pictured a cooperative struggle against nature, building bridges or fighting epidemics. Most social situations lack the unity of purpose given by a common natural enemy: the social "problem" is the exploitation of some people by other people. Like many Progressives, Dewey kept defining social problems in technical and technological terms, which evaded crucial considerations of power, class, and race.

The ambiguity in the term "adjustment" lay in the fact that Dewey meant two nearly opposite things by it. He meant a passive adaptation to the social environment, and he also meant mastery and control of it. In his educational writings Dewey sometimes talked about the need for workers to become conscious of the meaning of their work. This had a fine radical ring to it, but, put in terms of consciousness alone, it had a distinct oily flavor of "human relations" capitalism—ending the labor troubles in the cotton mills by treating the hands to edifying lectures on the history of the textile industry. Late in his life, when Dewey spoke of social adjustment, it turned out that he meant a revival of local democracy and workers' control of industry. That, however, was not always what he actually said. This ambiguous meaning of the term "adjustment" was a particularly serious drawback in the American context, because it reinforced the tendency of Dewey and other Progressives to conceive of social reform as a matter of assimilating immigrants into a society that despised them.

Many of the progressive intellectuals saw a new collectivism arising out of the central historical experience of their time, the industrialization of American life. Some were corporate collectivists, dreaming of rule by enlightened captains of industry. Others, like Veblen, dreamed of technocracy, rule by expert Bolshevik elites, scientists, and engineers. Unlike the technocrats, who made no bones about their elitism, Dewey remained a democrat; he was nonetheless profoundly influenced by Veblen, sharing Veblen's uncritical awe of the utopian potential of American industry. Dewey believed that modern technology promoted a rational, matter-of-fact industrial mentality among the masses, and like Veblen he bootlegged all sorts of hopeful moral, humane, and scientific virtues into his descriptions of the industrial order. Inevitably, he thought, a cooperative industrial commonwealth was going to replace capitalism.

Now it may be that, in the long run so derided by Lord Keynes, Dewey and Veblen were prophets; it may be that the imperatives of an advanced industrial order will move us all toward a society directed by intelligence. What was certainly true was that the Progressives, like more recent theorists of industrial development, drastically underestimated the strength of the corporate order and the grip of profit on American life. They hoped that planning would take the place of drift or the forces of the market, that the standards shaping social policy would be human needs and the welfare of the whole community; they were certain that history was rapidly converting these hopes to realities.

With the Progressives, Dewey thought that government and science would operate independently of politics. He shared their profound revulsion against politics, their weakness for technical solutions to political questions, their vain hope that institutions could do the job that only politics could do. The hope was reflected in Dewey's educational thought, for example, where, though he was a superb guide to the educational and social nature of the school community, he was a typical progressive reformer in promising that schools could solve basic issues of justice and equality. He thought he knew how schools could save society, when in fact all he knew were the conditions for getting decent schools.

With important exceptions in his ethics and educational writings —particularly chapter seven of *Democracy and Education* (1916)— the progressive Dewey took values for granted. Assuming that society was progressing toward good ends, he preoccupied himself with instrumental means and techniques. He criticized American life, but it was true, as Lewis Mumford charged, that he acquiesced in too much of it. In his own mind Dewey thought of himself as a populist radical, but from the outside he too often looked like a social engineer, preaching adjustment.

Two incidents illustrate the lack of critical political judgment in Progressive reform. The first is the strange case of the Gary, Indiana public schools. Both Dewey and Randolph Bourne, *The New Republic*'s cultural and educational critic, praised what came to be known as "The Gary Plan," a series of ideas put into effect by the Gary superintendent of schools. Dewey and Bourne liked these reforms because they made the schools lively and because they exemplified scientific principles of economy and efficiency—sacred words to Progressive ears. They were not prepared for what "scientific management" actually meant to most educators: in practice "The Gary Plan" boiled down to getting double and even triple use of the school plant by having twice as many children in one building and a rotating schedule of activities and rooms. The educators, in short, viewed the plan wholly as an administrative technique in the service of business and bureaucratic values totally at odds with any standards for a decent education. When the scheme was introduced to the New York City schools, Dewey had an opportunity to see a classic example of that exercise in bureaucratic manipulation, reform entrepreneurship, and ethnic and class warfare that Americans call education innovation. The reform mayor of New York and a motley coalition of reformers pushed the plan against the wishes of Jewish ghetto parents—who thought it was a plot to give their children a working-class education—and against the wishes of teachers and principals, who had never been consulted in the first place. There were riots all over the city —10,000 parents and children demonstrated in Brownsville—and the outraged voters threw the reformers out in the 1917 election. Dewey was slowly learning that school reform without the backing of teachers and parents was bound to be autocratic and reactionary. The reformers claimed to represent the public, but of course represented their own kind of interest group. This did not automatically discredit their ideas: it did make it imperative to analyze their class and ethnic biases.

Dewey was equally uncritical about war as a weapon of reform. He feared Prussian absolutism; when World War I seemed inevitable, he argued that the war effort could unite America, teach people how to cooperate, and bring about a new culture to replace the individualistic and capitalist culture. So for a time he was a booster for war, doing studies of alien populations opposed to the Allies, making the case for intelligently applied violence, and attacking pacifists like his friend Jane Addams for their sentimentality. What made Dewey's defense of the war so appalling was his opportunism, his identification with the warmakers, and his abdication of any responsibility to think clearly. Most of the *New Republic* staff shared Dewey's crackpot realism and his desire to be hard-boiled and effective; in fact they carried sentimental *Realpolitick* even farther than Dewey, tying their absurd dreams of national and international regeneration to such unlikely champions as Woodrow Wilson and the batty Colonel House. Dewey's enthusiasm for the war was brief and it was tempered by a habitual skepticism about great leaders and his growing alarm over the wartime suppression of civil liberties. In the end he had, however, committed the same sin as most of the rest of the *New Republic* editors: he had surrendered his critical judgment and his sense of common decency to a presumed direction that history was taking.

Randolph Bourne's famous attack on Dewey over the issue of the war is usually interpreted as Bourne's farewell to pragmatism. I think Bourne was making a point that Dewey later came to agree with: that instrumental values are only part of a complete philosophy; without a vision, an articulated set of values, and a grasp of politics, pragmatism could be twisted to serve any ends. Bourne was confessing that all the prewar reformers, including himself, had been insufficiently critical of American life. The men and women who had been raised in what Henry James called the "fool's paradise" of the prewar years had imagined that their private Utopias were being realized by what turned out to be questionable and sinister means.

Dewey finally saw that there was no conceivable relationship between his ideals and the ends for which the war was fought, and his basic vision underwent a change. This was the third phase of Dewey's career, beginning in the early twenties and continuing for the rest of his life, a period in which he was more publicly active than he ever had been before, producing an enormous amount of polemical journalism, as well as his two masterpieces, *Experience and Nature* (1925), and *Art as Experience* (1933). He changed his emphasis from the instrumental realms of science and technology to the human values to be served by science and technology, and radically deepened his critique of American life.

From being a progressive social engineer, Dewey became a utopian social critic, skeptical of progress, more and more aware of what was good about the good old days, and what was ominous about the industrial order. Morton White has pointed out that American philosophy before Dewey traditionally conceived of its task as the mediation of contrary realms of human experience; Romantic American philosophers like Emerson have characteristically vindicated morals, feelings, and esthetics against mechanistic and rationalistic science. In his progressive phase Dewey was a modernist rebel against these classic Romantic American traditions in the name of a new vision of science. Late in his life it became clear that Dewey's rebellion against Emerson and American philosophical tradition was strikingly Romantic and Emersonian in its aim: to make philosophy a criticism of experience from the standpoint of human aspirations. The late Dewey was trying to salvage the aspirations of American Romanticism without its craziness, to restore its deepest insights on a modest and empirical basis that did not exclude science.

The late Dewey continued to emphasize the scientific method as the only path to knowledge. He never abandoned his admiration for science as a model of all intelligent inquiry. He kept hoping that the spirit of science would pervade daily life. Yet now he drew an increasingly sharp contrast between the abstract, colorless instrumental realm of science and the intrinsic, richly human "consummatory" values of art, conversation, and shared experience. Once his inarticulate major premise had been the idea of scientific and industrial progress; now his central insight into industrial society was that it made people into machines. He still thought the industrial order could lead to a good life. He still believed in cooperation and planning; now he also insisted on workers' control of industry and a revival of local publics and face-to-face communities.

Art as Experience was the best statement of the late Dewey's chastened Romantic vision, with its profoundly esthetic core: good art was a paradigm of fulfilled experience, life at its most complete. Art was an exploration of imaginative possibilities, and hence ultimately, if indirectly, critical and moral. *Art as Experience* revealed Dewey's standards for a healthy society; it joined him to the great tradition of cultural prophecy attacking capitalism and industrial society in the name of an ideal of an integrated culture. From Coleridge and Arnold to the Leavises and T.S. Eliot, this has been in the main a traditionalist and elitist body of thought, although there has been a running socialist minority report from Ruskin and Morris, R.H. Tawney, Dewey, and, in our time, Raymond Williams.

In writing *Art as Experience,* Dewey was in fact reopening an important debate that started when Santayana, Henry James, and Henry Adams had attacked American life from an esthetic point of view, seeing art as a haven and a refuge from slums, immigrants, robber barons, boosters, bosses, philistines, and the consequences of unchecked technological growth. In the nineties, Dewey disliked the esthetes for their scorn for science, their escapism, their elitism, and their denial of the possibility or desirability of creating a democratic culture. By the 1930s he still disliked these things, but was prepared to acknowledge the penetration of the esthetes' critique of the prevailing forces in American life. This deepened his critical grasp of what was wrong.

There are interesting tensions in *Art as Experience.* One source of tension arose from Dewey's view of a common culture in which the arts would be a force, esthetic but moral too, educating the community and preserving and extending its better values in the face of greed, vulgarity, and ignorance. Dewey was committed to a humanist art, yet he was aware of the fact that much of the best, as well as the worst, modern art and literature has been produced by men whose values were far from being humanist or liberal. Dewey never reconciled his ideal of a healthy culture with the deep alienation of twentieth-century art.

There was another tension in the book. As a work of esthetics, *Art as Experience* was curiously reticent about standards of judgment; yet in a sense its entire theme was the need for critical intellectual standards. It reflects the cultural dilemma of every American democrat who wants to establish a basis for making artistic, intellectual, and moral judgments. On the whole, American democratic and populist traditions have tended to deny the possibility of ordering American life by any common values. The reason for this is obvious. Those who appeal to standards of any sort have usually been elitists; our history is full of ugly attempts on the part of elites to straighten out the masses. Thus, Dewey's intellectual ancestor, Horace Mann, argued that citizens in a democracy required the moral discipline of social institutions like schools, because democracy demanded more of human nature than other forms of government.

This was not a bad point, in theory. Given the actual class and ethnic realities of the American scene, however, a plea for social and moral discipline was a political weapon in the hands of ascendant groups against immigrants and the lower classes. Recent historians have done a good job of dissecting American reform, and we now take a more interesting and dour point of view about the motives of reformers in general. Having unmasked many benign figures in the traditional reform pantheon for the elitists and racists that they often were, those of us committed to democracy should be prepared to concede that American popular traditions have also left much to be desired. Some of the reformers stood for ideals that, however abused, were sadly missing from American life: the ideal of a public good that was more than the numerical sum of private goods; the belief that American life could be ordered in terms of values. Dewey was attempting the very difficult task of infusing American populist traditions with a concern for common moral, intellectual, and cultural standards. In the end he came to appreciate what most Progressive reformers missed, the enduring vitality in American pluralism: its revolt against any single group's definition of what was American. He leaned more and more toward traditions of local democracy and pluralism. Yet he also saw that a revival of these traditions would be reactionary without a commitment to universal values and shared standards. Standards would not be handed down by tradition or religious authority. There was no legitimate source of authority in the modern world except the rational, democratic process of thought and evaluation—the common social pursuit Dewey kept calling, vaguely and misleadingly, "the method of intelligence."

There are problems in reading Dewey today. One major problem is his writing style, which has the monotonous consistency of peanut butter. William James cursed it as God-damnable, and Justice Holmes once captured both the excitement and the difficulty of *Experience and Nature* by describing it as "what God would have spoken had he been inarticulate, but keenly desirous to tell you how it was."

Like many in his generation, Dewey was in revolt against lofty sentiments and fine writing, so his style was in part a rebellion against

Style. He was helped in this studied disregard of the graceful by a tin ear that simply could not hear the difference between "irrelevance" and "irrelevancy." Like Emerson he was at his best lecturing, but there was a lack of control and discipline even in the best lectures. The emotion filtered through the dry cracks at the wrong moments. In its energy, its mixed modes, its appetite for information, its chaos and dullness, and above all in its groping, muffled desire to say something about all of experience, a book like *Democracy and Education* resembles the formless, unfulfilled novels of Theodore Dreiser.

Among other things, a style tells you whether someone is thinking clearly. Dewey did not always want to think clearly. He wanted to erase many of the distinctions by which philosophy, common sense, and good style have sought to order discourse about the world, to reintegrate mind and body, self and society, truth and morals. He had a radically Protestant dread of idolatry, a sense of horror at the scandalous worship of words and images instead of the shifting, precarious, beautiful reality of actual experience. At his best Dewey was attempting to write a natural history of experience, to portray our logical judgments and moral decisions as they actually occur in encounters and transactions with other people. This enterprise took him to the borders of art, which is why *Art as Experience* is so important for understanding him, a guide to his ambitions and a key to the sense of incompletion and frustration that pervades so many of his works. The desire to do a natural history of living experience, thinking and valuing on the wing, lay behind Dewey's Socratic insistence that knowledge and virtue are one; it was probably responsible for his frequent confusions of fact and value, which also stemmed from something he shared with the late, metaphysical William James: a conviction that any healthy sense of virtue had to reflect our actual biological and social natures, which were subject to empirical investigation. This and the insight that in actual fact truth and morals are intertwined are aspects of pragmatism's legacy that are worth preserving.

In the realm of educational thought and practice, Dewey's legacy is still very much with us, and remains a lasting influence on our own struggles for better education. Although his progressive hopes sometimes made him a very misleading guide to larger macro issues concerning schools, he continues to be an extraordinary source of insight into the micro realm of classrooms, learning, and pedagogy. Thoughtful educators keep returning to Dewey's efforts to re-establish a high Romantic synthesis of science and feeling on a modestly empirical footing. The marriage of science and Romantic phenomenology that the best progressive minds sought remains a goal today, although we are certainly no nearer to it than Dewey or his contemporaries. He tried at first to make a clean break with America's Romantic past; later he attempted to come to terms with it. Each generation in our profoundly Romantic culture fights this same battle in different terms. Romanticism was as central to Dewey's educational thought as the issue of populism was to his social thought. Both are central issues for us today.

All the manifold varieties of Romanticism are protests on behalf of the concrete and the organic against the abstract and mechanistic. There is, however, a distinction between low and high Romanticism. In education and other realms, low Romanticism has traditionally exalted the heart over the head, celebrating the irrational and intuitive, and fearing science and rationality. It is a viewpoint and mood that is perhaps especially widespread today. High Romanticism, on the other hand, is the recurring search for a saving middle ground between the icy reductions of analysis and the undisciplined craziness of the solitary Romantic ego. High romanticism welcomes science and reason within their proper domains. Its real enemy is not reason, but scientism—all the partial, limited modes of thinking that deny the power and autonomy of the imagination and falsely claim to render a complete account of human existence. High romanticism is thus a quest for a mediating vision in which reason reinforces emotion in the exercise of the imagination. This was pragmatism's ultimate goal; it was a Romantic goal, even though no one was ever less of a Romantic by temperament than John Dewey. In the end, for all his commitment to the scientific method, Dewey was trying to be Emerson's heir in mediating between the abstractions of science and the values of concrete experience. *Art as Experience* was an effort to transcend the Romantic past and to preserve its best insights. Its difficult, unfinished program meant acknowledging the validity of the standards and instrumentalities of science as well as legitimating the intrinsic "consummatory" values of art and shared human experience. Dewey's grand educational synthesis was never completed; his educational views suffered by being a product of his middle years. *Art as Experience* contains the richest educational implications of any of his works; yet education is not listed in its index.

Dewey was trying to place man within the framework of a scientific universe and illuminate the ends science should serve; to naturalize man and to humanize science. For Dewey the activity of art offers some important hints at what a synthesis of science and feeling might look like. Art and science were both deeply intellectual realms to Dewey, calling for discipline, standards, and judgment. Each, however, was involved with different sorts of meanings. Science dealt with that class of meanings posing abstract claims to truth, or what Dewey ended up calling "warranted assertability." Art dealt with concrete meanings. Science mapped the world. Art told what it was like to walk through its greenness.

There is another point about science and education that the philosopher David Hawkins makes in a recent book, *The Informed Vision.* Hawkins, long interested in the education of young children and sharing some of Dewey's views, argues that the practice of science —the actual process of discovery, the blend of synthesis, guess, and analysis—is more akin to art than the actual results of science. It is true that scientific results have to be expressed in terms of abstract symbols and universal standards of verification; nevertheless, pursuing science as a concrete endeavor involves an interplay of hand, eye, materials, and intuition that has parallels with creative work in art. In thinking of science as something apart from the intuitive and the concrete, and in thinking of art as something divorced from thought, education has neglected the true richness of both science and art.

Dewey thought that the old idea of science as analysis and art as synthesis was a misleading simplification, having no more validity than the Cartesian fiction of the mind as a lonely ghost inside the body's machine. Not did he believe that science and art had to be in conflict, although he was painfully aware of the remoteness of the two realms in the splintered American culture. Art and science for Dewey were different points in the rhythm of the same dance of human imagination over experience. In both we come to understand the world by acting upon it.

As Hawkins also points out, Dewey was profoundly right to see an affinity between one style of scientific work and the active probings and explorings of children in good classrooms. Anyone who has watched the practice of art and science in such settings recognizes the quality of absorbed participation that reigns. Good learning in science and art and other subjects has common elements of freshness, absorption, and participation. The play between children's minds and materials illustrates the fleeting high Romantic goal of reasoned reinforcement of the imagination.

Like Dewey, Hawkins urges teachers today to look beneath the surface of achieved and codified scientific knowledge to the underlying life of scientific inquiry so few people ever take part in. Dewey looked with anthropological horror at the spectacle of a culture whose material base was profoundly shaped by science, but whose people did not understand science. This problem has grown worse in the years since Dewey wrote. Science has become an enormous, often malign force in our society. Although it raises the GNP, it also fights our wars, helps ruin our environment, and threatens us with annihilation. This is the side of science we see most clearly. Most of us are less able to perceive that science is also a way of thought that ought to enrich our lives. The fact that specialized science expresses a mode of living and thinking available only to an elite minority dismays Hawkins as much today as it dismayed Dewey years ago. The concern is political in part; if knowledge is power, as it surely is, then elite control of science is a threat to all of us. Politics aside, however, there is something disgraceful about a culture whose people are ignorant of their material and intellectual underpinnings; in which the sullen victims of the perversions of science and technology curse the day the genie ever left the bottle and stand superstitiously and passively awaiting the next catastrophe. Dewey took insufficient account of the fact that his ideal of science as an individual artisan's craft did not square with the bureaucratic workings of that highly political institution we might call Big Science. The progressive intellectuals did not anticipate the nightmarish potential of Big Science. Yet Dewey's contemporary followers are surely right in noting that science is all too rarely pursued for its own sake, as a way of informing and liberating our vision. Like education itself, science is made to serve too many questionable outside masters.

Dewey never reworked his later emphasis on concrete values back into his formulations of science—he seems to have been ignorant of the actual practice of science, and was thus apt to emphasize scientific method to the neglect of the actual content that all vital method must feed on. He understood, but sometimes forgot to mention, the intrinsic pleasure of science. Although today we find Dewey's efforts to understand science and art essential first steps in framing our own ideas about education, there are moments when Dewey seems singularly exasperating. Most of all, perhaps, we balk at the tone, the blandness, the rhetorical ease with which he achieves his harmonies and mediations of divergent realms. We grow impatient with the innocent limits of his social imagination, and his failure to see the way that schools are implicated in issues of power, social class, and race. Yet we keep coming back to his vision: we too work toward a style of education that would reflect a high Romantic synthesis of the values of reason and human community. We, too, are looking for a mediation of reason, feeling, and imagination, an education that, beginning in play and evolving into apprenticeship, encourages children to learn both a reverence for concrete experience and an active mastery of the proper place of symbols and abstractions in a scientific world.

The utopian complexity of Dewey's commitments means that each generation of his readers picks out a different set of emphases. Recent progressive thought and practice has not shared Dewey's interest in schools as social, democratic, and moral communities. This seems to me a pity. The reasons for our neglect of the social dimensions of learning are many; some of us are still spooked by the way classic progressive thought kept getting twisted into a rationale for conformity and groupiness. Much of the best recent work in Dewey's footsteps has concentrated on two problems: the high Romantic synthesis, and the challenge to make knowledge accessible to childrens active explorations along myriads of individual pathways. Both are aspirations; scarcely achievements.

Anyone speaking on behalf of even a portion of Dewey's grand program must speak humbly and doggedly, with what somebody once called the authority of failure. Plainly we must live with more pain in our hopes for the schools than the Progressives felt, or showed. In part the pain reflects America's continuing lack of two necessary perspectives on schools. We are, like the Progressives, still largely unwilling to admit that school is only one part of children's lives, and not the major part at that. We continue to make vast claims on the schools. And the very size of these claims leads us to the second error in perspective, our habitual neglect of the smaller, daily possibilities of our educational institutions. In the end, what allowed Dewey to shake loose from his grandiose Progressive utopianism was his hard-headed focus on the importance of the present moments in teachers' and childrens' lives, the day-to-day quality of life in the classroom.

Dewey would have been a friendly but severe critic of the second round of the New Education. He was deeply disappointed by the turn the first progressive era took, and he would have been critical of much recent work too. He was ever impatient with the New Education's chronic susceptibility to low, irrational romanticism, with its anti-intellectualism, it lack of confidence in legitimate adult authority, and its quite mistaken notion that its ideas invalidate all traditional practice and standards. Yet good recent, on-going work shows the strengths of progressivism at its best. Child-centered Progressives like Dewey believed that education's most radical step was helping children learn to think. Without discounting the importance of skills, they pointed to the significance of the kind of active learning that goes on in play, and showed in actual practice the effectiveness of pedagogies that move children from play to more disciplined work. They thought that childrens' present lives ought to be as important to their teachers as their futures are; that schools—in a valid, if much-abused formulation—were life, as well as preparation for life.

The child-centered Progressives had hopes for the social functions of schools as well. They wanted schools to become democratic, cooperative communities of adults and children. They worked against the historically conformist grain of American education, with its obsession for superordinate goals, its neglect of daily practice, and its search for a one best system to impose on teachers and children. They emphasized children's diversity and stressed the educational importance of the fact that childhood is a time of intellectual construction. Implicit in much of what figures like Dewey wrote was a dissent from an essentially economic view of the role of education. Dewey opposed the mainstream progressive educators; the administrative Progressives, as historian David Tyack calls them. They were busily intent on reordering schools along corporate and managerial lines; schools were to be sieves for sorting out students according to their future jobs. Since Dewey's time, child-centered thought and pedagogy has been a distinctly minority viewpoint in American education, generally more influential at the lower levels of schooling than in higher grades.

The New Education appears in fits and starts in educational theory and practice partly because we are a faddish culture and rarely build on the past in a cumulative way. It keeps reappearing, however, because it raises perennial questions. Each generation re-examines Dewey's complex educational legacy on new terms.

Dewey's progressive faith in science itself does not move us very much today. We are skeptical of his assumption that the anguish of living will diminish as knowledge grows. For one thing, the social sciences do not seem impressively cumulative in their wisdom; Dewey plainly underestimated the practical and moral problems involved in applying experimental science to people. He made a characteristic progressive mistake in neglecting the political character of all institutions, including science. I would agree with Dewey on the validity of the ideal of science. What else do we have to go by but science, broadly understood—the appeal to evidence, to logic, to inquiry validated by open public processes of criticism and debate? But the ideal is only fitfully represented by the institution called science. This is more obvious to us than to Dewey's generation. Every day we witness scientific rationalism harnessed to evil and even crazy political ends. In the middle of a panic-stricken flight from rationalism and the consequences of a perverted science and technology, it is useful to remind ourselves, with Dewey, that science ought to be a humane liberal pursuit, a path to liberation.

In social thought we are apt to prefer the late Dewey to the progressive social engineer. Dewey was wrong to ignore the politics of institutions—like the Bolsheviks, the Progressives kept forgetting that what they were mainly doing was building bureaucracies—but he was right about the need to create institutions. Being more conscious of the dangers of bureaucracy, we will want to fashion our institutions after the voluntaristic, pluralistic spirit of the late Dewey. Going beyond the world the Progressives left us will involve creating institutions on a human scale, and professions that truly serve clients. It will involve working for political coalitions to redistribute wealth and power, for without politics, attempts at reform will repeat the history of progressivism. Lacking politics, progressivism was in the end merely the ideology of liberal professionals and reformers. For a time Dewey looked like the ideal spokesman for the new bureaucratic order of professionals, managers, and experts. Just as John Stuart Mill outgrew the desolate calculations of Jeremy Bentham's Utilitarianism, Dewey transcended the bleak managerial scientism of the progressive outlook. Like Mill, Dewey will be remembered for the way he carried liberal thought to the edge of something quite different from what it started out to be.

Dewey's philosophy, which was really quite simple, reflected an enduring outlook—the outlook of Daedalus, the legendary Greek craftsman who built the famous maze, designed wonderful gold jewelry, and mastered the secret of flight. Daedalus is *homo faber;* he believes that we know what we can make and he scorns superstition, hero worship, and irrationality of any sort, glorying in the triumphs of artisans, builders, engineers, and artists. The temperament has practical strength and a number of theoretical weaknesses. It is not sympathetic to contemplation; it is suspicious of politics; it often does violence to nature; and it is afraid of the past. Dewey never conquered his fear of the past, which is perhaps why so many ghosts of old philosophical issues hover over all his work, and why his psychology has so little to say about the inner life. He never examined his own history, and he never understood the American past—the American history taught in Dewey's experimental elementary school was a pageant of technological cooperation, not the chronicle of violence and oppression that were equally part of the story.

Dewey's basic point of view was never tragic. It was comic, based on the healing potential of ordinary social experience, but it deepened and he came to appreciate realms he had once neglected. *Experience and Nature* is far in spirit from the technological imperialism of Dewey's earlier instrumentalism, suffused with a serene sense that man is within nature like Jonah in the belly of the whale. It turned out that Dewey's instrumental universe had room for many mansions, including the houses of contemplation, pain, and death.

In politics, after he stopped believing in technical solutions, levers to pull to bring about Utopia, he emphasized grass-roots change, and the necessity of diverse political coalitions to move a diverse and various country. He worked to build alliances between workers and professionals and the public in various ways, ranging from active support of democratic and highly political union movements to consumer and parents' groups and third parties, never quite settling on one means, never discovering a single source of social salvation, an increasingly lonely *philosophe* of a wispy revolution that never came about. He did not give up on the possibility of a democratic cooperative America. The wholeness of his late perspective, the cumulative nature of his concern, the steadiness of application, the lack of bitterness, made up for his terrible vagueness. He closed a late autobiographical sketch with these words: "Forty years spent wandering in the wilderness like that of the present is not a sad fate—unless one attempts to make himself believe that the wilderness is after all itself the promised land."

George Orwell once called Henry Miller "a Whitman among the corpses." He was pointing to the difficulty of working within the celebratory Romantic vein on the grim material of twentieth-century life. Dewey was struggling to be an Emerson among the dynamos, the bureaucracies, and the colossal wars of our recent past.

4

A Failure of Political Imagination

Daniel Bell's fat book *The Coming of Post-Industrial Society* is, as its subtitle says, "a venture in social forecasting," an attempt to predict some of the main trends in the twenty or so years remaining to us as we slouch toward the year 2000. Of all people Bell ought to be wary of the banana peel history enjoys tossing in the path of social forecasters. In the late 1950s and early 1960s he was a prominent member of a group of intellectuals who proclaimed "the end of ideology." The idea was that the historic antagonism of labor and capital was finished, at least in economically advanced nations; class warfare would no longer be the central feature of politics. Instead, neutral experts would benignly preside over a rational distribution of an ever-increasing Gross National Product. The traditional concerns of the left—from the demands of social democrats for justice and equality to the millenarian fantasies of the apocalyptic left—were retrograde and, historically speaking, irrelevant.

The second half of the sixties made a hash of these predictions. All the advanced Western nations witnessed intensely ideological student uprisings. (The fact that the mood of the time of troubles on the campus has melted away, leaving no trace except for painful memories, indicates nothing at all about the ideological fervor involved; the depth of feeling behind the various revolutions of 1848 in Europe cannot be denied, yet they too left little historical residue.) In this country there were unprecedented minority rebellions. And in all the industrialized nations there were waves of strikes and worker unrest, the likes of which had not been seen since the 1930s.

Events aside, there were also intellectual problems with "the end of ideology," genuine difficulties that were often obscured in the hail of illiterate and sectarian abuse that greeted it. The whole argument rested on assumptions that turned out to be themselves ideological. For one thing it assumed that individual choices in the free market were the best mechanism for establishing social priorities—an assumption suspiciously like capitalist ideology. For another it assumed (a corollary assumption that somehow didn't correlate) that experts could make proper decisions without recourse to moral or political values, the old deluded technocratic dream that science would end the need for the turbulent, messy realm of politics.

Now, as I read him, Bell appears to have reversed himself on a number of key points. *The Coming of Post-Industrial Society* is among other things a forceful attack on the technocratic doctrine that the rise of experts will bring about the fall of politics and usher in a new era of smoothly engineered social peace. Bell still thinks that in the coming order, which he calls "post-industrial society," there will be more conscious guidance of the economy, more expertise, and a greater social role for science and theoretical knowledge. He no longer however believes that this will fulfill the technocratic visions of St. Simon, Thorstein Veblen, or, I might add, Daniel Bell. Now Bell says that the market system is no longer capable of setting adequate social priorities. Choices once left up to the private individual will increasingly become political matters, questions of conscious, communal deliberation. So much for both capitalism and technocracy.

Bell arrives at this arresting reversal in the course of an extended analysis of the shift from industrial to post-industrial society. (These terms are theoretical constructs, abstract paradigms of social trends in the next three decades.) Up to yesterday, as history goes, we had been living in industrial society—Bell dates its end in the 1940s and 1950s. The central features of industrial society as Bell describes it were the industrial corporation as the prototypical social institution; the decisive impact of the machine on the character of work; and the persistent conflict of interest between labor and capital. In the post-industrial order, Bell argues, all these things change. The corporation becomes less central because competing institutions arise and because corporations themselves undergo inner transformations; control shifts from owners to managers, and big firms develop the capacity to capitalize future growth out of their own profits rather than outside investments. The primary image of work is no longer a man standing over a machine, but people dealing with other people. The relative size of the industrial proletariat declines, as new technical and professional strata grow in the service sectors, especially the government and nonprofit sectors, of the economy. The labor issue, which overshadowed all others in industrial society, is "encapsulated" in the post-industrial order; although there are still conflicts of interest over salaries and work conditions, politics is less a class matter and more a search for a general public interest for the government to pursue as it intervenes more and more in the economy.

Bell says that post-industrial society will be shaken by incessant conflict, not the old Marxist kind but one group after another appealing to the political realm to redistribute wealth and to substantiate conflicting rights and interests. In all the scuffling and tumult the main conflict will take the form of a clash between two opposed modes of thought, which Bell calls the "economic" and the "sociologizing." The economic mode stresses functional efficiency and the management of things; its prime value is economic growth, the corollary to which, at least in the capitalist West, has been increased individual consumption. The sociologizing mode sets broader communal, noneconomic goals, entailing reductions in output and loss of efficiency. In industrial society economic values prevailed; post-industrial society, Bell thinks, will represent the triumph of sociologizing.

Staring up at this vast panoramic canvas, the reader naturally grows curious to know whether Bell is right. In certain respects he is quite convincing, as when he forecasts a society wracked by competing demands on the political realm: to include previously excluded groups, to distribute income more equally, to readjust the relative size of public and private sectors, to balance individual and social goals, to square demands for increased participation with a greater degree of expertise and professionalism. In other respects Bell seems to me a misleading guide.

Take the whole business about labor. Much of his argument that the labor issue will be less central in post-industrial society rests on changes in the labor force. A majority of workers is no longer engaged in manufacturing or farming, but in the service sector: trade, finance, health, research, education, government. (One in six workers is now in the pay of one of the 80,000 or so units of American government.) By 1980 official estimates reckon that seven in ten workers will be in the service sector. White-collar jobs already outnumber blue five to four.

Bell thinks these dramatic changes decisively alter the labor issue, both because the "old" industrial working class is declining in relative numbers and because the "new" strata will not act the same way as the old industrial working class. I disagree. The relative proportion of blue-collar industrial workers is declining, yet in absolute numbers they are increasing. After some thirty years of post-industrial life, semiskilled work—the human cog in the industrial machine—is still the largest single job category. The 1980 projections are that 35 million workers will man Bell's post-industrial service sectors of the economy; there will still be nearly as many workers—33 million—in the old industrial areas of manufacturing, construction, and mining. This is certainly an odd way to exit from the stage of history.

Moreover, as he concedes, there are reasons for thinking that the industrial working class will be much more militant and social-minded in coming decades. The percentage of foreign-born is declining sharply, thus ending one of the historic sources of divisiveness among American workers. Workers will be well-educated in the future, most with high-school degrees and many with some college or junior college experience. For the first time in history, American blue-collar workers are approaching the classic Marxist picture of a well-educated, culturally homogeneous political force. And to judge from recent disputes, the growing agenda of working-class discontent will include many old as well as new demands. Better pay will certainly remain an important issue as long as a majority of the American people do not enjoy what the government defines as a moderate standard of living. Wretched and dangerous conditions of work—still outside the control of even relatively affluent workers—are likely to be a major point of dispute. What were once seen as fringe benefits will be more central: pensions, health insurance and care, vacations. Many of these latter sorts of demands involve what might be called the social component of the standard of living; they turn into political demands for amenities, rights, and services that only government can provide.

As a percentage of the total labor force, union membership is just what it was in 1947. Yet as Bell notes, the union movement is bigger than ever in absolute numbers, and—partly because of the politicizing of economic issues he describes—it has more political power than ever before in American history. The political potential of a class is in part a reflection of how easy it is to organize; as long as an important base of the economy is industry and industrial productivity —as long as factories exist—it will probably be easier to organize industrial workers than most other groups. (Small units of work and a high proportion of women have traditionally plagued efforts at organizing the service sector, although this may be changing.) As we move from a market system to one in which economic decisions are made through politics, it seems to me that the industrial working class will have more, rather than less, weight in the scheme of things, because it will be the best-organized counterforce to corporate power. Certainly unions will remain decisive in the hopes for the future of a majority of black and minority workers, since despite the phenomenal increase in black professional and technical workers in the sixties, most blacks are still in the ranks of the semiskilled.

Then there are the new strata of educated labor. Through sixty years or so of socialist debate about the "new" working classes, there has run a bright thread of wishful thinking, as one radical theorist after another has tried to locate historical successors to Marx's proletariat. Most attempts to identify the new social saviors have ignored the eagerness of educated labor for marks of status to set it off from blue-collar labor, and the degree to which educated and technically skilled workers continue to serve the goals of the institutions for which they work. Nevertheless, when all this is said, educated workers in many of the service, government, technological, and nonprofit areas of the economy tend to be critical of the system, feel no particular vested interest in capitalism, and favor a planned economy. Middle class in style of life and professional aspirations, they are subject to chafing industrial or bureaucratic discipline, and, increasingly, the threat of watching their wages vanish in the inflation whirlwind, or of losing their jobs entirely. Most important of all, they are rapidly being organized, and account for the bulk of new union membership. Whether educated labor will turn toward a defensive guild unionism mainly concerned with maintaining its position, or whether it will move to assert its very real interest in a different set of national priorities is one of the most interesting questions facing the American labor movement. We may get a glimmering of these various possibilities in the aftermath of the merger of the American Federation of Teachers with the National Education Association—which will create the second largest American union—and in the emerging self-definitions of municipal and government unions, health workers, and professionals.

Given the enormous political potential of both old and new working classes, it is hard to see why Bell thinks the labor problem will be any more "encapsulated" in post-industrial society than it was in the industrial past. To be sure, future labor issues will be charged with racial, ethnic, religious, and cultural complexities, but that has always been true of American life. If you had predicted many aspects of American history on the basis of social class alone, you would often have been wrong, which is not at all to deny the decisive importance of social class. Organized labor will not of course always embody everybody's interests in a largely unorganized society. In the 1960s important elements of labor were backward on key issues: race (especially the building trades), the Vietnam War, the Cold War. Similarly in the seventies it is quite likely that portions of the labor movement will be protectionist and ignorant of international issues such as the need to control multinational corporations, opposed to disarmament and blind to environmental questions. Nonetheless the old industrial and the new post-industrial unions are at the moment the only effectively organized part of the complicated political coalition that will have to be built to press for Bell's sociologizing goals. American labor, which so far has been a class movement to temper the effects of capitalism without changing capitalism itself, will have to become more consciously socialminded. Whether it will remains to be seen.

Though Bell does give us a stormy picture of strife in post-industrial society, and though that is in somber contrast to the placid future anticipated by "the end of ideology", there is still a corner of Bell's mind that recoils from conflict, longing for some automatic, apolitical means by which sociologizing values will tame the corporate order. Bell's discussion of the future of the American corporation reflects this optimism, relying heavily on the invisible hands tugging on invisible wires that were such an important part of the stage machinery for "the end of ideology." Somehow as new and more personal forms of corporate organization emerge, as new social types develop, and as rival institutions to business grow, the corporation will slide with effortless grace from the economizing to the sociologizing end of the spectrum.

Nowhere in the course of this agreeable fiction does Bell acknowledge that asserting a public interest over the corporations will require leverage against the corporations the political realm does not in fact now possess. This omission is all the more striking in view of Bell's clear sense that the era of social peace the corporations have enjoyed is not likely to return. The environmental issue is only the first of many issues that may awaken Americans to the divergence between corporate and public interests. The drawbacks to the corporate outlook are the same as those of what Bell calls the economic mode of looking at things. It is concerned with economic goods alone, whereas many of the goods that count for so much in our own reckoning of our well-being do not even show up in economists' calculations. The GNP measures wealth, not our true welfare, giving equal weight to expenditures on nerve gas and money spent for schools and hospitals. Indeed as Bell notes, a major problem with our present system of social accounting is that it only measures costs, not benefits, assessing health services for example in terms of money spent on drugs and fees and not by numbers of people cured. A second flaw in the economic outlook is that unplanned technological growth generates more and more of what economists call "externalities," costs of private economic acts passed on to the public, such as the air pollution from auto exhaust. Market prices do not reflect the true social costs of many of our goods, and Bell is undoubtedly correct in thinking that a major political issue of the 1970s will be deciding who is to foot the bill for these externalities. A third difficulty with the economic view is that it emphasizes individual, private consumption, which makes planning impossible and systematically creates an imbalance between public and private sectors. We are not as affluent as we like to think; our wealth is heavily mortgaged by unpaid debts to the poor, the old, the minorities, the victims of technological progress, and the starved public sector.

Bell is well aware that the major problem of post-industrial society is the unregulated character of the economy and the lack of public control over corporate power. Apart from his appeal to politicians, for whom he now has the dim reverence he once reserved for experts, he offers no plausible explanation of how a public interest can prevail over private corporate interests. His notion of sociologizing contains communal values, but is empty of sources of power to achieve these noneconomic goals; his notions of politics are similarly devoid of thoughts *about* power. Yet he has a good grasp of why politics will matter more as time goes on. The emergence of a truly national, interdependent society, foreign policy and the impingement of other nations on our daily life, the need for long-range planning and control of the economy, the growing social role of expertise—all of which in the end are products of technological change—help explain why the executive branch of government is now so powerfully swollen in all the advanced nations, casting its shadow over every aspect of life.

There is no doubt that politics will control more and more of our lives. The question is: who will control politics? Now we are beginning to recognize the danger to our rights posed by the clandestine national security machinery perfected in the Cold War. It is also obvious that the existing integration of corporate and political power is not in the interests of a majority of Americans. What we seem to be getting—what ought to cause Daniel Bell some anxiety over the redeeming potential of politics as it now operates—is an American style of bureaucratic collectivism, run for private corporate interests in very much the same way that Mr. Brezhnev and his colleagues preside over a collectivism run for the private benefit of the Soviet elites.

During the thaw in Czech intellectual life, a fascinating study along the line of Bell's book appeared. Radovan Richta and his colleagues argued in *Civilization at the Crossroads* (1967) that the advanced nations in both East and West were building a new class structure and a new ruling class. They foresaw a ruling class of professional and technical elites whose creative and free-wheeling styles of living and working would contrast starkly with the monotonous lives of working-class drudges. The Czechs, whose experience of arbitrary power is extensive, were particularly alarmed at the huge social cleavages that put the destiny of the masses in the hands of educated elites. For Bell this is not even a problem. Toward the end of his book he describes the new American attack on meritocracy—making some good criticisms of the excesses of the demand for total participation—but he misses what the Czechs see vividly: the problem of enormous disparities in wealth and power, and the resulting inevitable injustice and corruption.

The only way of arriving at "sociologizing" goals—and of serving the public interest in that manner—is to make American society more democratic and equal. My sense of justice is offended when I learn that the wage differential between the lowest and highest paid workers in American industry is 30 to 1, but apart from abstract outrage I recognize that this degree of economic inequality is also a political menace. As long as it exists, attempts to gain control over the economy will probably be subverted by the capacity of great wealth to veto policy or bend it to its will. The objection to enormous inequality is not simply the fact that some people take home bigger paychecks; the objection is that it sets in motion systematic processes whereby the effects of private and public spending are antisocial, and public policy benefits the wealthy and powerful. There is a tough core of Madisonian realism beneath the often perfervid rhetoric of the new egalitarianism, and Bell fails to come to terms with it.

This is mainly a failure of political imagination. Bell does not understand the argument for equality or the need for mass-based institutions to counter the private power of corporate wealth—unions, highly political professional groups, reformed political parties. For all his new faith in politics, Bell feels a distaste for such necessities; he is not comfortable with political realities or our political traditions. The revival of interest in defending and expanding people's constitutional rights upsets him, and he sees only the dark side of the new mood of populism, the sour-bellied paranoia, the contempt for intellectual standards and legitimate authority, the potential for demagoguery. He neglects the old hunger for equality and justice, and the determination to defend popular rights against arbitrary political and economic power.

One of the most intriguing ideas in the book is the notion that culture—the expressive and symbolic life of society—has achieved a certain degree of autonomy and is in fact hostile to middle-class values and capitalism. Conservative "structural" sociologists and radical theorists alike have long posed the idea of a social system, an interwoven totality of values, social structure, and economic institutions. Bell thinks there *was* a system but that now it is breaking down: the unity of economics and social character so pronounced in the flush heyday of capitalism is disintegrating. A sign of this is the gap between the social structure and the cultural realm. Mass production and consumption are destroying the Protestant ethic; the arena of work still exacts rigid industrial and bureaucratic discipline, but in the realm of consumption, prodigality, display, and self-expression reign. At the same time an important shift in intellectual history has taken place: the Romantic, antinomian and antibourgeois ideas of a handful of nineteenth-century artists and literary rebels now fill the minds of masses of people—Dostoyevsky's characters hitch rides in our streets. These changes, together with the sheer expansion in numbers of the intellectual classes, have produced a mass adversary culture especially attractive to the educated young.

Bell gives a more accurate anatomy of this new cultural consciousness than uncritical theorists like Charles Reich. At its best the adversary culture has created rather than destroyed form, but its worst traits are far from life-enhancing, and this needs saying too. The celebrants of the counterculture are committing the great historic sin of intellectuals: abandoning the responsibility to make critical judgments, letting some outside arbiter—the party, the movement, the status quo, historical trends—settle the crucial question of values.

The example of the cultural realm coming unstuck from the system is only part of Bell's general argument that the society we see emerging is less of a totality than bourgeois society, with its common values and social character. Bell is attempting to draw a pluralistic map of American reality to set against both radical and "structural" theories. I believe he is right in saying that life in America is growing more fragmented and diverse, more pluralistic and less part of a whole than before, and the contradictions and tensions he points to must be accounted for by any satisfactory theory. It is important to replace vulgar generalities about the System with precise information about the way that politics, the economy, and the culture operate in distinct and often divergent ways. Yet Bell offers no evidence that status, wealth, and power—to take three important categories of analysis— are more separate now than in the past, and his ultimately aimless pluralism fails even to explore the relationship of wealth to power.

This same sense—of questions blurred rather than defined—weakens the final portions of Bell's absorbing discussion of science in the new order. He draws a distinction between the traditional norm of science and what he calls Big Science—the difference between the ideal and the highly political and far from disinterested institution of science, with its bureaucracies, entrepreneurs, operators, and crooks. He defends the ideal of science as a norm of open public deliberation and rational thought, and I agree with him: the ideal needs particular defending at a time of panicky retreat from the consequences of perverted science and technology. Just as the Protestant ethic became an ideology concealing capitalist reality, and socialism in the Soviet Union came to mask the rule of the elites, so, he says, science risks displacement by politics as the ideology of the post-industrial order. For all the growing intellectual and social sway of science, the major changes in America in the last forty years—the managed economy, the welfare state, the military arsenals of the preparedness state —came about for political reasons. War as an instrument of politics brought planning, science, and expertise into government.

Bell notes this subservience of Big Science to the political realm, but fails to follow through and examine the problematic relationship of science and expertise to politics. Nor, apart from insisting on the growing influence of social science, does he analyze its political dimension or suggest that there might be problems ahead with the highly political institution we may one day call Big Social Science. He plausibly describes the university as a central institution in the new order of things, yet fails to give us the sort of political analysis that would illuminate the relationship between the ideal of the university and its institutional realities. In the universities as in the professions we are in for stormy years: valuable traditions, well worth preserving, are going to be threatened at the same time that indefensible vested interests need to be unmasked. To sort the one from the other will take a kind of political intelligence Bell lacks.

I would especially like to see Bell and other theorists of postindustrialism elaborate on the idea that education is itself the protypical "post-industrial" activity. Organized knowledge does seem to play a greater role in politics, yet the current shambles of our economic and political life makes it hard to feel that there have been great advances in our understanding of ourselves or our mysterious society. The university disciplines seem increasingly specialized; unable to inform general publics, let alone contribute to enlivening school curriculums.

The sheer expansion of mass schooling, and especially mass university education, is striking, however. Children and youth today spend much more time in school, for many more years than they used to. The revolution in American education in the last twenty-five years may turn out to be as profound as the initial development of mass public education was little more than one hundred years ago. One out of two high-school graduates now goes on to college. The clientele and appetite for all forms of education seems to grow, even in these hard times. Changes in the work force are interacting with changes in family structure and education: more and more women are taking on jobs and going back to school. The civil rights movement has altered the politics of education; in opening up segregated schools and universities it has launched another turbulent round of debate on education's participation in the inequalities of American life.

Developments in the teachers' unions offer a good example of the role of educated labor in the "post-industrial" order. My feeling is that we will not get a wholly new "post-industrial" set of emphases and issues, but rather a mix of old and new. A continuing "industrial agenda" has evolved—the fight for better pay, teachers' rights, classroom autonomy, and better working conditions—along with a novel "post-industrial" set of perplexities and options. The unions will have to decide, as they play the new politics of credentialed professionalism, to what degree they want to see themselves as workers, civil servants, or academics. The teachers, and other unions as well, will have the potential to align themselves with new forms of defense of small-scale scrabbled privilege, or to become part of coalitions pressing for new priorities in the society. The astonishingly rapid rise of militant teachers' unions in the last ten years and the picket lines around the country are some evidence that quiet post-industrial concerns have not pre-empted all the older educational issues.

Historically, education is the first of the long line of social services. Its dilemmas reflect in classic form problems of all the social services in an unequal society. Problems of fairness, access, stigma, standards, class and cultural chasms, professionalism, and bureaucracy that emerge first in the schools develop in other service sectors decades, sometimes many decades, later. A lovely book might be written about parallels between the history of schools and the unfolding politics and history of medicine, for example. However, the very fact that there is such a long educational history has to qualify our sense of post-industrial novelty.

A sense of the cumulative press of the past on the unfolding present must inform our thoughts about education. Consider the way that each new institutional expansion of education has opened up a host of issues that are novel and yet similar to earlier dilemmas. Around the turn of the century, when high schools began to evolve from elite preparatory schools into mass institutions, they became embroiled in many of the conflicts that had involved the common elementary schools—even, in muted form, the class and cultural wars between immigrants and Yankees. We forgot about the school wars of the past during the era of relative peace that ensued in schools during the era of professionalized calm—roughly the years between 1920 and 1960. Even the relatively quiescent years of professional control and dominance of the schools had its share of quiet tension. Conflicts between equality and meritocracy, between cultural plural-ism and universalism (or, which is not the same thing, conformity), and between education as an intrinsic value and education as prepara-tion for work arose during this period. In the compromises between academic and mass education, and between privilege and access to learning that the high schools represent, these remain continuing problems. It is, however, only in the last ten years that the schools have once again become important arenas of conflict. In a complex way, older patterns get repeated. Thus Bell's sense that the politiciza-tion of such areas in American life as social service and education is something new is a misreading of history, prompted by the fact that we have just ended an era of unchallenged professionalism. That era is now over, and education is back to being a storm center, as it was throughout much of the nineteenth century. At the same time the old issues are refought in institutions that represent a new, highly professionalized world of credentials and bureaucracies. The recent budget crises in schools and universities have only made it more painfully obvious that we are in for difficult and contentious times. The Progressives also debated over whether academic values and mass education were compatible; whether education could be made more equal and still encourage standards, merit, and careers open to talent; whether the "one best system" can become more pluralistic. Today it is the scale and sweep of the institutions that make our own dilemmas different; the substance of the problems themselves remains generally unchanged.

What is novel and perhaps "post-industrial" about our present awareness of educational problems is the growing appreciation of how organizational questions—professionalism, bureaucracy, administrators' and teachers' roles—affect the substance and politics of education. We are an organization-minded age, and we are right to sense that the problems of schools are in part reflections of problems shared by all institutions in an era of mass organization. Here again, however, fresh problems do not replace older ones; they merely add on layers of complexity. Another "post-industrial" contribution of expanded education to our politics is the spread of educated ideas, tastes, and opinions. One consequence of more education has been to widen the constituency of people concerned about educational issues and other issues that were traditionally left to elites.

The virtues of *The Coming of Post-Industrial Society* are many. Its scope and comprehensiveness are awesome. On every page there are glittering insights, and certain set pieces in it could constitute distinguished books all on their own, such as the brilliant intellectual history of speculation on the nature of industrial society. For those who disagree with Bell, as I do, there are important reminders throughout of the way the flux of historical change makes old categories and perceptions obsolete: earlier Marxist predictions of catastrophe were unhinged when the state intervened to save capitalism from its crises and when technology, for all its social costs, became—in Schumpeter's striking phrase—an open sea for the reinvestment of capital. Certainly this book challenges what might be called the thinking left to treat the role of both old and new working classes in a more complex way. I hope that Bell's discussion of culture (which he is elaborating in another work) will provoke more realistic assessments of cultural trends than the dreadful Romantic gush we have been getting.

Yet for all its undeniable importance, this exceedingly ambitious book is flawed. I have already stressed at length its main failing: its apolitical character, despite its repeated insistence on the primacy of politics. Let me quickly suggest three other faults.

Bell's sense of history is weak. His eagerness to point up the novelties in post-industrial society leads him to neglect the glacial and cumulative nature of the changes he is chronicling. Much of what he calls post-industrial society was present in the old industrial order, and much of the old order—industrial unions, for example—will persist in the new. Historians, who perhaps have an occupational weakness for stretching the present as far as possible into the past, often argue that the outlines of our present society were laid down in the Progressive Era, the period, roughly, between 1880 and 1920. For all our dazed sense of unending change, there are many respects in which we have been living for some time in a rather traditional order whose basic political, social, and cultural agendas have remained remarkably stable. Think of the precedents for our present society in the Progressive Era: new corporate forms; the advent of political capitalism and governmental interference in the economy; mass warfare; mass consumption; the rise of the great universities; the spread of education to the masses; the growth of bureaucracies, professions, and new technical strata; the beginnings of a new radical cultural consciousness among intellectuals. Bell himself points out that the basic machines of daily life, with the two important exceptions of TV and nuclear weapons, were all in place between 1850 and 1940: railroads, steamships, telephones, telegraphs, electricity, automobiles, movies, radios, airplanes. It would be foolish to deny the immense changes wrought by science and technology in the years since 1940, but it is not foolish to emphasize that the changes took place in a settled historical context. C.P. Snow, attempting to describe the infighting among Winston Churchill's science advisers during World War II, searched for a phrase adequate to what he conceived of as the radical novelty of the events he was describing. All he could come up with was—"court politics."

Bell assumes that the impressive changes he points to in the occupational structure transform society and its problems completely; it is equally likely that here again a new layer of problems is simply added on to the old structure. Bell says post-industrial society is less of a whole than the industrial order it replaces, yet insists that the educated workers in the new service strata are somehow more "central" and "typical" than the almost equal number of industrial workers still standing in the same tableau. This is both inconsistent and unpersuasive.

There is more historical continuity than Bell lets on; there is also a remarkable historical persistence to debates about the future. Bell is the heir of the Progressive intellectuals who watched the birth of a new order and decided, prematurely, that its advent meant the end of individualism and capitalism and the beginning of a new, collectivist America. They looked forward to an inevitable victory of what Bell calls "sociologizing" over economics. Like Bell, the Progressives underestimated the enduring power of profit, and never squarely faced the political questions of power and disparate wealth; they fooled themselves into thinking that historical forces would do the work that only people, acting through politics, can do.

Bell does not have the moral focus to be found in the best work of sociologists like David Riesman or the late C. Wright Mills. I'm not talking politics: Mills and Riesman come to very different, in fact opposite, political conclusions about American society, but their work is anchored to a profound moral concern for the fate of the worthy individual in a conformist and bureaucratic society. They have a test for the validity of social institutions—the degree to which they make room for an ideal of fulfilled individuality—and there is a kind of grandeur in their common assertion of liberal, rational, individual values in an illiberal world. Bell has no comparable moral center-weight. His criticisms of the intellectuals of the counterculture and the Left often hit the mark, but the reader is sometimes left with the puzzled impression that Bell really thinks the main problem facing this great, troubled country is its alienated intellectuals. He exalts the political realm and fears democracy. He vigorously and often persuasively defends his ideal of meritocracy, but is less vigorous in pointing out the degree to which American society is not meritocratic and does not honor real merit, and he can scarcely stir himself to acknowledge the unwarranted extremes of inequality in American life. For all his acceptance of the corporate order, he says he favors the new communal goals of the "sociologizing" point of view. Yet he attacks the egalitarian, socialist philosophy of John Rawls, which he thinks is destined to shape the thought of the last part of the twentieth century as individualistic liberalism molded the nineteenth and early twentieth centuries. His attempt at rebutting Rawls amounts to a reminder that these matters are all very complex, which is of course true. Socialists have not yet drawn a convincing portrait of human nature; the famous old slogan "from each according to his ability, to each according to his need" begs many questions, not the least being the precise definition of abilities and needs. Rawls's conception of justice as fairness leaves out many considerations of incentive, motives, and universal values, but in its consistent concern to preserve the best political values of liberal individualism in an inevitably collectivist age, it is surely a better and more appealing starting point for drawing up a new social contract than Bell's position, which is less a position than a set of warnings. There is a lack of balance in Bell's preoccupation with meritocracy that contrasts with Rawls's careful edifice of counterpoised principles. Bell is at his best as a cautionary sage, pointing to real problems and warning the gullible not to take any wooden nickels. The moral vision behind these warnings is truly complex, but the complicated calculations too regularly balance out on the side of complacency and the status quo.

Finally I would add my private disappointment at the remoteness of *The Coming of Post-Industrial Society* from the actual social texture of American life. To my mind the best sociology, however abstract and theoretical, renders our social existence more humanly vivid—as Max Weber does when he speaks of the iron cage of rationality descending on the modern world. Bell's assumption of the convergence of the various advanced industrial societies is characteristically ahistorical, and testifies to his indifference to the thousands of persistent cultural traits, values, traditions, and tics that make, say, Japan so different from France or America, no matter how contemporary the setting. His essential lack of curiosity about these matters, together with his lukewarm interest in social psychology, social types, and social character, make this book read like the work of a learned Martian. Some people once imagined that sociologists might replace novelists as explorers of the human complexities of the age. To judge by this monumental, chilly work, they were quite wrong.

5

Children and Youth in the Past

The lives of children, a subject often neglected by historians, get a full measure of attention in an excellent documentary collection, *Children and Youth in America*. The rich material in its two volumes is superbly organized and imaginatively selected, and a third volume will be forthcoming. Just as a literary anthology cannot help but be a work of literary criticism, collections of this sort are exercises in historical judgment and interpretation; in this case the result is a comprehensive and often somber presentation of the place of children in our national life—far and away the best chronicle of public policy toward children we now have.

Volume I deals with the nine generations of American children between the founding of the English colonies and the end of the Civil War. It is divided into three periods, each representing a stage in the development of policy toward children. In the first, 1600–1735, the documents reveal a concern for defining the nature of public authority over children who were subjects—not citizens—of private family governments. In the second, 1735–1820, they indicate a quest for the proper public response to children in an ideological climate stressing self-help, individualism, and self-interest. In the third period, 1820–

65, the documents demonstrate the growing complexity of public concern for children. A sense of crisis over the future of children and the family produced waves of institution building. We hear voices from the past discussing issues by no means settled today. How should the state and the adult public regard children in a society marked by turbulent political, social, and economic change and a high degree of geographic and social mobility? What should adults expect of children? What should they do for them? What should they deny them? Bremner and his colleagues illuminate the answers to these questions through a vast selection of materials, ranging from legislative debates and newspaper clippings to private diaries and memoirs.

Volume II, covering the period from the end of the Civil War to the beginning of the New Deal, reveals a more institutionalized, increasingly professional set of concerns, and therefore is less humanly vivid. It documents the remarkable rise in the status of children in American society, which Richard Titmuss, speaking of Britain, has rightly called the revolution in child care standards since the nineteenth century. Selections show how the renewed emphasis on the distinctiveness of childhood channeled reform and philanthropic energy into the provision of special facilities for children, and how an earlier generation's institutional answers to social problems became part of the problem for succeeding generations. There was state and federal legislation forbidding child labor, compelling children to spend more and more time in schools. With the approach of the New Deal, there was a growing, yet skittish and fearful, acceptance of the notion that the federal government has a responsibility for the health and welfare of the young.

Like the ancient Romans they admired so much, Americans of the past had a special passion for building institutions. The institutions were meant to mediate between older values and the tumultuous consequences of unchecked economic and technological growth. Institutions such as the public schools, prisons, insane asylums, and reformatories were supposed to shore up what were conceived of as declining older institutions such as the family, the village community, and the church. They often ended up as mechanisms for imposing an Anglo-Saxon, Protestant consensus on alien newcomers to society.

Living as we do in a world of ailing institutions inherited from this past, we are likely to look with jaundiced eyes on the consequences of institutionalization. We tend to see the ambiguities of particular reforms for special groups—children, blacks, the insane, juvenile delinquents. At the very least, the group in need has often ended up isolated from the rest of society; at the worst, institutions have become human dumping bins. It is difficult for a skeptical age to listen patiently to the evangelical rhetoric of so many figures in the American reform tradition. Reform ideology is often the same, the grandiose promises are similar, and the resulting cycles of disillusionment, repression, budget cuts, and reaction are all too familiar. Out of the reformers' mix of fears and hopes emerge the coral reefs of bureaucracies and unresponsive professions. But to point out these results is not to subscribe to the current anarchist mood of hostility to all institutions, reformers, and professions. Our revulsion against pathological professionalism and institutional arthritis is quite natural, but it need not follow that our main social problem is that we are overorganized, or that we can do without a reformed professionalism. Proponents of total deschooling and a dismantling of our social service institutions should take a hard look at Volume I of *Children and Youth in America*. In the seventeenth and eighteenth centuries many Americans lived in a relatively deschooled and deinstitutionalized society; Bremner's grim documents do not suggest that children were better off under this arrangement. Decent environments for people require institutions—pluralistic, voluntaristic, and on a human scale—but institutions nonetheless. And true professional standards to guide them.

The material in Volume II often is drab in comparison with Volume I, yet it has the same comprehensiveness and intelligent organization, and it is impossible in this short space to do justice to the many topics it deals with: the legal status of children, children's health, schooling, blacks, Indians, and other minorities, immigrant children, child labor, birth control, abortion, juvenile delinquency, developments in pediatrics, the fight against infant and maternal mortality, professionalization and the growth of bureaucracy, the Depression, the advent of the high school as a mass institution. Both volumes of *Children and Youth in America* are strong in two areas that have been neglected up to recent years: the history of education and the history of children's health. The material on education

· clearly profits from the current revival of interest in that subject which revisionist historians of education have sparked by their suspicions about the actual function of public schooling. The very welcome interest in children's health derives, in part, from the fact that this whole project is sponsored by the American Public Health Association. It suggests an understanding of the importance of children's health that continues to elude schools and legislatures.

Given the sources, it is inevitable that documents relating to childhood should record adult attitudes toward children; this is not the only realm in which our historical knowledge is limited to the beliefs of the articulate and the privileged. Nonetheless one would like to see ways around this. Perhaps Volume III could include material from some of the growing oral history archives, although no one, to my knowledge, has been following Robert Coles's lead in interviewing children and transcribing the results. Certainly it would be possible to include more material from literary sources, which Bremner and his colleagues tend to neglect. Images of childhood fashioned by artists and writers are important sources because they sometimes influence and reflect popular thought and because they often constitute profound, imaginative explorations of unacknowledged cultural dilemmas and tensions. Considering the wealth of photographs available, particularly for the period following the 1880s, the illustrations in Volume II are disappointing; one hopes for more and better selections for Volume III.

No one expects wholly novel ideas from a documentary collection of this sort. Its chief virtue, perhaps, is its potential for giving concrete examples of great historical abstractions. Leafing through these pages one can see how the shift from farming village to industrial city altered the American sense of community. Children were moved from a world in which the family was the main economic unit to one in which work took place in factories. As labor rose in value we see the consequences of industrialization for the new work force of women and children. Side by side with the new romantic and religious interest in the estate of childhood came the exploitation of the factory system. Stephen Knight, for example, describes his youth in a Rhode Island cotton mill:

My work was to put in the roving on a pair of mules containing 256 spindles. . . . The running time for that mill, on an average, was about fourteen hours per day. In the summer months we went in as early as we could see, worked about an hour and a half, and then had a half hour for breakfast. At twelve o'clock we had another half hour for dinner, and then we worked until the stars were out. . . . For my services I was allowed forty-two cents per week. . . . The proprietor of that mill was accustomed to make a contract with his help on the first day of April, for the coming year. . . . On one of these anniversaries, a mother with several children suggested to the proprietor that the pay seemed small. The proprietor replied, 'You get enough to eat, don't you?' The mother said, 'Just enough to keep the wolf from the door.' He then remarked, 'You get enough clothes to wear, don't you?' to which she answered, 'Barely enough to cover our nakedness.' 'Well,' said the proprietor, 'we want the rest.'

Through Bremner's materials on family life, we see the rise in the esteem for children in middle-class homes, and how this was connected with increased privacy, more property, and a keen sense of social divisions. The quick eye for class, ethnic, and racial differences seems to have been one of the by-products of a relatively egalitarian, competitive order. Foreign visitors document changes in the conception of authority, the declining power of fathers to decide the future of their children, and the slow extension of egalitarian and democratic ideas into every sphere of life. Bremner's visitors note the precocity of American youth throughout the nineteenth century; it is clear that the American youth cult had its roots in nineteenth-century America's emphasis on equality. Certain themes seem perennial: the pervasive assumption that each new generation faces wholly different circumstances, that each American life has to be, as Henry Adams put it, an education, because nobody can look to the experience of their parents for guidance. Also—and this grows more common as the immigrants arrive—children, being more at home in the new surroundings, come to act as cultural guides for their puzzled parents.

One finishes these 1522 absorbing pages with several thoughts. These volumes remind us that our pervasive sense of crisis concerning children and the family is quite traditional, being part of a worried national conversation that began in the 1820s and has continued to the present. They remind us, too, that concepts such as childhood itself, or youth, or adolescence, have evolved under specific historical circumstances and are not timeless universal truths about the human condition in every age and place. Children were adults in miniature until society perceived their distinct needs, set up specific institutions to cater to them, and developed a body of thought to account for their peculiarities. We can trace the glacial, yet sure, transition of children from perverse creatures whose will must be broken, to souls fit for redemption, to being valuable enough to care for, unique and precious beings. Volume I in particular reminds us of the remoteness of much of the American past from our present existence. A nostalgia for what Marx called "rural idiocy" persists, but we are now a civilization in which children are a distinct luxury. We see how defining childhood as a special stage of existence has had both good and bad consequences: the recognition of children's needs has often resulted in measures that cut them off from life. What was once a direct initiation into the world of adults, reality, and work, no longer holds. Along with our other ghettos we have created age ghettos where peers speak only to peers, and few young people learn what it is like to raise children, do productive work, or grow old.

The documents also make it clear that substantial gains have been made for children's welfare, despite well-warranted criticisms of our inadequate social service system. While it is fashionable to question the motives of many of our reformers—and they were a mixed lot—there is no doubt that without their efforts American life would be much more of a jungle than it is. At the same time, few readers will miss seeing the tenacious historical roots of America's public neglect of its children, at least compared with other industrially advanced societies. Even the relatively large sums of money spent on education seem to some extent to have been compensations for neglect in other areas, such as health. Throughout our history, children's welfare has been subordinated to economic goals, and institutions for children, operating in a context of market priorities and social inequality, have too often turned into scrap heaps. Social control of the alien poor has amounted to an obsession. Richard Titmuss has insisted that the central issue of all public policy is the sort of treatment we are willing to give to strangers. In America it seems that the problem of strangers and their children has been unusually hard, for they have been not only from a different social class, but from another people, and, often enough, another race. In this light, even proud and valuable American traditions of voluntaristic philanthropy can take on a sinister quality as one notes the systematic way in which private services have historically excluded the alien and the marginal. Individualism, the pervasiveness of the entrepreneurial and capitalist outlook, the lack of a social democratic tradition, the limitations of the reform mentality, the divisiveness of race and ethnicity, the rigid and self-serving nature of our bureaucracies and professions—have all worked against a public commitment to meeting the needs of every child.

Children and Youth in America is the sort of work we need to add substance to our current interest in children and the family, for it is a curious fact that these topics are now of enormous interest. The reasons for this are complex and partly historical. As a nation we have long—too long, perhaps—thought of ourselves as young, an identification which has often blinded us to the old, settled nature of many of our social arrangements. America's profoundly Romantic literary traditions have led many of our best writers to explore the world through the child's eyes; in recent decades what were the concerns of a handful of nineteenth-century intellectuals have become part of the general cultural property of masses of educated people. For the Romantics, new and old, childhood often stands, in Proust's phrase, for a return to the unanalyzed. Romanticism about childhood represents a complex of attitudes: hostility to logical analysis, a contempt for form, a suspicion of intellect, and a reluctance to develop a complicated reaction to society and life. It is an intensely private and solitary outlook. These are its vices. Its virtues are its integrity, its sense of wonder, its compassion, its humor, its refusal to be complacent. All this is part of the present cultural mood. For some Americans, childhood has become a kind of ideology, the last hope for the future, after successive creeds and intellectual idols have fallen.

Our absorption in childhood also reflects the fact that large numbers of middle-class Americans are wealthy enough and have time enough to devote themselves to the rearing of their children. The death of a child is no longer common. Perhaps this is the biggest difference between childhood in the past and childhood now, just as the reduction in the ravages of childbirth may be the biggest change in the lives of women. The reduction of the infantile death rate from 300 or 400 per 1000 births to less than 25 is an astonishing demographic fact, notwithstanding the persistence of disgracefully high rates among minorities and the poor. Before 1750 the odds against a child's completing five years of life may have been as high as three to one. We are apt to think of the nineteenth century's preoccupation with death and funerals, widows and orphans, as morbid sentimentality; but it also mirrored social reality. One would like to see more study of the psychological consequences of these facts; what we see as the callousness toward very small children of earlier times may reflect a simple reality: parents in a culture in which child mortality is high may not be able to invest much feeling in very young children.

Philippe Aries's famous work, *Centuries of Childhood* (Knopf), has provoked a series of debates which have made us realize how blinkered and parochial our ideas about childhood may be. Aries argues that childhood, conceived of as a separate stage of life, is a creation of Western society in the last three centuries; adults in previous ages saw children as tiny adults, not as beings with distinct needs and ways of thinking and feeling. Separate toys and games for children are, in the long sweep of Western history, novelties. Some of the new historical works, including Bremner's, remind us, too, that adolescence and youth as we now understand them did not really exist before the latter part of the nineteenth century.

The increased interest in children is not limited to historians. It is plainly one important reason the intense interest in educational reform of the 1960s has not died out; for all the budget cuts and racial tension, there is probably more change—both creative and faddish —in American schools today than ever before, and more public and parental involvement in school issues. What might be called the developmental approach to children's learning—emphasizing the stages in children's physical, emotional, and intellectual growth, the active nature of the child as learner, and the profound variations among individual children—has never received a more respectful hearing by American teachers, although it can scarcely be said to dominate classroom practice. There is much more of a sense among the educated that children's minds are not simply smaller versions of adult minds, as well as a recognition that they have adult-sized passions.

In the law, the movement for public interest advocacy has an articulate wing exploring possible extensions of children's basic constitutional and legal rights, examining, for example, the implications of labeling and tracking in classrooms. In medicine and psychiatry, stirrings toward public health and community medicine are focusing

on children's health and family practice, and sociologists and an-
thropologists are taking a new look at the family. Commissions of
inquiry are already at work trying to knit together these disparate
efforts, although one doubts that good synthetic scholarship will
suffice to produce compassionate social policy. All one can safely
predict is a flood of literature of mixed quality on the young and their
families.

Recent literature reflects the general testing of values and institutions that began in the chaotic 1960s and is continuing, in more
muted, scholarly, and restrained form, into the 1970s. Once again,
Americans feel that their distance from old certitudes is uncomforta-
bly great. There is much concern that public policy has weakened the
family instead of strengthening it; at the same time, the family as an
institution is under heavy attack. The women's movement is important in all this, but the women's movement itself is only part of an
intellectual process that has been in motion at least since the time
of the Progressive reformers like Jane Addams and John Dewey: a
widening of social sympathies among intellectuals and professionals
to include historic outsiders—immigrants, women, children, the old.
While American institutions have neglected outsiders and dis-
criminated against them, American intellectuals have often been
drawn to their communal values, using them to criticize American
economic institutions.

Nineteenth-century Americans were sentimental about families:
the realm of work was supposed to be a Darwinian jungle in which
only the fittest survived, whereas the family home was supposed to
be a haven for harmony, morality, and good manners. Americans
today are not free from this sort of sentimentality. The family is still
widely regarded as a refuge for noneconomic and preindustrial values,
a kind of pastoral realm of human feeling to hold up against a world
of conflict, minutely divided labor, and rationalized bureaucracies.
Yet for all our sentimentality, and our general reluctance to observe
the interaction of the family with other social institutions, it may be
a fact of some political consequence that family values are more
deeply rooted in American life than entrepreneurial economic values.
In the coming battles over national priorities and a new social policy,
children and their families may be more important as symbols than
ever.

6

Youth Deferred

Peter Pan ought to have traveled on an American passport, for in our booster moods we have thought that the rising generation would, by its innocence, redeem us. We have also, in more anxious moments, viewed youthful energy as a threat. It seldom occurs to us that concepts such as "childhood," "adolescence," and "youth" are products of historical circumstance and not universal truths about the human condition in every time and place.

Two important facts about modern youth separate us from the once-upon-a-time. The first is the economic irrelevance of children. Far from being the assets they once were in the agricultural and industrial past, the young are now economic liabilities or luxuries. The second fact is a result of the way we have responded to the recognition that childhood has distinct needs: increasingly, the young have been spending more and more time in institutional settings and age ghettoes. The once direct and often brutal initiation of the young into the world of work, reality, and grownups is no more.

Schools were designed by nineteenth-century reformers to mediate between older values and the consequences of economic and techno-logical change. Like prisons, hospitals, asylums, and reformatories, schools were meant to shore up what were conceived to be eroding institutions—the family, the village community, the church. But one generation's institutional responses to social problems have become part of the problem for a later generation.

As institutions for the young proliferated, certain ideas about education began to change. In the nineteenth century, before faith in education reached its utopian zenith, most people had understood that education was not limited to formal instruction in specialized institutions, that it was a lifelong process in which adults as well as the young participated. Its sphere encompassed workshops, libraries, working men's clubs, Chautauqua camps, lyceums, newspapers, jury rooms. The populists were characteristically American in believing that they could turn the political process itself into a kind of educational forum. Then, as formal education spread and consolidated itself into a system, these informal institutions of learning shrank in significance; "education" came to mean what went on in schools. Today, with criticism of formal schooling on the rise, interest has revived in the older, broader view of education as something that takes place in many settings over a lifetime. All these themes—the loss of a productive role for the young, their isolation in specialized educational institutions, and the quest for informal alternatives—are reflected in a fascinating recent report of the panel on youth of the president's science advisory committee; the guiding spirit behind it —whose intellectual influence is plain—is the group's chairman, sociologist James Coleman.

The main point of *Youth: Transition to Adulthood* is that it is unhealthy to cluster the young for so long in the bureaucratic institutions called schools, for by so doing we cut them off from experiences they need in order to become responsible adults. Since the report defines "youth" as the period between fourteen and twenty-four it includes colleges as well as high schools in its indictment of formal institutions of learning. So long as schools and colleges were only *part* of youth's existence, their academic emphases were not so harmful; now that they are the main places for young people to be, their preoccupations have imbalanced the whole business of growing up. Both in formal classes and in informal gatherings after school, students are thrown together with others their same age. But neither classrooms nor the peer culture do much to encourage the young to take initiative or to exert authority. The report envisages much broader experiences:

> This involves . . . either responsibility for his own welfare, or responsibility for others' welfare; it involves orientation to productive and responsible tasks; where it involves learning, it is learning through action and experience, not by being taught. Most of the proposed institutional structures also are designed to reduce the isolation of youth (14 to 24) from adults and from the productive tasks of society. This is intended to bring about a greater degree of personal responsibility of adults for the development of youth and to remove youth from some of the isolation that impedes the transition to adulthood.

The isolated, age-graded school has been convenient for professional educators, for it is relatively easy to organize and administer and offsets the traditional Darwinian advantage the large have over the small. Yet the critics are right to say that in most conventional age-graded classrooms the range of roles and activities is far too narrow; age is a grossly unreliable guide to extraordinarily diverse rates of physical, social, and mental development. Critics are also right to say that formal schooling organized into age groups denies students valuable contacts with people of other ages.

Fortunately we are at a turning point and can take time to reflect. Educators face a demographic moratorium during which the numbers of the young to be educated will remain constant. This is quite a change from the baby boom period from the 1940s through the 1960s, which put great strains on educational institutions. Between 1960 and 1970 the proportion of the population between fourteen and twenty-four jumped from 15 to 20 percent; in absolute numbers, the young increased by 50 percent, from 27 million to 42 million. But that extraordinary rise reached its peak in 1971. The decline in the birth rate means the ratio of young to mature will go down, first gradually, then rapidly. For the next five years, an annual wave of about a million highly educated workers will wash into the labor force —perhaps with turbulent consequences. The economy rather than the educational system and the army will now be contending with the children of the boom.

How shall we use the opportunities presented by this moratorium? In all probability there will be three sorts of responses. One will be to cut budgets: the powerful force of inertia will prompt many educators to continue the school business as usual, but on a suitably reduced scale. Another will be to take advantage of the respite from the dizzy spiral of expansion and to try to move schools from the quantitative and managerial concerns of the past and the present to new, qualitative concerns for diversity, individuality, and pluralism. A third will be to explore new realms of informal education outside schools.

Youth is on the side of the second two responses, especially the third. It makes a number of good suggestions. Within schools it favors more opportunities for older students to rub up against younger children, especially the very young. Too few young people, the report says, are prepared for childrearing. It would like more specialized schools in fields like art, drama, and science, so that students can commit themselves to one vital realm. It wisely reverses the conventional orthodoxy that bigger is better, urging smaller schools and the breaking down of hulking buildings that now predominate into humanly manageable units.

Yet *Youth*'s agenda for the schools is limited. Its emphasis is on alternatives for growing up outside the walls of formal institutions. To this grand end, it envisions a number of modest pilot experiments to develop special youth organizations and youth communities run by young people. It proposes lifting restraints on work for young people and the testing of a dual minimum wage for working adults and youth. It suggests a voucher experiment allowing students at age sixteen to choose between more formal education or job training. It recommends opportunities for sixteen-year-olds and older youths to do public service work.

One can be against some of these proposals in principle and still see merit in small-scale demonstrations. For example, I oppose a general dual minimum wage for teenage and adult workers, for in a time of serious under- and unemployment it might well reduce the number of jobs for adults; in any case it is unfair to the young (the parallel with the degrading dual wage system for women seems obvious). Yet I can imagine experiments that would explore job training and education for young workers, paying them something less than the prevailing minimum wage. Their value would, of course, depend on how useful the training or educational benefits proved to be.

Similarly I would on principle oppose widespread adoption of educational vouchers, which seem to me an abdication of our communal responsibility for education. Vouchers pose a real threat to professional structures of protection, to the support and autonomy that classroom teachers ought to and seldom do have. Even the most socially conscious voucher schemes, bristling with theoretical safeguards for the poor and minorities, run a practical risk of tipping society's balance even farther in favor of the better off and the better informed. They do not take into account the fact that the sum of all private decisions in the market is greater than its individual parts: this sum is a social system, in which disparities in wealth reinforce the position of the powerful and the privileged in a cumulative and dynamic way. Vouchers pose particular risks in a society divided by race and ethnicity, as well as by social class.

All this being said, it seems to me mistaken for opponents of voucher schemes to resist small-scale experiments under carefully controlled public auspices. Vouchers *could* be one mechanism for achieving wider choices in public education. I suspect, however, that if conscientious voucher reformers were given a wholly free hand, they would find themselves reinventing many of the familiar administrative structures of school systems, although one would hope on a more modest scale. It makes a big difference whether vouchers are conceived of as offering parents choices within a public school system whose officials are vested with authority to supervise, set standards, support and protect professional rights, enforce desegregation—or whether vouchers are thought of as a fundamental organizing principle of a privatized school system. From what I understand of California's Alum Rock experiment, it is the former: a plan carefully monitored by responsible officials and school professionals. At any rate, Alum Rock seems more promising than *Youth*'s proposal for vouchers for job training—a particularly pallid notion in the lurid light of the uselessness and corruption of many of the job-training swindles now being peddled by the private sector. But even here, we can't afford to reject a small-scale voucher scheme that incorporates honest job training alternatives into its framework. (Two members of *Youth* 's panel, Robert Bremner and John B. Davis, share my doubts about the dual minimum wage and vouchers in brief dissents from the majority report.)

Youth questions two assumptions that have long prevailed in education. One is that more and more schooling is necessary because society is more complex. The other is that more education automatically increases opportunities and enhances the personal development of the young. The report's greatest strength is its clear perception of the historical and social forces that have led to the segregation of the young in formal institutions. Growing wealth and leisure (widely shared, however unequally distributed) have changed family values about the benefits of full-time work for the young. Parents do not want their children to be exploited; adult workers do not want youth competing in the labor market. Child labor and compulsory attendance laws are on the books. Professionalization and bureaucratization of the schools has resulted in elaborate rationales for narrowing the range of human contacts for the young.

Youth opens a new round in a controversy that has been going on since the 1890s over the proper role of the high school. Out of debates between academic traditionalists and the proponents of "social efficiency" and "life adjustment" emerged the compromise known as the comprehensive high school, which tried to offer something for everybody. (Contrary to professed intent, the high school has not been notably successful in promoting social mobility for the poor; it has been an avenue up for many, but it has favored the children of the middle class.) A consensus was reached: everybody should go to high school; the college bound should take academic courses, while courses for those not going further should include more practical instruction. Courses in driver training and beauty aids attracted the sophisticated derision of the newly emerging university elites in the 1950s and there was some validity to their criticism. Yet "life adjustment" was a response to the inadequacy of older academic ideals when confronted with mass education. It *did* try to introduce the young to adult roles, though it thought of them mainly as future consumers. It was also profoundly anti-intellectual. Its underlying assumption seemed to be that the masses were ineducable, incapable of handling anything more than a curriculum based on secondhand versions of somebody else's practicality.

Well, if you wait long enough, the same idea gets repeated in a new context, because the dilemmas are enduring. "Life adjustment" reflected a genuine insight that the academic curriculum of the schools did not meet the full range of the needs of the young. But the progressive educators thought that a curriculum inside the walls of the schools could somehow become "relevant," could do justice to the realities of the outside world. And so they put an enormous burden on formal education, too much, as the authors of *Youth* are aware. Earlier debates on the role of the high school were between supporters of college preparation on the one side and "educators"— professors of education and school administrators—on the other. Now our official spokesmen on matters educational tend to be university academics: scientists and social scientists. *Youth*'s panel, for example, consists largely of sociologists, economists and historians. There is one school administrator and—an older and sadder story in these educational debates—no practitioners. One can welcome more scientific knowledge about the muddled realm of education, without applauding this current preponderance of social scientists in discussions of educational policy. For although we need to know a great deal more about schools, it is precisely the basic depth of our ignorance that makes it unwise to attach lasting significance to the products of researchers who are groping around in darkness. Regrettably the new spokesmen, like the old, ignore the realm of day-to-day educational practice.

It is intriguing to recall that in 1961 James Coleman published a study called *The Adolescent Society*, in which he argued that it was unfortunate that peer groups had become a central part of the adolescent experience, unfortunate because the teenage quest for status and popularity among peers was undermining youth's commitment to academic success. To restore the primacy of brains and grades, Coleman proposed interscholastic intellectual competitions along the lines of competitive school athletics. He was then very much a New Man of the emerging academic order, scowling at youth's earnest pursuit of loyalty, friendship, and romance. But for all his methodological sophistication, Coleman was naïve in imagining that academic contests could take the place of football or basketball or love, and practitioners and laymen may be allowed a smile as they imagine what the authors of *Youth* might now be saying if Coleman's 1961 position had been vigorously implemented over the last decade. The earlier argument has been completely reversed. *Youth* takes it for granted that schools and colleges are doing a satisfactory job with academic subjects, that they are stretching students' minds and meeting their intellectual needs. I wonder. Does the neglect of the life of the mind Coleman saw in high schools at the beginning of the 1960s no longer exist? I'm afraid it does, and the neglect stems in part from sources Coleman diagnosed earlier: the uneasy standing of intellectual values in American life, which has been reinforced in recent years by neopopulist and countercultural attacks on academic and intellectual legitimacy. It also stems from the malaise of many of the university disciplines, which have failed to work out a plausible and vital connection to the realm of education. History, mathematics, foreign languages, science, art, and literature are not flourishing in many of our high schools and colleges; the intellectual disciplines need all the help and support they can get—in traditional and in experimental forms.

I am not saying this to tie a tin can to Coleman's tail. There is a warning here to us all concerning the faddish quality of our debates and a caution that it might not be such a bad idea to maintain something of a divorce between social science research and social policy—a benign chasm, you might call it. Ultimately social science may help guide us to wise policies, but in the short run social scientists in policy realms often act like the clever man in the Isaac Bashevis Singer short story who set out to impress some villagers with his learning. First he propounded ten absolutely unanswerable questions to his wondering audience. Then he proceeded to answer each of them fully. And for a triumphant finale, he demonstrated that they were not questions at all. The villagers, Singer reports, were astounded.

In the early sixties Coleman stated the perennial view of many adults: The rising generation is going to the dogs. Others said: Well, if that's true it isn't youth's fault. There were those who held to the sacredness of that neo-romantic vision of youth first articulated by figures like Randolph Bourne on the eve of World War I: the young were victims of adult corruption; they were also potential saviors, the harbingers of a new culture. In *Growing Up Absurd* (1960) Paul Goodman emerged as one of the most attractive of these youth prophets. "My purpose," Goodman wrote, "is . . . to show how it is desperately hard these days for an average child to grow up to be a man, for our present organized system of society does not want men." Goodman argued that shabby jobs, rotten politics, and the atmosphere of mindless consumption were making it impossible to find arenas in which the young could develop a sense of honor, commitment, or responsibility. In 1962 Edgar Z. Friedenberg's *The Vanishing Adolescent* attacked the same issues from a similar perspective. Friedenberg was much influenced by Erik Erikson's notion that adolescence should be a time of self-exploration, free from the necessities that bind adult existence. He did not deny that the stage of youth was being prolonged—that more of the young were doing more time in schools—but he argued that youth's efforts at exploration were crippled by adult manipulation. Adolescence as a time for an often stormy quest for identity was disappearing in America, because adults insisted on confining the young in schools. The old painful and valid adolescent search for honesty and personal value was being replaced by a bland acquiescence in the school regime.

All parties to this controversy built their arguments on the quicksand of nostalgia. Goodman had his private past: Huck Finn and Jim delighting in radiant idleness on the raft, the incidental learning of children from adults in shady village workshops, the street-wise camaraderie of big-city urchins. Friedenberg's ideal of fulfilled adolescent individuality drew selectively on images of *Sturm und Drang* and on heroic individual authenticity from the era of what David Riesman and his colleagues called "inner direction." Coleman too seemed to see the destruction of a natural and harmonious way of growing up. But as the excellent historical chapters of *Youth* now point out, we should be wary of positing a Golden Age of youthful freedom or intergenerational harmony. There is no evidence it ever existed.

For a time the youth prophets held the floor; many otherwise intelligent people believed the young were leading us toward a New Jerusalem. (See *The Greening of America*.) We were handed a mystique of identity—identity being something the elect (young people) arrived at by a momentary conversion, rather than something we all search for more or less unsuccessfully over a lifetime. This mystique only revealed the enduring hold of evangelical and Romantic modes of thinking on American conceptions of adolescence. Whatever had been valid in Erikson's original sketchy discussion of youthful identity oozed into cant. Friedenberg's defense of elite youth's aristocratic values and rebellions turned more and more into a Menckenesque assault on the grown-up masses as a contemptible booboisie. Goodman was better prepared for the failure of the young to save society. In a sense he had been enrolled on the side of defeat from the start, for he had inherited the anarchist's lonely devotional task of writing the epitaphs for failed revolutions. His illusions about the young were in the end balanced by his Aristotelian sense of proportion, his common decency, and his respect for intellectual tradition, discipline, and professional standards.

Like the civil rights, antiwar, and ecology movements that nourished it and gave it a good deal of its force, the spirit of youthful protest was attacking much that needed attacking. But America's quest for innocence and salvation seemed much too heavy a burden to lay on the shoulders of those under twenty-five. In its late stages, the youth rebellion developed forms of corruption that mirrored the culture it was supposedly rebelling against: disdain for rational authority, drugs, contempt for law, a susceptibility to commercial exploitation, a penchant for violence. The notion that one's chronological age was evidence of either superior values or redeeming grace seemed less and less defensible. If youth turned out to be a mixed bag, grownups themselves turned out not to be a wholly malign species.

Still, to judge by *Youth*'s message, the radical youth prophets have made an impact on the conventional wisdom, an influence similar to that of child-centered pedagogy on Charles Silberman's *Crisis in the Classroom. Youth*'s vision is more balanced than Coleman's earlier schoolmarmish condemnation. The political stance of the young, it says, is "warmhearted, sympathetic, and open. . . . [It] focuses on certain principles like equal opportunity and civil rights, but ignores others, such as honesty, reward for merit, and the rule of law." Coleman, one judges, is now persuaded of *part* of what Goodman and Co. were saying: the path to adulthood is blocked not by the low status of academic grades but by the limited quality of experiences and human contacts schools offer students.

Another point of agreement between both youth prophets and *Youth* is the assumption that there is an entity called the youth culture. Goodman and Co. exalted its virtues and blamed adults for corrupting it. Coleman and his colleagues stress its pathological isolation from worthy grownups. Granted that the young are inward-looking, absorbed in themselves and youthful interests. Granted that they share certain media tastes and styles of consumption. But is there a deviant youth culture? Or do the young of various classes and groups also derive important values from their parents and adult institutions? There is as much evidence for the latter as the former. If the lives of youths and grownups are interwoven within the same social fabric, both parties to the debate have been oversimplifying; virtue and vice and their corresponding values and attitudes are not the exclusive property of any one generation. And so the tasks of education become more complicated than simply introducing the young to a healthy, educative world of adulthood that is waiting for them outside the walls of the schools.

Expressing disenchantment with the present system, Coleman and his colleagues expect little from formal schools with their compulsory nature, their passive definition of the student's role, their assumption that students are in class to learn, not to teach. Yet *Youth*'s vagueness about the alternatives is disquieting. It mentions continuing education for adults, which (it does not note) is taking on new life as more and more people are persuaded that education is a lifelong pursuit. Coleman and his colleagues cite Swedish efforts to promote "recurrent" learning by giving support to alternative periods of work and study. They touch on American efforts in "career" education, which are manfully trying to escape repeating the dreary and ineffectual history of vocational education. They tip their hats to the whole complex realm of work-study, citing cooperative education involving shared time between employers and schools. They note a variety of job training programs without going into any of them. They do not examine any of the efforts in what might be called the human service sectors of the economy—people helping care for others—yet some of the most promising training for new careers is going on here. There are many institutions—hospitals, juvenile asylums, nursing homes, schools themselves—where an emphasis on credentials, efficiency, and techniques has gone too far, where many of the problems are human, not technical, and where the young could contribute, both as volunteers and as apprentice professionals.

These varied and occasionally lively realms represent the interface between educational institutions and the outside world; they offer concrete examples of the dilemmas, drawbacks, and tradeoffs when we swap school environments for those of work. *Youth* ignores this existing practice in part, I suspect, because so much of it goes on in institutions called schools—high schools, junior colleges, colleges. One senses the old disdain of university academics for practical educators. In part, too, the report's neglect rests on its implicit assumption that much of our society is already geared for incidental learning and profitable mutual interchange between adults and the young—if only formal educational institutions would free their prisoners.

In its scholarly, cautious way, *Youth* at times skirts close to the exuberant errors of Ivan Illich and other proponents of deschooling, who sometimes seem to suggest that shutting down schools would be a positive step. Actually, though, all it would do is exchange the inadequate milieu of the schools for the more wretched ones offered by the streets and the job market. Illich and his followers are not interesting, intellectually, because they refuse to examine the complex problems of building and giving sustained support to what they regard as "natural" forms of human association and learning. They simply stand the old, misguided educational utopianism on its head: where we once imagined, naïvely, that schools could solve all problems, now the deschoolers imagine, with equal naïveté, that schools are the source of all evil. *Youth* is not saying we should close down the schools, but Coleman and his colleagues do share the deschoolers' lack of interest in thinking about crucial, day-to-day problems—the kind of help, for example, adult workers would need in working out apprentice roles for the young.

Youth views adult roles mainly in terms of work; it pays little attention to varieties of learning that do not depend on being on a payroll. *Youth*'s neglect of the potential of intrinsically educational areas, the arts, for example, smacks of anti-intellectuality. For all their rigidities, schools are in a better position than most work institutions to give students opportunities for such purposeful learning as goes on, say, in film crews, research projects, or theatre. Had Coleman and his colleagues examined existing educational practice, they might have pondered the grave difficulties the handful of high schools without walls are running into as they try to place students in outside learning settings. Recently I talked with Jan Rakoff, who has been going around the country looking at attempts to expand the world of learning outside schools. What he found was discouraging. Current efforts to break out of the pattern of formal schooling often are miseducative. Sometimes projects are organized simply for fun, rather than for what might be of more lasting value. Everywhere, the deschooling ventures suffer from a lack of adequate guidance and supervision of students and of adults with whom they are placed. Most students do not need the moronic apparatus of grownup scrutiny they now get in the schools, but they need advice, information, and encouragement, which are generally lacking in present-day alternatives to the schools. In most projects, Rakoff reports, there are no ideas on how to build and maintain enduring networks of adults willing and able to take part in the education of the young.

Another set of problems arises in trying to give institutional form to our cultural hunger for the local, the communal,. the spontaneous. Educational enterprises that rely on informal arrangements often fail the students who need the most help. Then, too, the less formal human connections are the more fragile and transitory. These are not arguments against informality, merely a reminder that informality and community need to be balanced by other values, such as universality. The deschoolers often speak as though we must embrace one of two counterpoised principles, when in fact our only realistic option is to live in constant tension between them.

Youth's animus against formal education also leads it to slight the extent to which the world of work as now organized is boring, alienating, and profoundly antieducational for adult workers. Few adults get a chance to profit from the kind of incidental learning *Youth* rightly prizes. How then will they be able to give such instruction to the young? What Coleman and his colleagues see as a "youth" problem is a reflection of the more general problem: our society is not organized to promote humane values. On occasion *Youth* glimpses this:

> Introduction of youth into work organizations of the sort we are describing will bring about a loss of efficiency in its central economic activity of producing goods or services. . . . It is important that the design of youth's schedule of activities and the implementation be jointly in the hands of management and workers' organizations, if that design is to be appropriate. This mixture of school and work in a work organization is difficult to introduce in American society because schools are in the public sector, while most work is in the private sector, in firms that are subject to market competition.

The report's discussion of the integration of the young into adult life reminds us, by its vast omissions, of what black Americans have learned since the *Brown* decision: true integration is harder to achieve than desegregation. Perhaps the oddest idea in *Youth* is the notion that mingling adults and young people will lessen conflict between them. Benefits there may be to integration—how the thing is done will be crucial—but there will inevitably be much friction. We don't know how to create opportunities and incentives for the various generations to break out of age ghettos. It is a subtle and tricky thing to manage.

Everywhere, as people push against the walls of the institutions we have created, they are crying out for more choices, flexibility, a smaller scale. Reformers dealing with schools, mental hospitals and prisons, and institutions for juvenile offenders and the retarded are pressing for alternatives, halfway houses and the like. The reformers are right to denounce pathological professionalism and the way many institutions function as human scrap heaps. Yet I don't think it follows that we can dispense with professions, bureaucracies, and hierarchies. The deschoolers and anti-institutional reformers are victims of our recurring hunger for earlier and simpler social forms— as Paul Goodman once described them, the sort of people who plug in their electric guitars in order to sing songs denouncing technology. The real issue is whether we can replace the swollen and pathological institutions we have with something humane, voluntaristic, and pluralistic.

One can anticipate a cycle of reform in which the anti-institutional critique of what exists triumphs in the public mind before workable alternatives are actually established, and the upshot of reform is slashed budgets and fewer services. It is one thing to argue for "alternatives" or "learning networks" if they have something like a public high school's budget, professionalism, and long-term political backing. Then we are talking about an institution that will last over time, that can hire professionals to guide students, help them plan work-study and apprentice arrangements, connect them to adults offering educational experiences, supervise them and their adult mentors in placement sites, and think about such mundane matters as transportation. It is quite another thing, infinitely less convincing, to speak of alternatives lacking these commitments. Must we build alternative institutions? Generally the political and human costs of innovation in brand-new settings are high. One successful innovation of the sixties—Head Start—was partially discredited because it failed to raise poor children's IQ scores; yet many Head Start centers combined a high degree of professional competence with substantial parent control and participation. In terms of services that satisfy poor clients' educational, nutritional, medical, and political needs, Head Start did at times compile an educational record that many school systems ought to envy. Sometimes it may indeed be necessary to start wholly new institutions—the old ones can be so bound by their rigidities that there is no possibility of change. Nevertheless, difficulties are immense. This point is hard to argue without seeming to condone complacency. Still, it is a risk that must be run, for our critiques of institutions have gotten ever more comprehensive, while our programs for improving them have gotten ever vaguer.

Any solid educational reform must be based on the realities of a particular group of adults and the young they are to teach. What is good in one context may be a bad idea in another. This, among other things, is why educational prescriptions that ignore practitioners are misguided and usually trivial in their effects. The language of "experiments" that still dogs so many of our discussions of educational reform is ludicrous in its false precision. There are no educational "models" that can be mass produced. It is a safe bet that the pilot experiments *Youth* proposes will be decisively limited in each case by the specifics of the youths they serve and the grownups who work in them. It is impossible to think of educational prescriptions that will meet the needs of students of different classes, races, cultural backgrounds, and religions. *Youth*'s framework is sociological, yet it is surprisingly indifferent to social differences within its broad category of "youth." Blacks and minorities, for example, are under few illusions about the present performance of the schools, yet to many, conventional high schools and colleges with good, conventional programs seem to offer more tangible advantages than vague "alternative" programs. Existing institutions, for all their inequalities, offer guarantees against even greater inequality.

Youth is too reluctant to examine the dilemmas posed by the diversity for which it argues. There is, for instance, a fundamental tension between freedom of choice and greater equality. School integration as the issue is now posed almost invariably means limiting freedom of choice in the name of racial integration. School integration may only be the clearest example of a conflict between diversity and equality that will beset alternative institutions as well as the schools. It may well be that diversity of choices will be easier to get within existing institutions than in new alternatives, which have a way of becoming magnets for the disaffected and lightning rods for outside criticism. Voluntary educational arrangements may be more workable under the legitimizing umbrella of high schools, junior colleges, and colleges; and precisely because more variety in education will mean less emphasis on equality, reform ought to take place within institutions that are broadly committed to public and egalitarian goals.

The pursuit of "alternatives" and "options" must center on public education, because that is where the students and the money for educating them are. The fate of private alternative schools like Harlem Prep and the firefly existence of so many of the "free" schools are poignant reminders of institutional necessities. Whether or not we can create decent schools on a mass scale is an open question. For all their manifest faults, schools in the sixties did change in response to new demands: think of school desegregation in the South, community control, paraprofessionalism, classroom reform, the development of open admissions. Of course schools in many places did not change. And true enough, the changes that took place were usually responses to outside pressure. But that is always the case. One reason schools are traditionally a focus of attack is that historic outsiders in our culture—minorities and the poor—know that it is sometimes easier to get concessions in education than elsewhere. Getting a form of community control in Bedford-Stuyvesant—however compromised and inadequate as a solution to the problems of educating poor children—is easier than getting your hands on the Chase Manhattan Bank. Just as politics, for all its corruption by disparate economic power, offers underdogs an occasional lever to pull, so education, for all its rigidities, offers them some purchase on the rest of the social order. This simple political truth has eluded us in recent years partly, I suspect, because there is a surprising degree of force in the old American legend that the private sector is better and more efficient than the public. This double standard of judgment for private and public institutions may not stand scrutiny. The bankrupt Penn Central Railroad serves the needs of a changing society considerably less well than the beleaguered Philadelphia school system.

In thinking about enlisting schools in the creation of informal alternatives, we will have to be more precise about their functions than are the authors of *Youth*. This is not easy, for schools do many things: they baby-sit, teach knowledge, skills, and work habits, give jobs to grownups, introduce the young to their peers, and provide them with the wherewithal to break free of family and locale. They also accredit one pool of students for elite careers and assign another pool to less august futures. This latter function is ignored in *Youth*, which sees the segregation of the young clearly enough but does not discuss the function of the schools as sieves for privilege. In the historic context of the inequalities of American life, less academic, more practical, more "relevant" educational offerings have a way of turning into tracks for the underprivileged. As far as I can see, this is a dilemma that faces education whether it continues in its present formal guise or branches out into the less formal networks advocated in *Youth*. Coleman and his colleagues briefly touch on the growing geographical division of American life by class and race, which entails a double kind of isolation for poor and minority students. But they do not anticipate the problems of privilege that less formal institutions are bound to share with formal ones, as long as drastic inequality persists.

What might be called the new, affluent agenda is represented by concerns expressed in *Youth:* the attempt to make life in schools and other institutions more varied and rich. But what of the items left over from an older, unfinished agenda, almost wholly ignored in *Youth*, the most outstanding of which is the struggle of minorities and the poor for basic skills, equality of educational opportunities, and access to credentials and jobs?

The rediscovery of how hard it is to move schools in any direction has tempted many to imagine that if schools cannot save society, then salvation must be found in some other realm. There is of course no single lever to pull. If schools do slowly change for the better, the transformation will be part of a whole series of changes in American life. Most of the time educators will be dealing with day-to-day possibilities, not salvation. Some larger perspective on schooling, however, may be useful to all of us. It will make an enormous difference to the vitality of informal alternatives to schooling if they operate in the context of a full employment economy in which the government guarantees jobs to all workers. Historically the opportunity for jobs has been decisive in the ascent from poverty. But full employment also alters the educational picture. The flexibility both adults and the young need to take advantage of informal learning networks, work-study options, apprenticeships, public service work, and the like will only come from full employment. During World War II vocational education, which is normally the sick man of American schooling, came to life, as formal and informal job training programs flourished. Full employment would also help guarantee that new, informal entrées to jobs would not introduce new forms of educational inequality.

A second vantage point on education is offered by a perspective on the family. The most puzzling omission in *Youth*'s exploration of alternative paths to adulthood is any discussion of what it means to be an adult. There is little about the changing roles of men and women, next to nothing about the family, and nothing about the old. One can applaud *Youth*'s proposals for informal alternative institutions and still argue that an essential part of sound policy toward the young will be giving more support to the most durable informal educational institution of all, the family. After all, a sensible reading of the situation *Youth* describes—the isolation of the young in impersonal institutions—would be that American families are not getting enough support for child rearing. There is little sense in *Youth* of the intimate connection between men and women in families in the economy, and patterns of relationships between adults and children. American youth does spend too much time isolated from adults, but what they are and what they become is still in some important part a product of interaction with parents. It is idle to focus on changing the estate of the young without thinking of changes in the estate of the mature. The "youth problem" is an "adult problem" as well, for the chances of ending the isolation of the young hinge on whether there can be changes in the relationship of adult men and women to work, families, and leisure. If the young are constrained by inflexible school schedules, the mature are hemmed in by job schedules. As long as the amount of time adults have to spend with the young is not theirs to decide it is unconvincing to speak of the incidental learning grownups have to offer. And it is probably true that adults will only want to spend more time with other people's children if they have more time to spend with their own families.

Recently Michael Young and Peter Willmott have argued, in their brilliant book *The Symmetrical Family,* that far from becoming less important in advanced industrial societies, the family is becoming more important as a unit of leisure and consumption. They point to a trend toward wives and husbands sharing both work and child-rearing. So far, they concede, this is happening mainly in families that are much better off than average. They also acknowledge real strains on the family: professionals in crack jobs spend more time at work and in forms of leisure that do not involve the family; and many more women of all social classes are working, including the mothers of very small children. As Young and Willmott put it, the technology that has revived the family and brought couples back into their homes may, in alliance with feminism and a heightened professionalism, take them out again. Certainly as women's aspiration for work increases, there will have to be substantial changes before "symmetry" ceases to mean the unsatisfactory East European formula of one job for husbands and two jobs for wives. Yet Young and Willmott are right to remind us both of the family's persistence as an institution, and the continuing widespread preference for it as a pattern for rearing the young. Support for families, they say, would mean policies that deliberately attempted to redress the current imbalance between support for work and support for spending time with the young. It would mean much more parttime work for men and women, more work at home, and more leisure. All of this will be costly, as Young and Willmott point out. People's margins for maneuvering free of economic constraints will increase if society's productive capacity grows, and we can generate full employment. Young and Willmott compare the advanced societies to a marching column. At the head of the column, the rich face a whole new set of social issues brought about by affluence, while the poor in the rear ranks are still struggling for their rights to a larger share of the wealth. The length of the distance between the head of the column and its rear must be shortened, they say. Present roles of men and women and their relations with the young are unlikely to change unless society's predominantly economic values can be reversed, and unless there is a diminished appetite for inequality on the part of those heading the column.

Discussions of the family are bedeviled by moralistic norms. Just as there is the statistical norm of the American family—Mom, Pop, Sis, Bub—there is also the moral norm, the father at work, the mother at home taking care of the kids, all parties happy in their roles. The moral norm has never done justice to the diversity of family styles; it has overlooked working mothers, female-headed families, families in which fathers contribute substantially to childrearing, and many other variations on the theme of family living. It is one reason American families, whatever their makeup, do not get the kind of support they need for childrearing. The norm has also been an agony to those who for their own good reasons find the family and its commitments oppressive. One of the best things the women's liberation movement has done is to publicize the truth that not everybody needs the family.

Yet prophecies of the impending demise of the family and a revolution in patterns of human relationships are not very convincing. Without either new political or religious ideologies to support them, communal modes of childrearing seem unlikely to spread very far in our society. Part of the recurrent sense of malaise about the family stems from a nostalgic picture of our ancestors clustered in the gregarious warmth of the extended family. The legend is false and historians are now showing that the nuclear family was the norm in Western Europe long before industrialization.

These reminders of the persistence of the family suggest further perspective on *Youth* and its concerns. After all, one interpretation of much of the recent sociological literature on schools would not be that schools are powerless, but that they operate in tandem with other powerful educational institutions, notably the family. I agree fully with what Coleman says about the need for alternatives in our near-universal system of education up to grade twelve. Many youths between the ages of fourteen and twenty-four would benefit by leaving their families for work, public service, or a stint in self-governed communities for the young. For those in families that are on the skids and in deep trouble, such alternatives would be especially welcome.

Youth's proposals for youth communities are among its vaguest, but it is right in saying there should be many more experimental opportunities for the young to manage their own affairs. Many young people, however, would also profit by spending more time with adults in their own families and neighborhoods.

In the fifties and early sixties, post-Sputnik educational criticism was largely the work of the academy. It was critical of bureaucracy, professions, and the educational establishment, all of which were highly vulnerable to criticism. The countercultural and radical critique of schools and colleges in the sixties was also largely a product of the academy and its disaffected graduates and students. It too made telling criticisms, although it was increasingly incoherent when it came to spelling out alternatives. *Youth*'s central, very nearly exclusive emphasis on freedom of choice reflects this largely negative recent history. There are many reasons academics are all talking about more choice, options, flexibility, and the like: the inflexibility of many institutions, the incredible variety of students' interests, needs, and talents, the awkward fit of older cultural and academic values with truly mass education, and the breakdown of society's consensus as to what education should be. This is a tangle of complicated historical phenomena. The collapse of the educational consensus as to what the young should learn, for example, will not be set right simply by determined effort, or still less by a return to those educational fundamentals that always look so golden through the dim mist of time. *Youth*'s genuine inability to state what the young should learn mirrors a general confusion; it will hamper all our educational efforts, in informal as well as formal institutions of learning. In the face of this general uncertainty we will probably have to be doubly wary of lapsing into a reductionism that agrees that all students' choices are equally educative. The idea that education should concern itself with what is intrinsically worthwhile has never had much standing in this society, and it needs protecting. The light, anti-intellectual flavor of *Youth*'s educational ideas—often its suggestions boil down to ways of providing the young with jobs, or their moral equivalents—may rouse the chronic philistinism dormant in American culture and hence in American education.

Youth's narrow set of answers is a start, but does not really do justice to the variety of problems facing American schools and colleges. The tension between diversity and equality strains all institutions. In some, the basic problems involve race and class, and education's participation in the systematic inequalities of American life. In others the problems are quite different—validating intellectual and academic values in the face of egalitarian pressures for mass education. In most, there are problems in getting support for good teaching, which remains a very low priority. It would be a pity if *Youth* signals a further shift in the pendulum of educational concern away from day-to-day teaching practice in schools and colleges. Schools without walls and the like could be adventurous new beginnings in integrating schools and life in communities. It seems to me both more practical and more hopeful, however, to view them as the next, natural step in opening up the education system, rather than as desperate alternatives to the discredited enterprise of formal schooling.

The new insistence that education is not just something that happens to the young in institutions presided over by credentialed professionals is welcome; the search for other paths to growing up is overdue. But unless the searchers are more realistic, ventures in informal education may end up with the same sort of disillusionment that now surrounds the enterprise of formal education, a disillusionment that is no less strong for being unwarranted. Modern psychology has not proved that we are incapable of self-government, any more than research in education has proved that the process of learning is an illusion. In both cases gloom arises from unreal initial expectation, not from some ultimately despairing truths about ourselves.

7

Measuring What Schools Achieve

Throughout the 1960s an organization called the International Association for the Evaluation of Educational Research (IEA) surveyed the achievement of school children in some twenty-two countries in mathematics and other conventional academic subjects. The results of many of these surveys are now being published, and recently a conference at Harvard met to discuss what they mean. With cross-national samples involving over 250,000 schoolchildren, the IEA researchers used the same sort of statistical procedures as those employed for the British Plowden Report, *Children and Their Primary Schools;* by the sociologist James Coleman in his report, *Equality of Educational Opportunity;* and by Christopher Jencks and his colleagues in their book *Inequality.* The data add an interesting international dimension to the long and often muddled debate over the relative effects of home background and schooling on children's achievement test scores.

On the whole, the IEA studies tend to confirm earlier findings: Social class and family background seem more important than schooling in accounting for differences in children's achievement test scores. There is one major qualification, however: Schooling seems to be more important in some subjects than in others. Both the Coleman and the Plowden reports dealt with tests for verbal and mathematical ability; the IEA surveys show significant school influence in science, literature, and second language teaching. In the case of literature particularly, the survey suggests that schoolchildren pick up very distinctive approaches to discussing literary works. Those in Chile, England, and New Zealand take an interest in matters of pure form; those in Belgium, Finland, and the United States talk about themes and content; those in Italy take an essentially historical approach. We don't know why. Nonetheless, the literature survey suggests that responses to literature—and presumably to other parts of the curriculum not tested by these surveys—may indeed be learned, and that the learning may well be the result of different sorts of school experiences.

This would scarcely be an astonishing revelation were it not for the heated current arguments over what schools can do. The IEA data suggest that in certain kinds of subjects schools do indeed make a big difference.

The most dramatic fact in the IEA surveys is the huge gap in achievement scores between children in the wealthy, developed nations and children in poor, developing nations. Differences in reading scores among affluent nations are not great, whereas reading scores in three developing nations—Chile, India, and Iran—are so low that fourteen-year-old students seem almost illiterate by comparison. In discussions at Harvard of the educational plight of the poor nations, two points were stressed. The first was their need to build up some kind of educational *system*. In developed nations a wide array of formal and informal educational institutions have existed for three or four generations, and egalitarian social policy has slowly—with some glaring exceptions—narrowed the range of differences between schools. This very systematization poses a new set of problems: standardization, bureaucracy, overly rigid professionalization. Poor countries do not share this affluent malaise. A rural school in Chile may have no books at all, and so the problem is not how well or how soon children learn to read but whether they will ever learn.

A second point made at the Harvard conference was that however great the need for system, it is an open question whether the models of schooling developed in the industrial West are appropriate for developing nations. No developing nation has thus far established an advanced educational system without exacerbating class and caste divisions, and without according brain work a higher status than hand work. This problem was debated in Bolshevik Russia in the 1920s; it is a pressing issue in China and many other poor countries today. Ivan Illich and other neo-Romantic proponents of deschooling and of a Tolstoyan nostalgia for rural life are right when they warn developing nations not to adopt wholesale educational institutions that are illsuited to the needs of a majority of their people. And yet our countercultural assaults on schools and reading have a shallow and elitist ring; there is something unedifying about the spectacle of the jaded and overeducated rich preaching deschooling to poor nations hungry for education. Representatives from poor countries at the Harvard conference noted that literacy and numeracy are coming to be reckoned as fundamental human rights, and although warnings about an overelaborated educational edifice are well taken, the problem remains: how to equip students in developing nations with practical, functional skills such as the ability to read a newspaper, political pamphlet, or tractor repair manual.

In economically advanced societies, the tests of fourteen-year-olds showed Japan, Hungary, and Australia first, second, and third in science. (The pitfalls of cross-cultural research were revealed when a Japanese gentleman politely pointed out that the IEA survey overlooked the fact that Japanese secondary-school students attend school six days a week; after momentary consternation, it was decided that this probably did not alter the results significantly.) In reading comprehension for fourteen-year-olds, New Zealand and Italy were first and second, with the United States, Finland, French Belgium, and Scotland all tied for third. (Some innovation-happy Americans were startled when a man from New Zealand suggested that one reason for his nation's high reading scores was the lack of abrupt changes of content and direction in New Zealand reading programs.) The United States ranked fifth in science; in literature its fourteen-year-olds scored second.

Now, achievement tests are a limited art form. Each culture has distinct educational aims; all cultures want much more for their children than a narrow range of skills that can be measured by achievement tests. Mass cross-cultural survey data probably should be taken with a pinch of salt. For one thing, the tests ignore important differences within each nation's educational system—most notably the proportion of students at a given age who remain in school to be tested. (The tests were given to ten-year-olds, fourteen-year-olds, and students in the last year of secondary school.) Also some observers accuse the tests of a Western bias, and it is true that students in poor nations are not as test-wise as the examination-ridden children of affluent societies. Few children in developing nations have ever even had the dubious pleasure of facing a multiple choice test on which the IEA surveys largely rely.

One illustration of why simple comparisons of test scores in a "cognitive Olympics" don't mean much arises from considering the US position in the science survey. Those who remember educational debates in this country in the fifties will recall that Admiral Hyman Rickover and others used to argue that the highly selective, elitist science education in European secondary schools was far superior to the science education of American students in our more or less comprehensive high schools. Now it turns out that the admiral and other critics were wrong. More students in secondary schools does not mean worse, although the results look wretched enough at first glance: The mean science scores of American students are lower than those for any other developed nation. However, it makes no sense to compare the performance of average high-school graduates in fairly comprehensive secondary school systems like America and Japan with the selected students who sit for *baccalauréat* in France, because the American and Japanese students constitute a majority, whereas the French students are a minority. If instead of comparing all science students you instead look at the performance of the best, the highest-scoring 1, 5, and 9 percent, you discover that they score about the same as their top European counterparts. Thus in the United States, which graduates over 70 percent of its students from high school, the scores of top science students come close to those of the best students in selective European educational systems graduating fewer than 20 percent of their students. The IEA data suggest that the performance of more able students is not hurt when masses of students are given access to comprehensive schooling. Traditionally those who argue for elite systems measure the quality of the surviving few; those who favor more comprehensive education focus on the quality of education given to all. Within the sharp limits of the conventional terms of achievement tests, the IEA scores are mildly reassuring on the first point for American educators, who, if they are candid, will confess that they have not squarely faced the second.

One other aspect of the science study is of interest: the clear advantage of boys in science across the board and across the world. Boys everywhere are more interested in science and do better on the tests. The gap widens as students grow older. Differences are most marked in physics and least in biology. The IEA science report hints here and there at innate sexual differences, but most of the scholars at the Harvard conference preferred the simpler hypothesis of sexual bias. (In reading comprehension and literature, girls did better than boys.) What has now been documented on an international scale is the degree to which much of science learning is a male preserve.

Because of the political situation within their own country, Americans at the conference were particularly concerned about the public response to this sort of research. One point that keeps getting blurred in American debates is that the research that has been done does not show that schools make no difference. What it does show is that by certain crude measures schools are very similar to one another.

We should not confuse discussions of the effects of schooling (about which we know very little) with research on the effects of differences between schools in a roughly uniform educational system.

As matters stand, the effects of schools on achievement tests are much alike—though their effects on the daily lives of the children who attend them may vary enormously. But matters may not stand still. Schools could change their ways of teaching, or—more plausibly in the current political climate—budget cuts and declining support for education might create significant differences between the schools that are adequately supported and those that are starved. The authors of *Inequality* speculated that if schools were shut down—or, presumably, if schools for the poor were to deteriorate markedly— what they call the "cognitive gap" between rich and poor and black and white would be far greater than it is now.

All the school research so far leaves unexplained a great deal of the variation in students' test scores. You may call whatever explains the leftover variation "social character," "as yet unmeasured characteristics of students, teachers, and schools," "luck," or perhaps even "love," as Lewis Carroll's Duchess might put it. Whatever you call it, it is a mystery to the researchers. Complex methodological issues lurk like carp beneath most statements about schools. Critics of the IEA surveys argue that the methods used inflate home effects and minimize school effects, a criticism that the economist Samuel Bowles and others have made of the Coleman Report and similar research. There was repeated questioning at the Harvard conference whether mass surveys of schooling have not reached the limits of their usefulness, and persistent complaints that particular research paradigms are too limited, covering over fundamental uncertainties with a misleading layer of numerical precision. Some educators argued that the IEA survey's reliance on standardized achievement tests runs counter to a growing international trend promoting individuality, diversity, active learning, and a variety of styles of thinking among students. Educators in many countries are beginning to see education as lifelong, not as steps up an achievement ladder. Although the IEA data contained noncognitive items on student attitudes, a number of scholars were also critical of a basic neglect of values. There is certainly a need to look at education from perspectives of people not normally part of the research and policy system: children, teachers, parents, poor people. There was surprising agreement at the conference that the various goals different nations have for their schools are far too broad and complex to be settled by the crudities of mass testing.

This subdued emphasis on complexities—the sense of how little is actually known—is probably the most important thing for the public, policy-makers, and practitioners to realize. By itself this ignorance constitutes a good argument for further research, research in a variety of modes. Yet many educational practitioners are coming to feel the same way about research as the exasperated student who, after taking yet another IEA test, wrote, "The money for this would have been better spent sending woolens to Africa." But as the process of framing educational policy becomes more self-conscious, the kind of research that is available and how it gets reported is important. The Plowden Report, for example, presented the British public with important quantitative research on the limits of schooling, along with qualitative material on classroom practice and educational philosophy that was of direct benefit to British practitioners. This combination is unheard of in this country, where educational discussions often manage to avoid the problems of practitioners altogether. It would be foolish pragmatism in our present state of basic ignorance to insist that all or even most educational research directly helps children and teachers, but it is not hoping too much that some of it will, and that some researchers will be willing to spend at least as much time working with teachers and children as Konrad Lorenz spends with his ducklings.

Part of the current animus against social science research on schools is the age-old desire to kill the messenger who brings unwelcome news. To the degree that these sorts of studies check the traditional American faith in the boundless power of schooling to effect fundamental social change, they perform a valuable service. For the dark side of the coin of our utopian faith is the despair that sets in when schools do not do the impossible. In this despairing mood, educators tend to exaggerate the baleful impact of research, forgetting the primacy of the political climate. Much recent American writing on the effects of schooling was intended as a critique of liberal sentimentality about the power of schooling, on the part of scholars who imagined that liberals would continue to dominate educational policy; the research reads strangely in an era when policy is in the hands of conservatives intent on dismantling the social services. It is, however, not the research itself, but the *Zeitgeist* that is mainly responsible for how particular findings get interpreted, emphasized, and acted upon. Arthur Jensen is, so to speak, always waiting in the wings, because the debate between conservative hereditarians and liberal environmentalists is perennial. It is only a political climate of despair and retreat from social commitment that puts the spotlight on him.

Meanwhile, in its endless concern for its schools, the American public might keep in mind two points made by one participant trying to sum up the IEA findings and other similar research. Home background is the best predictor of children's achievement scores, and yet the older students in school do successively better on the tests than the younger ones. The first point suggests the limits on the differences schools make; the second indicates that they may make a measurable difference on achievement test scores, as well as in more important, less readily measurable realms. Knee deep in computer printout, and profoundly divided on many of the research issues, the scholars are still far from having resolved this key ambiguity.

8

Children Out of School

Some time ago a group called the Task Force on Children Out of School tried to document the shocking number of children excluded from public education in Boston. The group, now the Massachusetts Advocacy Center, published its findings in a report, *The Way We Go To School* (1970), and has since been following up on it with a skillful combination of threats and wheedling to get school officials to act on the problem. It has pressed for more bilingual education teachers, more classes for kids with special needs, changes in school policies on discipline and suspension and rules barring pregnant girls from classes, and other related issues. This relatively successful local venture in advocacy has now prompted an organization called the Children's Defense Fund (a public advocacy group whose origins are in the legal wing of the civil rights movement) to try to assemble a national picture of the children excluded from school. Their report, *Children Out of School in America*, is sobering. Using a variety of sources—1970 US census data, data from HEW's Office for Civil Rights, official school surveys and rules, plus an intensive door-to-door canvass of families in selected census tracts in nine states—the CDF finds that nearly two million school-age children between seven and seventeen are not enrolled in school. Of these, more than a million are under fifteen and more than three-quarters of a million are between seven and thirteen. In thirty areas surveyed, the CDF found 5.4 percent of all children six to seventeen out of school. County-by-county breakdowns show some places where 20, 30, and 40 percent of the children are not enrolled.

There is reason to think that these figures underestimate the problem. For one thing, the CDF used the Census Bureau's rather conservative criterion for children not enrolled, counting only those who had no contact with school three months prior to April. The figures certainly do not include children expelled and suspended and otherwise thrown out of school for disciplinary reasons, the countless truants who elude census counters, children whose parents answer the census forms incorrectly because they don't comprehend English, or the handicapped children and pregnant girls listed by many school systems as receiving home instruction, although in fact they are being deprived of schooling. Nor, the report says, do its figures account for parents who won't admit to strangers that their children aren't in school, nor the more than 85,000 children not counted by the census because they were in detention facilities of one sort or another. And of course the report has no way of reckoning the numbers of children who are in school, but who sit at their desks in a state of what might be called functional exclusion—particularly children who don't speak English.

Children out of school come from every racial and income group. Of course, poor children are included in their ranks in disproportionate numbers. Minority children are out of school in greater numbers than white children, and rural children are out more than city children. The census figures say nothing about why these children are out of school. To find out, the CDF canvassers talked to parents, children, and school officials in selected communities. The eloquent yet understated case studies lead to this conclusion: "If a child is not white, or is white but not middle class, does not speak English, is poor, needs special help with seeing, hearing, walking, reading, learning, adjusting, growing up, is pregnant or married at age fifteen, is not smart enough, or is too smart, then in many places school officials decide school is not the place for that child."

The common denominator of these children is that in one way or another they are different. Most of them are out of school not by choice but because they were kicked out. Case after case testifies to the extent to which too many school officials get rid of children as a matter of course, in effect taking it on themselves to decide that certain groups of children are educationally expendable. Kids are kept out of school for reasons ranging from pregnancy to inability to afford clothes, textbooks, lunch, and other school fees and transportation costs, to being diagnosed as handicapped in some way for which there are no educational services. In Floyd County, Kentucky, local CDF canvassers discovered that 21 percent of the children were out of school because they couldn't afford textbooks or other school fees. In Portland, Maine, poor children in a housing project two miles from the nearest schools have to pay two dollars a week to ride to them.

The plight of children with special needs makes up an important part of the evidence gathered in *Children Out of School.* In a great many places children with special needs of one sort or another—mental, physical, emotional—are denied entry to public education. Where they are admitted, they are often wretchedly served. And apart from the talk of special programs, there is the separate yet intertwined problem of misclassification. An appalling vacuum in services is compounded by the fact that existing special education classes are often dumping bins. Just as tracking systems can be used to resegregate schools, so can special classes. The Office for Civil Rights has been gathering data in 505 school districts in Alabama, Arkansas, Georgia, Mississippi, and South Carolina with an eye to seeing whether there is racial discrimination in classes for what are called the educable mentally retarded. It has found that black children in these school districts are twice as likely as white children to end up in special classes. In some southern districts, a black child is five times as likely as a white child to end up in a special class. Similar, if less drastic, disproportions of minority children in special education classes can be found in many parts of the country.

School suspensions and expulsions are another problem. Office for Civil Rights data show that in the 1972–73 school year, over a million children were suspended from this country's schools. High schools suspended students twice as often as junior high and elementary schools. Here again, the Office for Civil Rights is looking to see whether the figures show racial bias. (The case studies in the CDF report document individual instances of bias.) In 1972–73 schools suspended 6 percent of their white students and 12 percent of their black students. In high schools blacks were suspended three times as often as white students. Yet it would be a mistake to think of school suspensions as a minority issue, any more than children with special needs or misclassified children are a minority issue. Half a million of the children suspended in 1972–73 were white.

These figures probably also understate things. Many school systems do not report suspensions, or they call them by other names. The city of Los Angeles, for example, reported no suspensions in 1972–73, and New York City's school suspension figures have a widespread local reputation for self-serving whimsicality. In its surveys the CDF found that 65.4 percent of all suspensions are for offenses that are dangerous neither to persons or property. In fact, 24.5 percent were attributed to truancy or tardiness, for which suspension seems an odd remedy.

The arbitrary character of many expulsions and suspensions comes through in the case studies. In Macon, Georgia, a sixteen-year-old black student was expelled because he could not pay five dollars to replace a ruler accidentally broken in shop class. In New Bedford, Massachusetts, a seventeen-year-old white boy was suspended for two days when he left the school grounds to help an old man change a flat tire. When his mother called to find out about the incident, she was told that the boy had done a good deed, but the rule was that anybody who left school grounds had to be suspended. School officials often told the CDF canvassers that suspensions are a way to get parents in to talk about a difficult student. Yet in a third of the cases surveyed, suspended students returned without a parent conference.

Some groups are excluded from school in such disproportions that the next step is clearly litigation. Yet in a sense the deeper problems raised by *Children Out of School in America* are so universal and complex that they are not all that accessible to action through the courts. Schools that carelessly mislabel poor children as retarded are very likely going to mislabel middle-class children as dyslexic or hyperkinetic. Inadequate special education services hurt children across racial and class lines. Schools unable to tolerate diversity reflect our tenacious cultural assumption that it is wrong to be different.

An exercise on the part of lawyers and activists, the report quite sensibly focuses on exclusionary practices that are unconscionable by any reasonable standard: kids kept out of school because they are poor, or labeled retarded because they are black, or suspended for wildly capricious reasons. Beneath the straightforward abuses lurk more complicated issues.

Take discipline, for example. There is a growing body of litigation and local agitation on this in many communities. Students' rights are expanding, and there are efforts afoot to give disciplinary procedures in schools some semblance of due process and accountability. Even when the gross abuses have been dealt with, however, discipline still remains a tangle. The fact that many school systems have never thought through, let alone spelled out, their policies on discipline has meant the growth of a vast area of unsupervised power on the part of school officials. One problem is the absence of policy. This may be one rare area where schools are not bureaucratic enough, in the sense of having orderly machinery for fair decisions and appeals processes. Thus courts generally permit suspensions of three days or less without hearings. Instead of holding hearings, however, many schools now in effect expel kids by successions of short suspensions. When black students in newly integrated schools complain that they are being suspended or expelled in disproportionate numbers, there is seldom adequate machinery—parent-professional advisory boards, or whatever—even to hear their complaints. Discipline *is* a problem. Teachers in a lot of schools are very scared. The contrast between the complexity of the realities of life in classrooms and the frequent simplicity of reformers' attacks on the schools makes many teachers angry. Yet practitioners and school officials have to realize that attempts to assert their legitimate authority and control of turbulent classrooms will continue to be undermined as long as widespread abuses of the sort documented by the CDF continue to flourish. The discipline problem illustrates the ongoing, terribly vexing process of making professionals accountable to the clients they are supposed to be serving; here the process is complicated because there are genuine claims of necessity and professionalism to be served, as well as legitimate complaints that school disciplinary procedures in many places stink. The vague yet insistent demand for participation, which was so vociferous in the late 1960s, is not in fact going to go away: it is now reappearing in the form of local and national demands for accountability, more parent representation, review boards, and the like. One hopes this time around—in contrast to the disasters of the community control wars—that some coalitions of parents and professionals might form, but the precedents are not auspicious.

Similarly, the issue of the educational rights of children with special needs is not simple. In many of the relatively advanced states, parents, advocacy groups, and coalitions of social service professionals are taking steps through courts and legislatures to expand the educational rights of these children. The long-overdue rights being won—for educational programs, for inclusion, where possible, in regular schooling—are making new sets of demands on schools and teachers. The demands are enormous and unprecedented, and unless practitioners in schools can get commensurate support for new efforts, they will probably employ their formidable powers of resistance to make sure that little changes significantly. The whole field of special education is rich in parallels with other areas of the social services. People are asking society to be more tolerant of a greater range of differences among children. This is not just a matter for school officials and teachers, of course; it includes everyone. For more than a century, one of the main enterprises of social policy was constructing vast institutions, defining certain groups as special in one way or another, and segregating them in these institutions. Now many of us are questioning the institutional legacy we have inherited, although we are very uncertain about workable alternatives. Along with the institutionalization, professionalization, and the spread of new forms of social isolation is a slowly growing respect for human variety and the diversity of childhood itself. There is a search for alternatives to the machinelike institutions we face, and a growing bias toward keeping people where possible—it is certainly not always possible—in homes and community alternatives to mass institutions. In some states there are moves to deinstitutionalize institutions for young criminal offenders and the mentally ill. Criticism of many of our large-scale institutions has rightly insisted that they are human scrap heaps. Yet there is a real fear on the part of some observers that deinstitutionalizing and the quest for alternatives may not generate the increased political and financial support workable alternatives will need. Asking the schools to undertake new responsibilities for handicapped youth, to integrate those who can be integrated, and asking the social services to build community alternatives, where possible, to big institutions, adds up to a very large set of demands.

Children Out of School in America does not have to address these complexities, or those in other areas. (Misclassification, for instance, goes to the heart of the way schools function.) Instead it provides initial documentation of indefensible abuses. One lesson to draw is the need for more local and national information. The rock-bottom ignorance on which many social programs operate ought to be a major scandal. Most federal agencies involved with various services for children have no idea at all how many children need the services, how many actually get them, and how many are excluded from them for one reason or another. Local agencies are even more ignorant. Facts alone are more or less neutral, to be sure. However, where there are no data at all it is readily assumed that there is no problem. Conversely, the generation and publication of new facts can help focus attention on urgent problems few knew existed. This may now be the case with children out of school.

A second lesson is that different kinds of educational issues coexist and overlap like geological strata. This is one reason why most truths about education require more than a single sentence to get across without distortion. Along with a host of new demands on the schools for openness, for alternatives, for options, for more attention to individuals, there is an older, unfinished agenda. Poor people, immigrants, and minorities have been struggling hard to get inside classrooms since public education was established in this country. The CDF shows the dismaying extent to which this basic fight is still going on. Reformers with an itch for panaceas in education—such as the terrible simplifiers now bent on abolishing compulsory education or child labor laws—will have to develop more of an eye for these overlapping complexities.

There will be additional CDF reports on related issues: a volume on school discipline, and reports on labeling and treatment of children with special needs, the use of children in medical experimentation, children's rights to privacy in school and juvenile court records, the juvenile justice system, and day care. The CDF hopes to get the same kind of sustained advocacy for children that the NAACP Legal Defense and Education Fund started giving blacks many years ago. It and many other advocacy groups now concerned with children's rights represent a long-delayed professional response to the slow, yet persistent rise in the esteem of children and youth in this culture, an ongoing shift in cultural values that is real even though it has scarcely begun to budge our mass institutions or alter our budgetary priorities. In part these efforts are attempts to give legal force to a largely rhetorical tradition involing children's rights. The increased interest in children's rights also reflects a reading of recent history by some veterans of the victories and defeats of the civil rights movement and the poverty war: unless you can make social services and programs a matter of right for all children—black and white, rich and poor—no enduring political constituency can be maintained to support them, and in fact gains may be reversed when the political climate changes for the worse. The challenge for national and local groups like the CDF will be to keep up the legal pressure on schools and other institutions in situations where rights are obviously being violated, and yet break out of the narrow confines of litigation and legalism. We are learning the limits on what schools as institutions can do; we are also learning the difficulty of changing what goes on in them by means of levers outside the schools. Lawsuits and injunctions are a proper (often the only) remedy for the trampled rights of various groups, but cannot guarantee redress at the level of day-to-day life in classrooms and institutions. What is needed is a whole range of levers: more money and services, litigation, and the sustained work of local citizens' and advocacy groups such as the Massachusetts Advocacy Center. Legislation and the federal courts have a role to play, but real change, if and when it happens, will come in local communities, and it will involve what now seems very hard to imagine: coalitions of reformers, parents, and practitioners.

9

Notes on Practice

One of the things I discover in trying to teach a course in the history of education is how little we know about teachers, children, and educational practice in the past. We are getting a better sense of the contours of children's lives through being more aware of the way ideas about childhood have been time and culture bound. But except for an occasional glimpse of the classroom triumphs, and political troubles, of a gifted practitioner like Francis Parker, we don't know very much about the history of teaching or learning.

I have the feeling this represents something more than the genuine difficulty of unearthing practice from old records. It also reflects the fact that our culture has not set much of a value on practice. Some reasons for this are the low status and pay of child-minders in many cultures, the fact that most teachers are women, the essentially administrative priorities of the schools, and the lack of an adequate educational theory. Another factor is that—although they would not have put it in these terms—Americans in the past generally paid more attention to the macro realm of education than to the micro realm. It seems to me that nineteenth-century Americans were a windy group, more comfortable talking about the macro realm: they were also preoccupied by the social aims of schooling. There were exceptions: sinister developments such as the Lancasterian school-machines, and more hopeful phenomena, such as Horace Mann's musings on pedagogy, the Oswego movement, the kindergarten reformers, or figures like Parker. An interest in pedagogy was exceptional, however.

Education was very much bound up with people's hopes and fears as they faced modernity: schools were a response to what was felt to be a crisis in the culture, part of a new urban order's reckoning with the existence of unprecedented strangers and immigrants. Bernard Bailyn's fascinating essay, *Education in the Forming of American Society,* argues that, from a very early period, Americans looked to schools to take up the slack for other, supposedly failing, institutions transplanted from Europe to the New World. In the last decade or so, Bailyn's essay has prompted a lot of discussion. Responses to it have varied—recent work on the history of the family is making a fascinating issue of whether the family was in fact decaying, or merely shifting its social functions—but no one to my mind has pointed out that Bailyn's general argument is, besides being a reading of the past, an echo of the classic American line of thought about education. More often than not, people talking about schools have stressed their ulterior social purposes: they were for something else, usually to shore up older pieces of the culture that were believed to be collapsing. It is a curious fact that one of the major collective enterprises in an intensely individualistic culture has repeatedly emphasized the social functions of schools, at least as much as their benefit to individual students. The idea that education exists to serve intrinsically educational purposes is rather a minority point of view in the history of American education.

An exception to this generalization is the Progressive Era—roughly the period between 1880 and 1920. The mainstream Progressive educators—some historians think of them as the administrative Progressives—were very much concerned with the macro realm: they were bent on making the schools into efficient servants of the new, emerging corporate order. Opposed to the administrative progressives, with their essentially bureaucratic and economic values, were the child-centered Progressives, who argued the case for the intrinsic values of education and took a profound interest in the micro world of pedagogy. One reason we are still fascinated by the Progressive Era is that its educational and political agenda looks recognizeably like our own. The conflicts seem similar: disputes over schooling as work or preparation for work as opposed to schooling for play and intrinsic values; the idea of education for homogeneity as opposed to education for cultural diversity; the central tension between equality and meritocracy; the tensions involved in extending older, academic models of secondary schooling to masses of students, which still persist, being repeated again in higher education.

Recent histories of progressive education stress the bureaucratic and administrative emphases of the mainstream Progressives and their attempts to mesh schools with the corporate order. The best description of the micro world of practice that emerged in the Progressive era is still Lawrence Cremin's *The Transformation of the School*. Cremin's categories for the varieties of progressive classroom practice—democracy, science, and child-centeredness—may not jibe completely with our sense of the variety of practice today, but there is a rough fit. Our problems in practice are not new. The pendulum of debate between the new education and the old is, alas, still swinging back and forth to extremes, slogans of freedom alternating with slogans of discipline and order. The debater's simplicities continue to mean little to most practitioners, who have to exist on the muddled intersections and borders of counterpoised realms.

In one sense it seems discouraging that our efforts to improve practice have not gone beyond the formulations of the Progressives. The general lack of cumulative development makes a good deal of our educational reform seem terribly faddish. In what I sometimes think of as the United States of Amnesia, we keep rehearsing the ideas and dilemmas of the past, and I suppose we will continue to start from scratch each generation until we develop a sixth sense of the past to add to our other five senses. In another way, though, the most recent waves of classroom reform have been encouraging; the best work has been at the proper level—individual classrooms and schools—and my sense is that the upshot in many schools has been a greater tolerance for variety than existed before. If I'm right, this sense of the variety of good practice is a real achievement, outweighing the failure of child-centered pedagogy to sweep the schools and establish itself as —heaven forbid—a new orthodoxy. In one way or another, it seems to me that the issues raised by the newest round of the new education will continue to be very much alive. This time, like last time, the most thoughtful new educators are trying to encourage teachers to gain more control over their classrooms, and children to take a more active part in learning. It may be, too, that our growing appreciation of the diversity and variety of childhood depends less on short-term fads in education (which come and go, as cynical educators know) and more on long-term shifts in the culture. Historians are beginning to get a clear sense that in the long run the family has changed from being an economic unit of production to being a unit of leisure, consumption, and childrearing. I believe these changes underlie the long-term shift in the status of children from being quite marginal and exploited figures to being something close to culture heroes (a position not without its own drawbacks). Where the extension of schooling and the bits and pieces of child-centered practice fit into these trends is a puzzle.

Basically two opposed lines of interpretation are emerging. One holds that mass schooling and increasingly child-centered families both represent different facets of what Richard Titmuss (speaking of Britain) has called a revolution in standards of child care since the nineteenth century. An opposite point of view—that of a historian like Philippe Ariès, for instance—holds that the shift toward child-centered families and more and more formal education both reflect long-term loss of community in the West, a thinning-out of the richness and diversity of a medieval order in which adults and children lived and worked together and shared a common world outside the bounds of the private family. There seems to be some truth in both these accounts. At this stage of our knowledge, we can leave it as something of a paradox to be resolved that the growing sense of the value of children has resulted in their spending more and more time in bureaucratic institutions called schools. It also seems clear that the culture's slow movement toward more child-centeredness has prompted many of the new criticisms of the schools. Masses of people now hold views about education that were once the property of a handful of romantics, eccentrics and rebels. More and more often frustrated parents and teachers share an appreciation of children's variety that runs against the grain of many of our settled institutions.

One reason many of us have turned to asking broad, macro sets of questions about the schools is that we believe that the macro realm can limit decisively the opportunities for good classroom practice. Discussions of practice have often ignored the decisive constraints of social class and race, and the way they reshape educational ideas. But although the macro realities exist, the form they take is always local and particular, and this is why our broad ideas about educational reform so often break down. The quest for a poor people's pedagogy —the one right way of teaching poor children—has always floundered in the face of the actual diversity of the children in a given classroom. If there is one slogan to be salvaged from the aftermath of recent school reforms, my nomination would be: "Differences within a given group are always more educationally significant than differences between groups." What may be a good idea in one setting is not necessarily good in another. There is something ludicrous about the false precision with which we speak of educational "models" and "experiments." In reality there is no such thing, only more or less promising approaches and ideas.

Recent historians tend to take a dour view of the macro social functions of schools in the past, but they continue to focus on superordinate aims: socialization, keeping the poor in line, the quest for community and order, economic productivity. There is no doubt that the broad questions need asking. In the field of educational history this probing has been equivalent to the kinds of structural questions about schooling that surfaced in the school controversies of the late 1960s. It is important to know, as Diane Ravitch has shown in her marvelous *The Great School Wars,* that the nineteenth-century New York City schools were a Protestant poverty program to shape up the children of the Catholic poor, just as it is important to have the general perspective on schooling offered by James Coleman's work on equality and schooling. However, raising big questions in the macro realm is not the same as answering them. It is odd that in the aftermath of a period of intense debate over the social functions of schools, our ideas are still very tentative and shaky. There is a kind of elephantine comedy to our basic ignorance: different disciplinary traditions lead economists to grope around and pronounce on the great importance of schooling, while many sociologists, fingering the same beast, minimize its effects. In history, a student is now in a

position to read thoughtful interpretations of the Progressive Era that
seem as wildly at variance with each other as the different characters'
accounts of the crime in *Rashomon.*

This rich and perhaps promising basic confusion prompts several
thoughts. One is that we seem to be at a point where good synthetic
theorizing is in order. At the same time we should not be in too much
of a hurry to translate the theory that emerges into policy. (One
suggestion is that we publish it in German.) Another suggestion is
that the intellectual neglect of classroom practice may be one of the
sources of some of our general conceptual problems in the macro
realm. It seems to be much easier to pose overarching formulations
than to connect them in practice to the lives of teachers and children,
and the sense one has in general that our theories are overdetermined
and much too simple is reinforced by the extraordinary variety of life
in classrooms. We need synthetic theory. We also need to use much
smaller nets, or we may find ourselves in the position of ingeniously
refining and overelaborating techniques for sifting through the same
old sorts of junky data.

Susan Isaacs, who has had a good influence on British classroom
practice, used to say that what she was trying to do was to understand
and to help. It isn't always possible to do either; and our culture
today, with its denigration of practice, makes it especially difficult to
help. Our knowledge of many fundamental things about education
is so poor that it would be a foolish pragmatism to reject all research
that is not of direct use to working teachers. On the other hand, it
is not asking too much to say that more researchers should be involved with teachers and children. I sympathize with the impatient
feeling on the part of most practitioners that much educational
research is not a help, although practitioners' resistance to thought
is not an attractive trait.

In the recent past the most prestigious universities have not done
very well by educational practice. This has been as true of the educational practice in courses for graduates and undergraduates, as of
teacher training. The priorities of a university largely organized along
the lines of graduate disciplines do not lend themselves readily to an
encouragement of teaching. Debates here, as elsewhere in education,
sometimes revolve around ancient and false polarities: research vs.
teaching being a favorite, or the old snobbish distinction between

educational methods courses and "real" academic courses. Although mandarinism exists in the universities, it would be a mistake to see the general neglect of teaching as a mandarin plot. Education at all levels has fallen in between the cracks of other, often legitimate, concerns. Some people have just wanted to get their work done. Others have been busy defending academic values from countercultural and neopopulist assaults. And still others have discovered that educational innovations takes a very great deal of time and effort. I'm now planning a third round in a social policy course I teach with two colleagues, and I'm struck by how long it has taken three congenial friends to begin relating our material to each other's interests. This is one reason, I suppose, why there aren't more of those interdisciplinary courses we keep saying should be offered.

Another reason the university has often had problems in its involvements with classrooms is that it is, in fact, very difficult to mesh the culture of the universities with the culture of schools. Teachers live in different worlds from those of the researchers and academics. Their status is lower. This is not necessarily something the researchers need to feel guilty about—guilt being an overwhelmingly useless emotion—but it does pose problems. Teachers who come to the universities are probably right to resent the neglect of practice, but they are quite wrong if they think they have nothing to learn, and equally wrong if they imagine they have nothing to teach. Much of what they have to learn is academic and theoretical in the good senses of those words. What they may have to teach is some ways that university discourse might inform educational practice, assuming the university can listen. The academics need to touch base with practice, and to reflect more consciously on the ways that teaching faces common problems on many levels, including the university level. Teachers need something more than the day-to-day horizons of the classroom, whose limits are one small part of why so many good ones are going crazy. All this sounds very pious, but truisms are sometimes true. A school of education not in touch with classrooms is in danger of losing an important part of its mind—the necessary understanding of the world of practice—and its soul as well.

We do know some things about teaching. We know that the key figures in schools are principals and classroom teachers. Policy or reform that seeks to bypass them is futile. The general staff, top-down model of school reform is part of the professional pathology of education, and the resistance to change and innovation on the part of many teachers often can be a functional form of self-defense against this pathology. Giving practitioners the mixture of autonomy and support they need, and so seldom get, ought to be a central priority. Support for the professionals means money in a day of shrinking budgets, and it means advice and help. I'm always struck by two things about teachers in our schools. One is how harassed they are by what the army calls "chicken shit." The other is how lonely they are in their work. At all levels the educational system needs people able to act as advisers, sitting in on classes and talking with instructors. In England, the shift in the role of government inspectors—essentially they stopped being punitive inspectors and instead thought of the job as advising—was a great help to primary-school reform.

The utility of the sort of macro research that has been done is to point out something that should be obvious, but seldom is, at least in the light of America's utopian educational traditions. Schools are, after all, only part of children's lives, and not the major part at that. But what is still missing is an appreciation of the fact that life in schools is very much a day-to-day and local affair. It is the quality of the micro life of teachers and children in classrooms that is most neglected in our discussions of education. At the end of *36 Children*, one of Herbert Kohl's Harlem students told him that "one good year is not enough." We need to understand both the bitter truth of that, and the way in which one good year in a classroom is, after all, a great deal.

10

Among Schoolteachers

Dan C. Lortie's *Schoolteacher* is one of the most interesting and thoughtful social portraits of the teaching profession since the appearance of Willard Waller's admirable classic, *The Sociology of Teaching* (1932; 1961 edition by Russell and Russell, New York). Lortie is a sociologist who is fascinated by the way occupations mold and season people. He has already written about doctors and lawyers, and in many ways *Schoolteacher* is a meditation on why teaching is a profession and is not. Lortie's own central value seems to be an ideal of professional technical expertise which he finds notably missing from the enterprise of education. Not all scholars or practitioners will agree with all his findings or his notion of what the profession should be but anyone interested in education can profit from his intelligent work.

Lortie's chief source of new information is a long questionnaire he gave to ninety-four teachers from five towns in the greater Boston area. (Boston was not one of them.) He also has a written questionnaire filled out by five thousand teachers in the Dade County, Florida, schools. And here and there he draws on mass polls of teachers' attitudes and opinions done for groups like the National

Education Association. He makes excellent use of his very open-ended interviews. The teachers' voices come through clearly; what they say richly illustrates his main themes. He is able to pull the material together without suppressing the variety of responses. The greatest virtue of the study is the glimpse it offers of how life looks to teachers as they gaze out the classroom windows.

He finds teachers' professional lives marked by three essential qualities. He thinks they are *conservative,* with a distinct preference for doing things the way they have been done. He sees them as *presentist:* Few plan to teach for a long period of their lives, and most seek their psychic rewards from the immediacies of day-to-day life in the classroom. And he thinks of them as terribly *individualistic:* at the core of their professional existence is the time they spend alone with their students in their classroom.

These three traits—conservatism, presentism, and individualism—are the outcome of many complex forces and constraints. Some are historical, as Lortie insists in his opening chapter: His grasp of the long-term historical continuities in the teaching profession is refreshing and altogether rare in either social science or education. History does have a lot to do with the way things are in our schools. The historic status of teaching has been, as he puts it, special, yet shadowed, a job associated with lofty ideals, yet underpaid and difficult, with a high turnover of people. Professionalism of a certain sort has developed, but lay boards still control schools, and the status of teachers within schools and in society at large has remained suprisingly stable. Teachers' organizations and unions have begun to challenge the power of administration, but classroom practitioners are still outranked by professors of education and administrators. Nor has the economic standing of teachers changed all that much from the past, despite improvements in pay scales. The average teacher goes on teaching longer than teachers in the nineteenth century, but critics still complain that teaching is not a lifetime career, or indeed a full-time commitment, for many teachers. Teaching remains today what it was in the past: a partial profession in which practitioners find entry easy, methods of teaching generally the same, and the work very lonely.

The nation's two million schoolteachers do not share a single type of personality, yet there are important commonalities in their lot.

The way an occupation attracts new members, teaches them its culture, and sustains their commitment over time gives a definite shape to it. Lortie's teachers say they are drawn to the trade because they like children and working with people, because teaching offers a form of upward social mobility for some, because they like to be of service, because the job is secure, and because the pay and the hours are attractive. Salaries are certainly not high, but, relatively speaking, they are good for women and can look good to men moving up from poor families. The teachers Lortie interviewed approve of the prevailing system of education, and they sometimes, he feels, lack a sense of complete commitment to their profession and its affairs.

In retrospect, few teachers think their preparation much of a help for the job. In the solitude that Lortie sees as so pervasive, beginning teachers are left to sink or swim. The schools of education often promote lofty goals without giving students any practical means to accomplish them. Lortie notes the education profession's pathological discrediting of past practice, the general absence of cumulative development of technique and pedagogy, and the lack of any systematic codification of practical experience. The repudiation of past and collective experience is in part responsible for a characteristic style of reform discourse that dwells on aims and fails to give help on daily problems. Lortie's teachers are Robinson Crusoes, monarchs and prisoners of an island existence. The isolated, fitful, and various patterns in which teachers learn their trade and ply it makes it hard for them to think in collective terms about it. And this inability, in turn, constantly threatens their standing with the outside world of parents, school boards, and critics of education.

In comparison with other professions where rewards and satisfactions are staged over a long period of professional development, teaching is singularly lacking in stages. Teachers say they learn to teach by teaching, yet within a school the differences in status between those in their second year on the job and those in their tenth are usually minor. (In fact, older teachers are often thought of as dead wood.) The rewards for accumulated experience are slight. A gifted practitioner like Frances Hawkins argues that it takes five or ten years to learn to teach; generally, however, the education profession does not seem to agree. Even the teachers' unions have focused on getting high beginning salaries; seniority scales aside, they have paid much

less attention to the needs of experienced teachers. The relative lack
of rewards and respect for those who do stay on is frustrating to many.
Teaching is hard. The hours are not as short as the public imagines:
Lortie's teachers spend a mean of 47.4 hours a week at it. The job
seems especially tough on younger men and unmarried women. The
married women Lortie talked to seemed to have the most favorable
balance of rewards. They work slightly shorter hours—a difference of
about half an hour a week—and seem more satisfied with their lot.
Thinking about this, Lortie wonders whether teachers who give the
most end up being the least satisfied. (One wonders whether this
would hold true if sex and marital status were controlled.)

Teaching does seem to be a pretty good career for married women
with children. (In the 1930s Waller complained of the practice of
keeping married women out of the schools, saying that the culture
was trying to make teachers into its Vestal Virgins.) They don't mind
the isolation of the classroom as much as single women, nor are they
as resentful as men over the pay. It may be, too, although Lortie
doesn't say so, that teaching is one of the few trades in which you
can make professional use of training as a parent. Being a parent can
teach one a lot about children and the vagaries of learning and
development, as well as affording perspectives on schooling. Many
young teachers, impressed by the awesome needs of the children in
their classrooms, chafe guiltily at their own limitations and those of
the schools. A teacher who is also a mother or father may be in a
better position to appreciate the peculiar, if limited, benefits someone
outside the family can render children.

There is a modest yet quite real set of differences in the values
teachers bring to teaching. Some think of it in moral terms; the point
for them is helping to develop children's character. Some think of
teaching as mainly a matter of connecting students to a particular
subject or to education itself. Others stress their efforts to reach all
the students. Despite the different goals they set for themselves, they
all face similar tensions. Teachers are uncertain about what they are
accomplishing, and the uncertainty is compounded by a number of
important facts about the teaching situation: The relationship of
teacher to student is mostly involuntary, the job entails extracting
certain amounts of work from the immature, and education mostly
takes place in crowds of people. Teachers at all levels feel torn by the

need to exert the kind of authority that gets students to work under these difficult circumstances and the kind of warmth required to sustain good relationships. They learn, as Waller put it long ago, that teaching is an uncomfortable affair of stepping on and off one's high horse.

Questions about the outcomes of teachers' work got very charged answers that seem to have embarrassed Lortie. Plainly many of his teachers anguish over the question of whether they are doing a good job. They have high ambitions for helping students—too high, Lortie suspects—but there is the possibility that their efforts may have only a temporary effect or no effect at all. Research in education, like most social science research, has concentrated on measuring the short-term effects of schooling, and rarely has it been of much help to the practitioners themselves. They are becoming defensive about the meager results of their work. It may well be, as Lortie suggests, that the style of thought currently dominant in the social sciences may not be really appropriate for those who must take responsibility for the development of children.

The strained sense of having to control difficult situations and suppressing a part of yourself is also a constant in the interviews. Teachers work with people; yet they are seldom trained to consider their own feelings and to take them into account in the work. As Lortie says, the ideal stance—for survival, if nothing else—would be an appreciation of your own limitations within some context of self-acceptance. Yet the tone of many of the interviews is self-accusatory: "Teachers seem lonely; they fight battles alone with their consciences, and, it seems, frequently lose."

Teachers lack the status and power to do their work as autonomous professionals. In a sense they are stage managers, yet they lack the independence of theatre directors; they manage classrooms, with much less discretion and fewer resources than managers and supervisors in industry. Their work resembles therapy at times, with much less recognition and support than therapists, psychologists, and analysts. They care most about what goes on in their classrooms. Yet even here control is precarious. Teachers often have a desperate feeling about time: They race the clock. Lortie says that their intense anger over interruptions—the P.A. system booming out in the middle of a lesson—is all the deeper because the intrusions characteristically reveal the system's lack of respect for the core of their enterprise. So many teaching choices seem zero-sum games, impossible to win; if you take the pressure off William so that he can relax enough to learn how to read, then you must start worrying about how far behind he might be next year, in which case he will face another sort of pressure. And so on.

Lortie concludes with some speculations about the future of the teaching profession. He sketches three plausible "scenarios," future projections of current trends. One possibility is a continuing quickening of the pace of cultural change. The erosion of tradition in and out of schools, the spread of alternative ideas, and higher expectations of schools by the public may force teachers to adapt to an educational climate alien to their conservatism. If this turns out to be so, then Lortie hopes teachers can develop new forms of collegiality that will go beyond simply banding together for self-defense. A second scenario stresses the growing importance of unionism and collective bargaining, and the enlargement of the scope of negotiations to include classroom and pedagogical issues. The organized teachers' movement must deal with a decline in the "ritual pity" for the teachers' lot, and new demands for "accountability." If this trend continues, Lortie sees a need for greater professionalism and the legitimacy conferred by expertise; among other things, the unions will have to develop cadres of their own educational specialists, researchers, and experts. Lortie's third scenario pictures continuing centralization, in which teachers may find themselves dealing with bigger and fewer school districts and much stronger state educational authorities. Teachers will have to define themselves either as civil servants in the bureaucracies of the public sector of the economy or as academics, but in either case, Lortie says, they will need new forms of collegial authority and expertise to offset new threats to their independence and conservatism. Some overlap of all three scenarios is most probably what we will see. Lortie's suggestions pose impressive challenges to the unions, who have yet to form policies in a number of the realms he touches on.

Lortie's diagnosis for what ails the teaching profession is in the end fairly simple: What is wrong is the extreme quality of teachers' independence, presentism, and conservatism. His cure is also fairly simple: Teachers need to develop a more collegial profession equipped with a developing body of shared technical expertise. His earlier studies were of law and medicine; these fields are the model of professionalism he often uses.

There are two drawbacks to all this. One is that it is very hard to understand just what he means by a body of shared technical expertise. Teaching practice is so complex, and our modes of knowing about it so limited, that it is difficult to believe that any emerging paradigms of technical knowledge will be anything but scientistic mumbo jumbo, concealing their essential inadequacy under a veneer of statistical precision. A second objection is perhaps more basic. Although the schools do suffer from a lack of a sustained, shared concern for practice, the main trouble is not a lack of technical expertise; it is the fact that schools are often not good human environments for children and teachers. If the main problem with schools is the quality of their human relations, then the cure may not be more hard-nosed professionalism. After all, neither law nor medicine gives any evidence of augmenting the humanity of their practitioners, whatever their degree of expertise. Hospitals are not markedly better environments for people than schools. A growing number of patients and professionals in the hospitals are, in fact, coming to feel that medical technique, bureaucracy, and professionalism are getting in the way of humane care. As with the schools, some of the biggest problems are human, not technical. And, as with the schools, a professional style that values impersonal technical innovation over human relationships can create serious imbalances.

Lortie is right when he points to the lack of collective and cumulative experience in the teaching culture; there should be more common discussion of practice and more attempts to build on existing good practice in a cumulative way. Actually, more of this is being done than Lortie lets on. The movement toward informal and open classrooms has been a very mixed bag, but it has generated much discussion of pedagogy and materials. Many more teachers are aware of the possibilities in math and science materials and children's writing than they were. A few teachers' centers have opened up here and there. One promising development in the last decade has been an unprecedented number of first-rate personal accounts of teaching by—of all people—practitioners. Caleb Gattegno, Sylvia Ashton Warner, Elwyn Richardson, Herb Kohl, John Holt, Frances Haw-

kins, and many others have helped ease many thoughtful teachers'
sense of isolation. They have also had a considerable impact on
educational thinking outside schools. At one point, Lortie asks a
rather snobbish question: "How many famous teachers . . . can the
reader think of?" Lortie does not think that even the famous have
made "technical contributions to the art of teaching." This may be
true enough by his lights; by ours, the contributions of the writer-
practitioners of the 1960s have been a great help.

True, teachers would find life easier if their craft possessed the
authoritative "mysteries" of law and medicine. The absence of recognized expertise certainly hurts them in their dealings with parents,
school boards, and critics of education. There are, however, advantages, even in a highly professionalized age of mysterious technique,
to a profession that speaks of its work in plain English. It is very
interesting that Lortie's teachers do not use any educational jargon.
Lortie thinks this a sign of weakness. We think it is a sign of strength,
particularly in a field that is not always immune from gobbledegook.
There are vices as well as virtues in the private language and inturned
habits of the professions. Indeed, the history of progressive education
was marked by the dominance of a certain style of educational professionalism and its jargon. The result was that education became exclusively an affair of educators, who spoke educationese; school reform
calcified as it lost contact with parents and the public. One growing
struggle in an age of splintered publics, expertise, and professionalism
will be to foster public realms in which common discourse is possible.
Teachers' lack of technical language may become an advantage in a
time when consumers of all the professions are beginning to inquire
more closely into the social cost of the mysteries.

Professionalism is certainly bound to grow. The forms it takes,
however, need not be the old ones. If older varieties have not promoted decent institutions—and there is widespread dissatisfaction
with the human workings of many of our institutions—then perhaps
we need to look for some alternative models. In doing this, it would
be wise to pay more attention than Lortie and most other students
of education do to the realm of daily practice. The presentism of
teachers hurts them in thinking of careers, but the present moment
is, inescapably, the main locus of learning and teaching. Like therapists, teachers have to be present centered, because the only hope for

growth is in the present moment. The presentism of teachers is also a response to the insistent futurism of bureaucracies and the general culture, which undervalue the significance of events and feelings in children's lives here and now, and rush them on into the future. Teachers sometimes feel that the bureaucracies are always focused on next year, and that they alone are tuned in on the day-to-day lives of children. Teachers' presentism often coincides with children's perspective on life.

Lortie's lack of respect for the perspective of classroom practitioners is all the more apparent because it clashes so openly with his sympathy for teachers. He sees isolation and conservatism as defects in teachers, and not as responses—often sensible ones—to schools as unhealthy social organisms. Teachers' resistance to change can be infuriating, but their suspicion of "innovation" is, after all, often justified. Our schools' historic patterns of reform do not generally respect practitioners. Lortie's ideal of professionalism does not speak to the problems of harassment, intrusion, and the general lack of support for teachers. Lortie comes close to what is called "blaming the victim." He doesn't seem to understand the aspects of the work that most interest teachers. When they point to the enormous satisfactions involved in reaching one difficult student—the fine feeling of getting William to read—he accuses them of elitism, which seems very odd. One senses that Lortie's ideal of professionalism excludes many small matters that teachers care about. It may be, however, that it is precisely the small daily things that count; good teaching draws on values that are not widely respected in a professionalized culture increasingly haunted by the future.

Lortie's general lack of a sense of schools as institutions may reflect the small-town and suburban bias of his long interviews. His teachers do not talk about red tape, curricular meddling, shortages of books and supplies, and administrative hassles. Teachers in big-city schools will register skepticism. One also misses the defiant esprit of the sort of teachers who explain to you, "There's nothing really wrong with my principal—just a little marginal brain damage." Lortie's teachers in Boston suburbs and Dade County feel lonely in their work. Teachers in despotic and overbureaucratized systems often feel that a little more loneliness would be an improvement over harassment. Lortie's teachers do not speak of discipline as a problem, and they do not discuss race. Some of this restores a certain perspective; not all schools are in the big cities, not all are convulsed by disciplinary and racial problems, not all are beleaguered. It is worthwhile remembering how varied our schools are. Nonetheless, these interviews lack the dimension of life in classrooms where crises, shortages, and tensions are constantly generated by outside forces.

Although we are skeptical of Lortie's hope for a new technical expertise to bind teachers together, we very much agree with his view that they need much more support and collegiality than they are getting. He makes some good suggestions on this latter score, and others would add to his list: There should be more shared and less top-down authority in schools, more time set aside for visiting each other's classrooms, more principals who conceive of themselves as heads of teaching staffs, more advisory work, and, in general, more opportunities in schools for people to collaborate voluntarily. (Team teaching, which is a good idea, has too often been forced down teachers' throats.) Teachers at all levels need to develop a greater awareness of the many common dilemmas of the job and share their feelings about these problems. More technical knowledge and less uncertainty would help, but clearly loneliness is not a technical matter, and trust is not easy to engineer. As it stands, the teaching profession generally does not reward good formal preparation or rich experience. Many teachers believe that it is impossible to be a first-rate teacher for very long. Good ones, especially, often feel they must take a break of some sort to avoid being scooped hollow.

Lortie's portrait updates Willard Waller's *Sociology of Teaching;* in some ways it also shows how little has changed. Waller's book was published in 1932, after the close of the period of mainly administrative reform vaguely called the Progressive Era. From a teacher's point of view this was an era of administrative tyranny and small-town conformity. There is a touch of Sinclair Lewis's rebellion against Main Street in Waller's account; his largely midwestern teachers are victims of the intense moral scrutiny and regimentation of small communities. Lortie's study reflects our own metropolitan and often suburban order. The tyranny of small communities has diminished; instead professionalization and the spread of professional modes of thought have increased.

Waller wanted to free students and teachers for personal growth.

He sought independent, vigorous people as teachers; one of his main concerns was the problem of sustaining creativity in a profession that was peculiarly draining and given over to what he called "formalism." Lortie, as we have seen, is indirectly concerned with the question of self-renewal, but he tends to look for technical answers that would strike Waller as formalistic. Perhaps this reflects our more highly professionalized era. At any rate, Lortie's central concern is not the independence of teachers—to him this is a problem—but rather the need for a common technical culture. Where Waller saw the school itself as an ever-intrusive presence, and teachers' colleagues as creating a social milieu that encouraged deadness and "teacherishness," Lortie sees only isolation, and looks for more collegiality to break down the walls separating teachers.

Both start by assuming that life in schools is a complex affair; they are attuned to the tensions and constraints in teachers' working lives. Lortie locates the tensions within the minds of lonely teachers. Waller describes the school as a social organism, and sees many of the conflicts in teachers' roles as an outgrowth of the conflicting demands of community and profession placed on them. One wonders whether the absence of community in Lortie's account reflects a greater social distance between schools and communities today, or whether Lortie has been too narrow in focusing so exclusively on the inside of the classroom. Waller's sense of the power and influence of the surrounding community and the different ways teachers and parents see children is still valuable. He was particularly good on the different perspectives of teachers and parents: Parents see children as unique; teachers inevitably see them some of the time as part of the general category "student." Someone following in Waller's footsteps today might cast certain of the conflicts he described in slightly different terms. One thinks of Margaret Mead's notion that American expectations of schools and teachers are complex overlays of historical residues and legends. One set of expectations derives from our nostalgic sense of teachers as moral representatives of cohesive communities served by little red schoolhouses. In another part of our minds we look on teachers as bearers of academic traditions and standards. And in yet another part of our minds we see them as agents of acculturation, especially for the poor and the alien.

Waller's lively curiosity took him into many realms where Lortie fails to tread. His more personal style of sociology led him to look at sex roles and affairs of the heart in schools, for instance; the splendidly gossipy quality of his portrait contrasts with Lortie's drabness, but we cannot, of course, turn the contrasts in two styles and temperaments into a commentary on school, in two epochs. Lortie's silence on these matters should not necessarily lead us to conclude (as Americans today are apt to do) that we live in a flatter and drearier time, although the costs and benefits of greater professionalism do involve more impersonality.

Teachers in the twenties and thirties were treated as genteel navvies; except in the worst schools, they are generally less oppressed today. Waller attacked the prevalent custom of barring married women from the schools, and criticized the way the category "teacher" meant something alien and straight-laced. Waller described how barbershop conversation died out in the presence of a male educator: "It has been said that no woman and no negro is ever fully admitted to the white man's world. Perhaps we should add men teachers to the list of the excluded." Waller's debunking irony was a perfect response to an age of unrivaled sanctimoniousness concerning education. Sanctimonies abound now, of course, yet one senses a difference. Schools are still repositories of ideals the community does not actually practice. Our culture has its hypocrisies, but it is generally less moralistic than Waller's. Countercultural, Bohemian, and radical ideas about schools have achieved mass audiences, and news of the defects of schools as institutions has traveled far and wide. Today, unlike Waller's day, the intellectually iconoclastic thing to do would be to defend schools. Our ideas about the culture schools should transmit are in disarray. This, in part, is why we so often end up concentrating on academic skills. The school culture that embalmed Emerson and Longfellow and Sara Teasdale in the same watery gray fluid is vanishing; *Silas Marner* is perhaps the last remaining monument of the old order. For all its rigidities, and its formalistic emphasis on technical skills, the culture we live in is less dogmatic and more pluralistic. There are drawbacks to all this; there has been a diminution of the notion that education is somehow sacred. The Cathedral of Knowledge is emptying of believers, and schools, like universities, have lost a certain amount of their legitimacy as a result. The uncertainties of an era when old idols have crumbled can be genuinely painful, and often most bitterly so to the teachers really committed to academic subjects. Nonetheless, it is better that we no longer demand that our teachers kneel at the altar of Culture, serving as moral exemplars in schools that were supposed to be, in Waller's deadly phrase, museums of virtue.

Waller was, like Thorstein Veblen, a disturber of the intellectual peace. He was a cynic; he was saddened into cynicism by watching the way life can defeat people's hopes. For all the ironic fun he poked at "teacherishness," he liked teachers. He had taught high-school French himself and his father had been a small-town school superintendent in the Midwest. It was his respect for the craft, if anything, that made him so outraged at the way the commercial culture of the twenties and thirties—with its preoccupation with business and success, and its machismo—denigrated the teaching profession. In Waller's day, unlike ours, there were almost no intellectual alternatives to the reigning philistinism.

In its early, less professionalized days, sociology looked at the world with a child's eyes and asked profoundly simple questions. Most people, then as now, took the social order for granted. Waller didn't; he was apt to wonder what in the world kept it all going. He began with a vivid sense of schools as imperiled orders. Here were adults, teachers, and here were children, at once the most tractable and the most unstable members of the community. They confronted each other in institutions called schools—fragile, artificial orders, built on despotic principles, and in a state of perilous equilibrium. (This sense of ongoing peril is oddly missing in Lortie, whose teachers rarely even mention discipline.) Given the drama of the daily clashes between teachers and students, each group operating under different constraints; given the tensions and discontinuities; given the ever-recurring possibility of chaos—what in the world kept them going? Waller's answer was to record the way tensions balanced and the participants struggled daily in a dramatic recreation of order in the face of endemic conflict. The struggle between the need for authority and the claims of friendliness at the brink of chaos was a daily event; the unchanging surface of life in classrooms added up to a dramatic achievement, not something to take for granted.

Waller was trained in the pragmatic sociology of the Chicago school created by such forgotten figures as C.H. Cooley and W.I.

Thomas. His aim was to do a natural history of life and institutions, to capture the ebb and flow of human existence. (He once wrote a study of divorce that tried to chart the course of loves and hatreds in married life.) The natural-history approach was not simply a method with him. The Chicago school was influenced by figures like John Dewey and Thorstein Veblen. Waller's ideal of writing a living narrative represented a commitment to a particular style of social criticism and certain almost mythic values. Veblen's criticisms of the lifelessness of leisure-class culture in *The Theory of the Leisure Class* and Dewey's criticisms of the formalism and deadness of education represented a whole intellectual generation's pursuit of "organic" social institutions that would promote growth and self-renewal. Waller inherited this tradition at a point when its myths were still potent. In tracing conflicts within the schools, then, he was writing about a mythic confrontation between the organic and the formal, Youth and Age, and even Life and Death.

The natural-history method was in itself a pursuit of the qualities that made for living things. Waller thought that the key problem of the schools was the menace posed by formalism to the spontaneity and creativity of students and teachers. Like Dewey and Veblen, Waller was in pursuit of life:

> Something happens to ideas when they get themselves organized into social systems. The ethical ideas of Christ . . . have . . . been smothered by churches. . . . An idea must be organized before it can be made into fact, and an idea wholly unorganized rarely lives long. Without mechanism it dies, but mechanism perverts it. This is part of the natural flow and recession—the life principle in society.

He tried to describe how institutions age, for he thought of schools as living organisms that somehow keep generating dead tissue: "Where the structure has become too intricate, or too rigid, or the idea of function has faded from the minds of functionaries, we speak of the institution as suffering from formalism." Waller packed a thousand meanings into the word "formalism." It meant institutionalism, traditionalism, conventionalism, ritual, bureaucracy. It stood for all the ways that the mechanics of the business kept interfering with the adaptation to human needs. There was a perennial tendency for means to become ends; the institution began to work for its own benefit rather than for its intended functions. Waller thought that schools were especially prone to formalism because of the large element of dominance and subordination in the relations of teachers and students. (He was shrewd, however, in seeing that in any human relationship, including teaching, those who care less have great power over those who care more.) Domination and its attendant problems cut students and teachers off from each other; they were both fighting to live. Waller realized something Lortie misses—the fact that, for better *and* for worse, students have a considerable hand in shaping the social environment of the classroom. As Waller put it, "Students as well as teachers put up walls, as many a teacher has learned who has tried to form a real and vital contact with his students on a common human level. . . . Then the teacher is thrown back on the formalism in his classroom and upon the primary groups of the teaching profession."

Waller's criticism of schools of the 1930s meshes in part with Lortie's complaints about our schools today. Waller thought they were barren ground for the cultivation of human personality. The complaint itself has been perennial, and Waller was not always immune to the weaknesses of many antiformalist and neo-Romantic attacks on the schools. Like Dewey, he could sometimes sound anti-intellectual in his pursuit of Life and his mystique of Experience. The insistence that the school stop trying to be a machine and "realize its destiny as a social organism" could become a slogan, too, and reflected pragmatic intellectuals' tendency to fashion idols made in the image of the social life of small groups. (One imagines that this was because they were village minds trying to frame social ideals for a new metropolitan world of mass institutions.) Today many of us sense the necessity for some balance between the organic and the formal (as Waller would put it). We would use different words, probably—freedom and structure, human and professional, or whatever. What lifted Waller high above the level of most neo-Romantic educational criticism was his sense of life's complexities, and his ability to see common dilemmas of teaching at all levels. Many of his examples are drawn from college teaching; he was perhaps ahead of our time as well as his own in seeing the similarities.

Unlike Lortie, who has no views on what schools ought to do—besides reflecting the latest technical consensus among the professionals—Waller believed they exist to develop students' personalities. It was not possible, he thought, to develop students without giving teachers ways to develop, too. He believed that education should reproduce the patterns of life itself; he admired the project methods of the child-centered progressive educators. At the end of every chapter of *The Sociology of Teaching* (which was intended as a college text) there are ingenious suggestions for students to pursue on their own, making the book a kind of manual of do-it-yourself sociology. Waller wanted to recruit vigorous teachers and keep them vigorous, able to combat "the relentness march of growing teacherishness." He wanted teachers who could be stronger and more independent than the harassed and persecuted teachers he saw in the schools. (He pointed to the vigor added to the profession by "stepping stone" teachers who pause to teach on their way to some other goal.) He was mainly concerned with self-renewal, a problem that is still very much at the heart of the problem of teaching today. Teachers now are probably much less of a recognizable social type than those in the midwestern schools of Waller's time—"teacherishness" is less of a spinster's phenomenon—but from kindergarten through graduate school they are fighting daily against becoming someone fitting Waller's definition of a pedagogue: one who can wax unenthusiastic on any subject under the sun.

For Waller the answer was more freedom in and out of school. Lortie has a more professional set of suggestions; in some respects he is more sophisticated than Waller. Waller's era was not yet at home in a world of organizations, professions, and bureaucracies; for all its fascination with social groups and institutions, it sometimes simplified them. Lortie is right that freedom for teachers is not enough, although many teachers need more than they get. They also need, as he says, more professional support. Waller asked that teachers be treated like human beings, not "teachers." Lortie is taking an opposite tack; he thinks schools would be better if teachers treated each other as "teachers," professionals. Certainly in an age of professionalization, some mixture of both roles is inevitable. Professionalism and humanity can overlap at many points; Lortie is right in arguing that schools would be more comfortable places if teachers were more assured and less anxious about the basic uncertainty of their tasks. In the end we lean toward Waller; we think that even more possibilities would open up if teachers could be treated like human beings. Waller's study is a reminder that Lortie and other critics who focus on the conservatism of the profession need to look further. It is still true today, as Waller wrote in 1932, that "most programs for changing schools founder on the rock of teacher resistance. For the most part we consider this resistance well placed." He would agree with Lortie that teachers need more self-knowledge and insight into the common constraints they work under, and he would add that they also need to understand more about the complex social realities of life in schools. For all his irony, Waller seems more optimistic, more of a meliorist than Lortie, perhaps because he had faith in people, if not professions; the heart of the matter was the human climate of the schools. We need to compare Waller and Lortie because their enterprise is common, because too many discussions of education lack any historical perspective, and because Lortie himself is an apt illustration of his own complaint that our educational thought does not consciously build on the work of the past. He mentions Waller, but his book would be richer and more complex if it engaged in a debate with Waller. In the United States of Amnesia we are always starting out from scratch. We teach, write novels, explore sociology as though nobody had ever done any of these things before. That, in small part, explains why our ideas on education do not develop in any cumulative way. For the rest, it is unfair to fault Lortie for lacking Waller's rich, mythic complexity, and his Dreiserian grasp of students and teachers as people. Lortie has not written a classic, but he has written a very useful book. *Schoolteacher* should be put on the shelf next to Waller and to Philip Jackson's *Life in Classrooms* (1968). The fact that it is a rather gloomy book may depress some of the practitioners who read it, but its depth of understanding may help them—as Waller might put it, with his wry gallow's humor—in their efforts to keep a good class and hold on to their jobs as well.

The more we learn about other lives the more we understand how painful and full of trouble life is. Freud once spoke of analysis as one of three impossible professions (the other two were being a leader of a nation and being a parent). Lortie, like Waller and Jackson, convinces us that teaching is a fourth impossible profession to add to the list. It may be, though, that more people endure impossible demands than we think.

11

Participation Revisited

It would be more convenient for us all if periods of educational history actually coincided with the decades marked on the calendar —if there really were entities like the 1960s and the 1970s. In fact, most of the educational issues raised in the turbulent school battles of the 1960s continue now, albeit in more subdued and local forms. This is the case with the vague demand for something called "participation," and the equally inchoate quest for "community." Often these abstractions come in tandem with a third, "accountability," which is another conceptual swamp. Under these phrases, people discuss everything from reworking the governance of local education with such ideas as decentralization, community control, and voucher schemes to new varieties of citizen involvement, including the creation of new citizen groups and counterprofessions to balance and monitor the educational professions.

The issue of participation arises from two historic trends that are very strong, and by no means confined to education. One is the continuing expansion of what might be called the "human service sectors" of the economy—professionals helping people. More and more of the work of our society is in the service—and often the public service—sectors: schools, hospitals, government. The other trend is almost a dialectical response to the first: as services expand, those who use them organize to make them more responsive and accountable. Often the initial set of issues around which consumers organize involves what I call the pathological professionalism of many of our social services, which often seem designed to insulate the professionals from the public rather than to provide decent services.

In education there is a particular force to the demand for participation, because our political tradition mandates local lay control of the schools, and also because our traditional style of school reform often takes the shape of citizens' movements. In the schools, unlike other areas of the service sector, an expectation of substantial public participation antedates the vexing issues generated by the increasing professionalism of all areas of American life. There is, moreover, a set of historic precedents for turning the schools back to the people whenever they lose their legitimacy—when they lose what the Chinese elegantly term "the mandate of heaven." Although almost nobody realized it during the events of the late 1960s, there is a history to be learned. The failures of schools to educate the urban poor are not new. Nor is our sense of social crisis new. Both attended the origins of our city schools in the nineteenth century. Then, we faced the problem of absorbing and contending with the influx of immigrants —"strangers" to American culture. The problem was doubly complex, for the strangers were not only from a lower social class but also from another people, and, often enough, from another race. When schools insulted and failed America's historic strangers, they often fought back through local politics. In the past, schools—especially city schools—sometimes reworked patterns of government in response to these challenges. The school wars of the nineteenth century made education one of the main arenas in which the hopes of the immigrant newcomers and fears of the natives clashed. Sometimes Yankee elites and reformers won the school wars—the successful fights to centralize the big-city school systems whose rigidities plague us today being one such victory—and sometimes the immigrants and outsiders won, in the establishment of ward and local neighborhood systems, for example, or in the seizure of city hall and the machinery of educational government, or in the recruitement of immigrant teachers. Schools were an important part of the mechanism by which

America's outsiders fought for—and gained—a relatively more inclusive culture. From time to time in the past the rules of the educational game got redrawn; new rules sometimes included new forms of citizen participation. These traditions ran so deep in the culture that they even survived into the era of highly centralized and bureaucratized school systems of the late 1960s—as the tragic battles over community control in New York City showed. Once again we found ourselves living, as we still do today, in an era of school wars.

The 1960s witnessed a drive for equality and new rights on the part of previously excluded and oppressed groups. An important, not wholly successful part of this push was a series of reworkings of the idea of participation. Some of the impetus for this came from the civil rights movement, which played inventively back and forth with novel lower- and working-class modes of protest and traditional middle-class styles of action and reform on the part of concerned professionals and citizens. The result, as everybody knows, was an unprecedented national movement aimed at reversing the historic status of blacks and other minorities. Demands for participation were, however, not usually the main items on the agenda of protest. Unfairness in the realm of education was often the first step, because education itself is so central a part of what Gunnar Myrdal called the American Creed. Violations of the right to education were particularly important as an issue after the Brown decision of the Supreme Court in 1954, which in effect helped create a mass movement by legitimizing the educational grievances of southern blacks. At some point educational grievances also came to include a demand for parent participation in schools. This was, I think, often a kind of second- or third-order item on the black protest agenda, something educational (and, of course, political) that people pushed for after other demands failed. It was in the aftermath of the signal failure to integrate New York City's schools, for example, that people around IS (Intermediate School) 201 began connecting the new talk of black power to the realm of education, and there was discussion of community-controlled schools.

The Bundy Report proposing decentralization of the New York schools and the participatory slogans of the Lindsay regime distantly echoed these debates within the black movement, but stemmed more from developments outside of black and minority circles. There were many sources of new, participatory ideas. The notion that alienation and powerlessness were central ills of our society, to be cured by something called "participation," had surfaced in the academy and the foundations among reformers dealing with problems like juvenile delinquency. It also arose from middle-class radicals like Paul Goodman, and theorists like Jane Jacobs and Hannah Arendt. Participation was a central item in the creed of what used to be called the New Left; it became a slogan in the campus uprisings and helped shape the rising student movement, which was in part a product of the clash between the expectations of affluent students and the rigidities of the institutions they encountered, and in part a response to national issues like the civil rights movement and the Vietnam War. All these stirrings influenced the architects of President Johnson's poverty programs, partly in a pure and rather naïvely idealistic form, and partly because a number of the poverty warriors saw local participation as a kind of end run around recalcitrant state and city governments and educational authorities, a prerequisite to any real reform. Participation in one form or another became one of the distinctive features of the war on poverty, at least until that war was killed off by the other, less metaphorical war in Vietnam. Head Start, the community-action and model-cities programs, and a number of other educational and social measures included one or another form of participation. The poverty programs were both a cause of the widespread demand for more participation and a symptom of it. It is terribly important in the 1970s to remember that the hunger for more responsive institutions was never solely the creation of a small group of academics, radicals, students, and government officials. Participation as an ideal struck a much more general chord. Many of the people who migrated to the suburbs in the postwar period did so because—among other, no doubt weightier reasons—they were eager for human-sized scale, the possibilities of participation, and decent public services that were in some degree responsive to the people they were supposed to be serving. There was a good deal of nonsense talked about participation in the late 1960s. It was an age of rhetorical excess, and many of the demands in the name of participation were foolish. Nonetheless, the general notion that institutionalized professionalism had developed severe pathologies was sound, and fueled the demand for human-scale institutions that society was not meeting.

Nowadays, the excesses of the time seem part of a remote past. A compromised form of community control came to New York City after tragic confrontations between teachers and the black community; slum schools were not transformed. The leak of funds away from the poverty programs often brought participants to the point of bitter fights over bones devoid of meat. Participation, it turned out, was not an effective substitute for things like money, jobs, and housing. This does not mean that the participatory ventures were meaningless. The historian of the social and educational reforms of the late 1960s will be able to write a fascinating chapter on varieties of extraordinary social inventiveness. Head Start at its best is still one of my favorite examples of how substantial amounts of parent participation can in some communities be reconciled with professionalism and educational standards. The money for Title I of President Johnson's 1965 ESEA bill did not exactly redeem the education of poor kids; students of its impact tend to be dubious about its effects. Yet it helped out a good many distressed schools, and its mandate for parent participation, however honored in the breech, is plainly a clear and continuing influence on many recent participatory reforms. The exercises in participation of the 1960s were often a kind of political education, a Tammany Hall for poor outsiders and previously apolitical middle-class parents and professionals as well. Like the peace movement and recent political party reform, the poverty wars and the battles that ensued over them taught a good many people how to organize, hold meetings, run mimeograph machines, and make trouble. Local government in this country will probably not be the same. For many of the poor as well as the middle class the enduring legacy of these often inconclusive participatory reforms will be the difficulty of running social service programs in many areas without involving the people they are supposed to be serving. This in itself is an achievement.

Although much of the furor has died down, it is apparent that the obituaries written for many of the participatory and educational reforms of the 1960s are premature. As the national wave of reform has ebbed, local agitation and change have continued in many places, if not in others. For all the national climate of gloom and despair, it is still true that many localities are living through their own educational reform eras. If the United States were a tightly knit national society, then we could discuss education in simple national terms. The fact is, however, that the clear emergence of national forces, institutions, and a national stage on which some educational dramas are enacted and described by the media has blinded many of us to the fact that, educationally, we still remain a profoundly regional and local society. Understanding the profound importance of local contexts and local actors is crucial, and the variety of the current educational scene makes it hard to generalize. An illuminating example of this fact is a statement from Zeke Wigglesworth's essay in *Schools Where Parents Make a Difference* (1976) about current participatory efforts in Minnesota:

> I can't say here that what will work at Marcy or the Free School or Pratt-Motley is going to work in other schools in Minneapolis, let alone the rest of the country. We are trying to see what can successfully take place here, in our area. I am not at all sure that what we have learned here is exportable. There is only one truth, I guess: what works for one group may not work for another. The community involvement and response of parents may not be proper anywhere else in the nation.

In some places budget cuts and racial tension have put an end to any sort of reform. In still others the aftermath of a reform era is a period of educational reaction. There is a dark side, as well as a democratic side, to our populist and participatory traditions; it is sometimes visible now in the form of a sour reaction against all experts, professionals, and outsiders—and the universal, cosmopolitan, or elite (not necessarily interchangeable adjectives) values they represent. Thinking about ideal ways to involve parents should not make us lose sight of the fact that the Boston School Committee in its opposition to integration and the textbook protesters in Kanawha County, West Virginia are both in their way exercises in local participation, too often drawing in debased and demagogic ways on valid ideals and complaints.

The variety of parent involvement is extraordinary. One must be very careful neither to discount its genuine local significance and vitality nor to romanticize it. My own feelings about some of what's happening are mixed. It seems to me that many of the things parents and schools are trying offer glimpses of new possibilities for social democracy and for professions that really serve their clients. At other times I'm bothered by the way people march into unprecedented situations armed with a load of nostalgia for ideals of lost democracy and community that may in fact have never existed in this country in any satisfactory form. I'm suspicious of the chronic tendency of American reform tradition to couch its goals in terms of loss and the promise of a restoration of a better past. The quite valid criticisms of the pathological professionalism of many of our social services are not made any more valid, it seems to me, if the critics are mainly haunted by images of a happier past. On the contrary. When I look at the educational world pictured in a book like *Schools Where Parents Make a Difference*, it looks to me to be a more open and pluralistic world than that of most of our educational past. People are making a good many more options for themselves and their children. The educational scene is somewhat more tolerant of diversity and variety, and has slightly less of the often obsessively monolithic quality of its traditional pursuit of what the historian David Tyack calls "the one best system." This is not to say that the news is all good. Such interesting work as the parent involvements in the Louisville schools or the Milwaukee Federation of Independent Schools takes place against a somber background of urban decay. The mountaineers in West Virginia and the Chicanos in Crystal City are doing impressive things, but their struggle is desperate, and victories in the schools are only a small part of it.

I think we have to learn to think of things like participation and democracy in ways less clouded by simplicities and nostalgia for the past. The various efforts of parents and citizens to make a difference in schools all take place within a complex modern, professionalized social order made up of mass corporate institutions. We may be able to make these institutions smaller, more humanly scaled, more pluralistic and voluntaristic—I hope we can—but they are not likely to disappear. Demands for participation have to be squared with the realities of a huge and populous order that is not only national in scale, but, increasingly, international as well. Participatory demands themselves often represent something genuinely missing from the existing order of things. Yet it may be that our older visions of democracy and participation—which are still turfbound, localistic, and individualistic—need reworking.

In reworking them, we need to transcend simple slogans and see the genuine complexity of an educational order that is a very uneasy blend of local democratic tradition, entrenched privilege, and aloof professionalism, fitfully accessible to people and fitfully controlled by no one, in which citizens have a role to play, but in which the modern, impersonal realities of mass organization also coexist. For all our nostalgia for the simpler, more readily understandable institutions of the past, there may now be more citizen participation in education in many communities than ever before. (One thing our nostalgia misleads us about is the extent to which the older democratic localism in many places was in the hands of the local elites.) The positive effects of participation are obvious—examples of successful parent involvement in schools, the ease with which neighborhoods in many cities have blocked highways and renewal projects that would have been encouraged in the urban era symbolized by Robert Moses. The drawbacks of an increasingly participatory order are also obvious, in education as well as in politics generally: The sense of paralysis of many of our city governments is not only a matter of budget crises, but also a reflection of the fact that a system with more and more openings for participation is less and less geared to action. Fortunately for those of us interested in education, schools lend themselves better to the possibilities of participation than, say, regional sewage systems, or air traffic control.

I have a sense that the participatory agenda of poor outsiders often has a different, less utopian and more pragmatic character than the participatory strivings of the emancipated middle and professional classes. For outsider groups like Indians on reservations where community control is an issue, or for the Chicanos trying to gain political power in Crystal City, educational issues are real both in themselves and as ways of organizing powerless groups for political power. Educational demands open up—besides gains in education—new possibilities for jobs, leadership positions, and a sense among the group that change is possible. Poor and politically weak groups in such situations must constantly think in terms of tradeoffs; weighing the advantages and disadvantages of organizing tactics that result in short-term separatist gains but perhaps cut off the possibility of future coalitions with other groups. The whole ongoing, never-resolved separatist-integrationist dialectic between American educational institutions and outsiders has a much more complicated history than we realize, and it is re-enacted in each generation.

The accounts of middle class participation here do not contain quite the same urgencies or dilemmas. I'm struck by the spread of new standards and concerns among educational consumers. The higher standards parents have for schools are probably in themselves an important byproduct of the extension of education, which has created new tastes for education among masses of people, as well as new ideas and dissatisfactions. The tolerance of diversity and the growing notion among teachers and parents that there is no one right pedagogy for all teachers and students is one of the really important after-effects of recent classroom reforms in many places. Its advantages, I think, outweigh the considerable disadvantages of packaging teaching approaches into readily identifiable categories and slogans. It is a good first step perhaps to think of, say, three equally valid approaches to teaching instead of one, but that should be the beginning, not the end, of the story. It would be a pity if parents ever came to rest on the notion that a few packaged categories themselves do justice to the variety of good practice.

Both formal and informal, the varieties of participation that are developing seem very healthy, and do not, I suspect, do more than touch on the possibilities for more parent involvement in schools. But it is precisely those of us in favor of more participation who need to be clear on its limits. The chief limit, I think, is that our older conceptions of local democracy need reworking; they are not adequate to build a national politics capable of exerting democratic control over education, let alone controlling the private corporations that dominate the country. A decisive limit on local citizen participation as a central focus for social change is the increasing shift of many major democratic issues from a local to a national political scene. Most local school reform movements today do not link up with national issues. This is both an advantage and a disadvantage. It frees people to move on a local stage. But it circumscribes the stage in important ways. Local politics is still vital; it is especially important in many communities as a key arena in which disputes over cultural values and symbols often take place. Yet the atrophy of many of the traditional democratic forms of educational governance, such as school boards, is one reason why so many people—including many parents and professionals—are searching for alternatives. The reasons for this decay are complex: the growth of the power of the states, the emergence of unaccountable national institutions of education, such

as testing, accreditation, and curriculum design, and professionalization itself have contributed to it in education. It is true of local
politics generally: national and regional economic forces, the power
of entrenched local privilege, the patchwork of jurisdictions and their
profound inequalities in tax base and status, the accessibility of national politics to the discontented and oppressed, have all turned
national politics into the main arena for most of the major democratic
issues we face. Yet it is just here that older turfbound and individualistic visions of democracy and citizen participation simply don't seem
to fit very well. Movements like Common Cause and Ralph Nader's
various crusades are brave efforts to explore new possibilities, but it
is hard to argue that they have hit upon enduring answers. The
question is whether we must scrap the old ideals and start from
scratch, or whether they can be reworked.

I think the best chance of reworking older ideals is to see participation as a needed, often missing, fluid element in a complex and often
overly rigid modern educational order. Any participatory forms we
develop will have to mesh with the true political complexity of an
educational scene that is, like an archeological dig, a mixture of the
old and enduring and the new. This sense of complexity is lacking
in much of the current quest for "accountability"; take as an example
such proposals as voucher schemes and community control. Both as
usually proposed seem to be fairly simple political answers to problems that are generated by exceedingly complex collisions of social,
economic, and political forces. Vouchers are, I think, exercises in
nostalgia in attempting to substitute the workings of a vanishing free
market for the complex politics of education that now exists. Proposals for community control have very varied sources—in part they have
been a rather despairing tactical response to the ongoing relative
failure of school integration in the North—but in part they too are
exercises in nostalgia; they try to restore vanished varieties of urban
"community" by simply shrinking the size of the turf. Both ideas are
responses to genuine needs that are not being met; but both as usually
formulated attempt to do away with the complex mixture of formal
and informal politics that has emerged to deal with our society's
education.

I don't know whether we are up to being as socially inventive as
Americans in the eighteenth and nineteenth centuries, who had such

a passion—at times such a genius—for building institutions. I'm clearer about what I'm against than what I'm for. What I'm against is our current habit of talking as though we can do without organizations, professions, and institutions; I think that what we misleadingly call "the welfare state" is in fact very badly organized and much in need of more institutions to reach people and give them support. I'm also proposing that we attack rigid bureaucracy and pathological professionalism, although not professionalism itself. Some of the really good work I've seen in this country and others has been a result of the kind of support and autonomy that healthy educational professionalism ought to provide but seldom does. And thus I propose thinking about the possibilities of participation within the context of an acceptance of the fact that we live in a world of professionals.

Thinking about participation in modern contexts, I'm left with a strong sense of at least two sorts of possibilities. (I'm sure there are more.) The first is coalitions between professionals and parents. I'm struck by the fact that many of the most promising educational ventures today include school administrators in alliance with parents. Often enough the key figure is a good principal, a fact that New York City's community-control movement understood very well. In a professionalized system, professionals will usually end up with a disproportionate amount of influence. Citizen groups are often essential for starting changes in rigid school systems, but unless they win allies among the professionals, the changes are unlikely to last or to be built on. The challenge for parent and citizen groups, therefore, is to redirect the priorities and allegiances of the two key sets of practitioners in schools: principals and classroom teachers. What the politics of education badly lacks is coalitions of parents and practitioners. In some embattled school systems this idea seems laughable; in others it seems quite possible.

A second promising path offers another way to square participation with professionalism. It might be described as using the machinery of a kind of quasi-professionalism to overcome the pathological professionalism of school systems. Essentially, this is the sort of work that is taking place in Boston's City Wide Educational Coalition, the District of Columbia's Citizens for Better Public Education, the Queens Lay Advocate Services, and the Madison Educational Forum. These are groups that work professionally—up to professional standards, although often staffed by volunteers—to counter school bureaucracies and professionals. These and other similar groups in different cities inform the public, uncover hidden issues, keep the professionals honest and responsive, help with parents' complaints, defend students' rights, litigate, and so on, working against the school system's inherent tendencies toward inertia. As I say, even when staffed wholly by volunteers, they work on a professional basis. They have their counterparts in public service and citizen groups in such areas as law, medicine, and television. They are a kind of counter-profession designed to balance the power, secrecy, and rigidity of existing professions. Over the next decade or so, we will probably see a great variety of similar attempts on the part of citizens and professionals to set up such counterweights. Their frequent adversary style will no doubt make our world even more contentious than it has been; it may also produce more variety and mechanisms for redress for consumers of public services of all sorts, especially outsiders, the poor and minority groups. Such lay and often volunteer groups are, I believe, forerunners of the increased professionalization of our society; they combine older forms of citizen participation with a quasi-professionalization of reform itself. (Nor, of course, will professionalized reform be immune to the ailments of professionalism.)

Besides parents (and, of course, children), the people neglected in our discussions of education are the classroom practitioners. Parents need to understand that the pathological professionalism that exists in many of our schools is hurting practitioners too; it fails to give principals and teachers the mixture of support and autonomy they need. Parents are cut off from schools, and their efforts to find out, to help, or to complain are often seen as a source of further harassment. Patterns of school reform have not helped this. In the educational past, as in the present, reform movements have in fact often widened the gulf between practitioners and parents. Top-down, general staff patterns of administrative reform are resisted by classroom practitioners, who are equally resistant to the sort of grass-roots citizen reform that often looks from the classroom window like the educational equivalent of a lynch mob. Surely the patterns are self-defeating. The growth and shape of the teachers' union movement may influence the possibilities of coalitions and bargains between the counterpoised groups of service professionals and consumers of services. Whether teachers will be able to respond creatively to the needs prompting citizens' and parent movements, and whether lay movements can come to understand the problems and legitimate concerns of practitioners, is, of course, an open question. Our reform history is not promising. Perhaps we can transcend it. My own feeling is that the more internally democratic—participatory, if you will— the unions are, and the more they can think in terms of alliances with parents and principals at the individual school level, the more promising the future will be. Individual classrooms and individual schools are the ultimate focus of change; this is the level where one would most like to see an end to the traditional adversary relationships. This is also the level that is most difficult to reach in ways that help, rather than exacerbate matters. Prediction is, however, a mug's game. The only safe prediction is that a society ripe for possibilities for participation will continue to see many variations on all these themes, in many different communities.

12

Boston Desegregation: Thoughts on a Bicentennial City

This has been a troubled period for Boston, enmeshed in the problems of court-ordered desegregation. Phase I of the court's plan touched off demonstrations, boycotts, and bloodshed until cooler weather brought a lull to the racial violence. Although many of the city's schools have quieted down and attendance figures have climbed steadily, resistance to busing continues strong in many white neighborhoods, particularly the Irish enclaves of Charlestown and South Boston. Mothers have staged marches against busing, prayed, and sat in the streets. At night white youths threw rocks and baited the police. Supporters of desegregation, or at least those obedient to the law, are now better organized in the city. The city's leaders, who had equivocated on busing, now stand four-square against violence. The legal technology for enforcing desegregation has expanded into a formidable machine—city, state, and metropolitan police, units of the National Guard, federal marshals, the FBI, officials from the Justice Department, all entered the scene at one time or another.

US district court judge Arthur Garrity has issued a very complicated desegregation plan. Besides busing, it involves new districts, a large citywide magnet district with special programs to draw students from the neighborhoods voluntarily, and a complex series of advisory councils to monitor the whole operation. The judge is making an unprecedented effort to link desegregation with improvements in education. His notion of pairing schools with businesses and universities still has to be worked out. The distinguished array of institutions of higher education around Boston stays aloof from schools; strangely enough, it is by no means clear what crack universities can offer the city's schoolchildren. Apart from student assignments, the most visible effect of the judge's planning is the presence in the system's 162 schools of more black and Spanish-speaking teachers. Boston's students are 52 percent white, 36 percent black, and 12 percent from other minorities, such as Spanish-speaking children and Chinese. Desegregation here, as elsewhere, has sharpened each group's awareness of grievances: Spanish-speaking parents worry that it has thrown bilingual services into confusion, and some Chinese parents conducted a boycott to resist busing.

Judge Garrity has in many respects taken temporary possession of the school system. No one supposes that a federal judge should be doing this, yet the situation is not of his making. It results from the fact that for many years both the school administration and the school committee have deliberately segregated black schoolchildren, maintaining what is in many respects a dual school system. Both the administration and the committee have been defying challenges on this issue for a long time. The school administration is a mainly Irish hierarchy that looks back to better days; its inbred loyalties have produced a style of professionalism even more pathological and vacuum-sealed than that of other big-city systems. The Boston School Committee, though it often speaks to the genuine concerns of its constituents, has been a scandal. It was largely responsible for the present situation, three of its members profited politically and in more direct ways from the prolonged school crisis, and thus had a vested interest in keeping trouble brewing.

A new, more moderate school committee has been elected; Boston's voters seem to have realized that the old committee had taken them for a ride. Judge Garrity may have performed a real service in opening up new channels in the city's moribund educational politics. Citizens and parents have begun to participate in the newly activated district councils and advisory groups, and it seems likely that the new school committee and the school administration are going to get more attention from parents and people active at the school level.

The imperviousness of the administration and the small, dangerous wiles of the politicians only make up a fraction of the city's problems, but they give it a particularly local twist. Social forces outside the schools, years of conflicting demands for compensatory education and desegregation, the fears of the city's whites, the bitterness and frustration of the blacks, have all gone into creating a war that no one feels confident of winning.

Meanwhile Bicentennial visitors arrive in town to see the sights—Bunker Hill memorial is just across the way from Charlestown High—and pay tribute to the two hundredth anniversary of the republic. The Bicentennial is on many people's minds. The contrast between its ideals and the frightening actualities of the present, and between memories of recent decades of relative peace and the present turmoil, feeds a sense of loss. There is something elegaic in the air, as when Judge Garrity wrote in the past tense: "Boston became the bridge not only to liberty but to the ideal of the free, universal and inclusive public school." The antibusing people speak a nostalgic language of rights and redress for the wrongs of an oppressive government. Black activists and the lawyers for the NAACP are fighting for rights, liberty, and an ideal of schooling, although they don't have much to be nostalgic about. To the worried whites and blacks who are not activists, people who live in very similar neighborhoods and projects, there doesn't seem all that much to celebrate.

It is a bad time; many feel it to be the worst of times. The memory of the bitter ethnic and religious wars of the past is fading, and people have forgotten that Boston's history in the nineteenth and twentieth centuries is a story of chronic, sometimes violent conflict. The struggles between Yankee Protestant Republicans and Irish Catholic Democrats formed the major fault line, but successive cleavages opened up as each set of older groups faced each wave of newcomers: Italians, French-Canadians, Jews, Portuguese, and now blacks and Puerto Ricans. Blacks go back a long way in Boston, but their numbers were small until the 1950s. Within the memory of many citizens, Roxbury was a mainly Jewish section of town; it is full of abandoned synagogues. Now the older ethnic quarrels take second place to race, without, however, disappearing.

Our pleasant legends about schools in the past lead us to ignore the fact that they, too, were involved in the wars. These days a number of what are sometimes called "revisionist" historians are looking into the past of institutions like schools, prisons, and asylums. The revisionists have only a mood in common; the mood is skeptical. They peer at the motives of the founding fathers of such public institutions, and find them more mixed than many of us think. American traditions of reform and institution-building have a dark side, it turns out. It might interest Bicentennial visitors who come across the statue of Horace Mann to know that Mann cuts a rather different figure in the historians' accounts from the public figure portrayed in earlier boosterish histories of public education. He begins to look more like Melville's monomaniacal Captain Ahab than the benign figure of reform legend.

In a sense, Mann and the founding fathers of many of our urban institutions were obsessed by what we now call the crisis of the cities, which has been going on much longer, at least in the older eastern cities, than we generally imagine. Boston's schools in the 1830s and 1840s were a first venture in what we now speak of, rather grandly, as the framing of social policy. They were one facet of a complex institutional response to modernity, part of a whole array of institutions designed to redress the imbalances generated by unchecked economic growth and technological change.

From the beginning, city schools were bound up with the reckoning with industry, technology, divisions of labor, and new impersonal urban institutions. The reformers hoped they would take up the slack for other, supposedly failing older institutions, such as the family, the village, and the church. They intended schools to renew a sense of community in cities where community was felt to be collapsing. Building common schools was a real achievement in cities whose inhabitants found it very difficult to act collectively. Nineteenth-century civic reformers found it hard to wrest services such as water, sewers, and even police forces from a profoundly individualistic culture given over to a frenzy of capitalist enterprise. In the chaotic American cities, whose slums appalled foreign visitors like Charles Dickens, schools were sometimes the only collective and communal enterprise Americans seemed able to agree on.

Modernity made Americans strangers to each other in two ways whose consequences we still live with. First, the Industrial Revolution made strangers out of country and village people who were going to have to work in factories, new realms of social distance and divided labor. And second, native Yankees confronted a flood of alien immigrants. In America a crucial fact about industrialization is that it coincided with immigration. Americans were doubly strangers because they belonged to different social classes and because they were drawn from different countries and from different races.

The reformers who faced this twin urban crisis tried to make the schools into what one historian aptly calls "culture factories"; they were supposed to right imbalances, restore lost community, and keep order. Schools were also part of the social machinery with which the Yankees attempted to deal with the threat the strangers posed to their rule. Among other functions, schools served as poverty programs to shape up the children of successive waves of newcomers.

In reacting against the legends that paint education as the pillar of democracy, the revisionists show the power of the American love-hate polarity when it comes to schools. Once, implausibly, schools were thought to be all-powerful agents of social good. Now, in the revisionists' hands, the old legend gets turned on its head and the schools sound, equally implausibly, like malevolent elite conspiracies against democracy. (An echo, perhaps, of the curdled nationalism that imagines sin to be uniquely American.) The revisionists generally think of themselves as radicals, yet they usually write elite history, in the sense that they concentrate on the motives of the Yankee reformers. They tell the story as a melodrama in which elites work their wicked will on the passive immigrant masses. We still lack an adequate history of what ordinary people made of schools, but there are bits and pieces of a more complex and interesting story at hand. It is significant, I think, that the first articulate rationale for public education in places like Boston and New York came from the working-class political parties whose vigor so impressed Karl Marx. Where the elite reformers stressed the role of schools in promoting social order, the workers argued that the citizens of a republic needed education to preserve their liberties against the threats of power and privilege. (Early on, workers were less enthusiastic about the high schools, which seemed to them to benefit the middle class.) You would not gather from the revisionists that immigrant outsiders themselves placed a high value on education, and badly wanted schools to do their part in helping raise literate children. Nor would you gather that immigrants wanted schools to Americanize their children—only on their terms, and not those of the Yankee elites. They did, though.

The reformers did want to impose their values on the children of Boston's strangers. Yet to desire is not to succeed. The dreams of social and cultural control through schools often turned out to be pipe dreams. The truth is that big-city schools rarely worked well, for good or evil purposes. Throughout much of their history, for example, they were never able even to catch up with the numbers of immigrant children whose parents clamored to enroll them. Schools excluded the poorest and most unruly of what were called "the dangerous classes." They enrolled the children of the deserving poor, when there was room.

As radicals skeptical of today's politics, the revisionists tend to ignore city politics in the past, which is a great mistake. Although politics was and is often a charade and a comic opera, it is also important. Our city history is not a tedious melodrama in which the elite villains have always had their way. It is a story of conflict, in which the "masses," far from being passive, fought back. It is among other things the story of how ordinary people acted on their own behalf, battling with some successes and some defeats against narrow definitions of what it is to be American. Often, as Diane Ravitch has shown in *The Great School Wars*, battles over city politics and institutions like schools were the arenas in which the hopes of the immigrants confronted the fears of the Yankees.

Thus the schools stood in an ambiguous relationship to the city's strangers. An extraordinary consensus emerged as to the value of schooling but, like the larger ideological consensus of American society as a whole—the common agreement on the sanctity of private property and the Constitution—it masked profound conflict over who would define the purposes and content of public education and whose definition of America it would serve. (The awkwardness of those bicentennial TV programs about our past derives from the fact that a central issue has always been who would be included as one of "us.") The growth of the Catholic parochial schools—still a critical, if generally ignored part of Boston's educational scene, enrolling just under a quarter of the city's schoolchildren—was a response to the Protestant nativism preached in the public schools. The creation of separate Catholic schools marked an extreme of religious dissent from bigoted and narrow versions of education as great as that of black separatists and community-control advocates in recent years.

When schools insulted outsiders they fought back; the result was the school wars that Diane Ravitch chronicled for New York. (Boston's wars remain to be described.) Sometimes elites and reformers won, as in the successful effort to centralize the big-city systems whose rigidities plague us today, and sometimes immigrants and outsiders won, as in the establishment of ward and neighborhood systems, the hiring of immigrant teachers, or in the capture of city hall and the machinery of local government. As the fortunes of war shifted, power was reshuffled up and down and to different levels of political jurisdiction; and as they won or lost, cycles of separatist and integrationist political impulses touched the outsiders.

It is at this point in the story that blacks, sensing that historic parallels are about to be drawn, demur. Such parallels bear a heavy symbolic weight these days. Blacks insist that their story, the record of their oppression, is different. And these days, many of the social historians agree. In his admirable book *The Other Bostonians,* Stephan Thernstrom has talked about the various strangers who struggled for a living in nineteenth- and twentieth-century Boston. Many things he describes are novel and fascinating; the high rates of social and geographical mobility belie our picture of the past as more stable than today. (To read historians like Thernstrom is to find out that our urban malaise was probably never less than it is today; in many periods it looks decidedly worse.) Thernstrom asks why different immigrant groups rose from the bottom at such very different rates, the Irish and the Italians who now predominate in Boston being slower than many others. The reasons are complicated: a mix of history, culture, religion, previous city experience, and a good many other factors that Thernstrom and others have yet to explain. The historic position of blacks is striking. In a city of upwardly mobile immigrants, their place lay squarely and permanently on the bottom. For a long sweep of Boston's history they remain the only group to resemble a permanent proletariat. Certainly they are the only group in America requiring a national political movement to begin to alter their historic status. In recent decades, Thernstrom cautiously concedes, their status has in fact changed somewhat. From World War II on, a combination of prosperity and political activism did produce gains. For this period, Thernstrom guesses, it might be possible to draw some parallels between blacks and other groups. Most of the time the parallels don't hold at all.

Nineteenth-century blacks in Boston and elsewhere struggled first for families and churches, then for schools. It seems to be an axiom of educational history that strangers and dissenters—those barred from formal educational institutions—must lay all the more stress on informal ways to pass on culture and tradition, such as families, synagogues, and churches. The struggle for families, according to social historians, was far more successful than the social scientists who speak of the legacy of slavery and black family pathology generally realize. The long struggle for access to formal schooling came next. (The infamous old doctrine of "separate but equal," which the US Supreme Court endorsed in Plessy v. Ferguson, owed a good deal to the handiwork of a Massachusetts judge in a pre-civil war Boston desegregation case involving a five year-old black girl named Sarah Roberts). It is partly a consequence of this history that faith in education tends to be even stronger among blacks than other groups. In point of cold statistics, education did not in fact serve blacks all that well. Schools often kept them out, North and South; the separate education they did get was radically unequal, and premised on racist assumptions. Educators offered them a secondhand version of somebody else's idea of practicality and vocationalism. Many blacks in the past got schooling without making gains in other realms. Thernstrom points out that the low standing of Boston's blacks is not explained by a lack of education. In 1950, for example, Boston's blacks had more education than the Irish, Italians, and French Canadians, yet were lower in occupational status.

It is tempting to conclude from this that the traditional black preoccupation with access to schooling was misguided, a diversion from more fundamental issues. This would be a mistake, I think. Blacks inherit more than their share of American faith in schools; but in the past this was grounded less in naïve idealism than in a shrewd assessment that schools were the only game in town that would let them in, albeit on condescending racist terms. Schools kept blacks out and oppressed them; but separate black schools and colleges served as havens, turfs, and sources of jobs. The reasons for black separatism have been truly complex. (Reasons for white support of black separatism, which were once quite simple, have also become more complex.) There is a complex, dialectical quality to the whole story; segregated churches, for example, led to the spiritual autonomy of black protestantism, and segregated schools and churches provided a base for those who led the attacks on slavery and segregation.

Today's dialectic between integration and separatism has deep roots in Boston's past. The fascinating duality of this history lies in the fact that the intentions of white society have never wholly controlled the use blacks have made of the racist institutions offered them.

Schools were the way up for black leaders and professionals, and they seem to have become more important in today's professionalized world of credentials and degrees. One crucial fact presses on the school situation today in Boston, illuminating another difference between immigrants of the past and the urban poor today—the lack of adequate work. It was not education that lifted most people in most groups—although some did use the schools to rise—but jobs. The immigrant kid who left school became a worker; black students who leave today are part of the unemployed dropout problem. When all the long, moralizing analyses of group character and social pathology are rehearsed, the difference in the past between those who were able to climb out of the dangerous classes and those who weren't probably boils down to the availability of steady work.

Schools in the past, as today, were arenas of conflict; they were, and are, more accessible to outsiders than most other institutions. The same ambiguous quality—the legitimacy conferred by access—that pervades the American political system suffuses the history of education. Politics and educational politics have mediated the symbols of ethnic, religious, and racial conflict. It's exasperating to see the way these problems have consistently overshadowed the pursuit of economic justice and a redistribution of power. The responsiveness of schools, like the responsiveness of politics itself, has certainly worked to defuse class conflict. Yet it has also been an important set of levers that our historic strangers have used to win a more inclusive consensus. The revisionists and neo-Marxists are quite right to point out that in many ways the traditional focus on politics and education is a poor substitute for fundamental economic change. The school wars never challenged the mainly economic values and priorities of the society; and thus in many respects schools have been marginal to the main business of the American past, which was business. And in classic form, the historic dilemmas of the schools reflect the problems of all social service institutions in an unequal, competitive capitalist society. The egalitarian promise conflicts with the realities of inequality.

Yet to the historic actors the symbols involved in urban politics and school wars have been fundamental, sometimes worth dying for.

Religion, ethnicity, and race overshadow and complicate the class politics of American cities. The educational history of Boston is terribly complicated because its participants, the poor and the working class, as well as the elites, believed that the central fact of American life was the diversity of its peoples, and not the existence of clear-cut, homogeneous, counterpoised social classes.

This urban history has left a legacy of strengths and weaknesses that affect life in the city to this day. The main strength is the historic leverage that successive groups have been able to use to gain a wider and more inclusive consensus. In fighting back, the strangers used the mechanisms of American city politics, including school politics, to force the culture to adopt a wider and more pluralistic definition of itself. Each group has adopted political tradition, the language of rights, and the machinery of local politics and reworked them to its greater advantage. The result, for all the bigotry that has surfaced in Boston today, is a more pluralistic society than many nineteenth-century Americans would have thought possible or desirable. (Because the central Boston cleavage pitted Yankees against the Irish for so long, Boston's rather weak civic culture has been much more of a latecomer to urban pluralism than in cities where a diversity of groups emerged earlier.) To describe all this is not to say, in the words of the banquet orators, that the system was sound. There was nothing automatic about what happened. It was not an abstract, benign "system" but people acting on their own behalf that created changes. Ruling groups didn't send out engraved invitations to outsiders; strangers forced their way in.

One legacy from this past is a style of politics that lays peculiar stress on symbols. From the standpoint of jobs and bread-and-butter economics, it can look like a politics of shadows, devoid of substance. In an earlier Boston the Irish working class was captivated by symbols of national and religious identity. These were never empty symbols: they were symbols that people all over the world live and die for. Yet the power of symbols made the Irish here, as in Ireland itself, vulnerable to shadow politics; Irish and Yankee elites in Boston often worked out symbolic accommodations at the expense of the Irish poor. Now the symbols are racial, and once again they seem quite fundamental, but a certain lack of substance remains. "Ireland will get her freedom, and you will still break stones," Yeats had his Parnell say to the cheering workman.

A history of school and city wars created a more pluralistic, tolerant, and egalitarian city culture than that of the past. It never produced anything quite like the legendary melting pot, but the city historian Sam Bass Warner, Jr., is right to argue in *The Urban Wilderness* that elements of a common urban culture emerged. Working-class voters in Boston and other cities may be far ahead of the country's leadership in recognizing the need for basic social change guaranteeing people jobs, homes, schools, and adequate medical care. The way the present symbolic fight over the schools diverts everyone from such egalitarian goals gives you a sinking feeling that even the winners, if there are any, will end up breaking stones.

The history of the school wars is forgotten. In part, this is because after the 1920s, when the main features of the present centralized and professionalized school systems were in place, it became plausible —though never entirely convincing—to think of schools as the apolitical province of neutral experts and professionals. Second- and third-generation immigrants forgot their parents' fight. For several decades there was relative peace. The revisionist historians are right to point to the enormous significance of the organizational changes that took place. Whatever else the progressive educational reformers left us—and their legacy is an ambiguous mixture indeed—it is clear that they were cementing professions and bureaucracies that have often taken on a life of their own. And it is clear that the world that they built is very different from the highly political world of the nineteenth-century schools. Yet, as we are finding out in a new era of school wars, schools are still a very political matter. The present politics of education is so complex precisely because it represents a fusion of older political styles, traditions, and institutions, with the realm of bureaucracies, statistics, experts, courts, unions, and national educational policies. Some would argue that the new order has totally usurped the old, making a mockery of the democratic machinery of local school governance. There is a good deal of truth in this; Judge Garrity's constituency of lawyers and other federal judges is not the same as the constituency that elected Mrs. Louise Day Hicks to the Boston city council. Yet the political role of Boston's schools today —as the arena of confrontation between the city's older and new groups—does bear a resemblance to the role of the schools in the less complex and professionalized past. (Similarly, the battles over community control in New York City bore an eerie resemblance to earlier school wars.) Much has changed; there is no doubt that in many areas of education there is a growing chasm between the machinery of local democratic governance and the highly professionalized, often national forces that play on the schools. But some things remain the same.

Historically, symbols of religion, ethnicity, and race take precedence over those of class. This is true today in Boston, where many have the feeling that what is going on in the schools is largely symbolic; the have-littles and the have-nothings are set to fighting over bare bones, while the haves look on and shake their heads. Class emerges when people speak resentfully of the elites who send children to private schools and make decisions in favor of busing, or of the suburbanites, whose lives are exempt from the consequences of such decisions.

The common culture of Boston is plagued both in the past and in the present by two historic weaknesses. One is the continuing acceptance of the legitimacy of a society run as a lottery with big winners and big losers. The ready acceptance of enormous differential rewards for the privileged has crippled the culture's egalitarianism. The egalitarianism of American life is real, but it easily turns into what Richard Hofstadter once called an equality of greed, rather than fraternity. This is why the fitful populist impulse of this society is so vulnerable to entrepreneurial radicalism, slogans, and reactionary styles of populism that attack everything but corporate privilege and the enormous disparities of wealth and power. Reactionary populism has a particular susceptibility to the second great historic threat to the common urban culture—its racism.

The acceptance of gross inequality and racism both frame the contexts of the current crisis, which involves another set of strangers. Once again the symbols are crucial, and far from empty, yet there is not even any guarantee of solid improvements in education, let alone in the economic status of either working-class blacks or whites in the city. Beyond teaching staffs, schools do not have all that many jobs to offer. They cannot create new jobs or break down the walls of residential segregation or repair existing housing, or build new homes. They can give blacks in the city the exact amount of symbolic and educational leverage they have won through the history of the court decisions in the twenty-one years since the famous Brown case, but at a potential political cost and a potential sacrifice of real populist possibilities to reactionary populist demagoguery. Boston is twisting in the ambiguous momentum this society has taken since the Brown decision.

Things appeared less complicated in 1954. When the Reverend Oliver Brown tried to enroll his daughter in an all-white school three blocks away from their home in Topeka, school authorities instead bused her to an all-black school twenty-one blocks away. The Reverend Brown sued, and ultimately the Supreme Court declared that separate schools were inherently unequal and therefore a violation of black children's Constitutional rights under the Fourteenth Amendment. (Ironically, the Brown residence was later demolished to make a path for a freeway leading out from the city to the suburbs.)

The Brown decision and its successors struck crippling blows to the southern system of dual schools. The struggle for desegregation in the South led, in turn, to many regional and national gains for blacks and other minorities in a host of realms.

Contrary to much of the current defeatist thought about education, schools can in fact act as powerful instruments of social change. Not by themselves, of course, but in alliance with other social forces. The Brown decision shows this. Together with postwar prosperity and the civil rights movement, the events touched off by the Brown decision led to the destruction of many historic obstacles to equality, altering the terms of the country's most enduring dilemma, the relations between the races. Brown helped sweep away the legal underpinning of the South's Jim Crow system. It was part of a whole series of modernizing forces that transformed today's South into something very different from a one-crop, single-party region gripped by poverty and racial oppression. The federal civil rights acts—particularly the voter registration laws—are altering the political face of the region. Southern public education is now more integrated than northern education. In some parts of the South, as politicians like Reuben Askew and Jimmy Carter have noted, the school issue has disappeared from politics. And North and South, the black middle class —especially new professionals and white-collar workers—has expanded. American society is far less monolithically racist than it was. Yet the Brown decision and the civil rights movement that both prompted it and fed on it were failures, too, in important respects whose consequences we are living with today. Neither changed the lot of the poor all that much. Schools in the North are still very segregated, and some of the larger southern cities are resegregating along patterns familiar in the North. (At the time of the Brown decision no large city had a majority black population; the vast migration of rural southern blacks to the northern cities was still under way.) Everywhere in the country residential segregation has increased. The national trend toward increasingly black central-core cities and mainly white suburbs has continued apace.

Thus the balance sheet on Brown, like that of the civil rights movement in general, has to be complex. Sometimes you hear it summed up in an argument between the generations. "Remember how bad things used to be, how far we have come," the old-timers say. And the young insist: "Look at how bad things still are." Both have a point.

At any rate, it's clear in Boston in 1976 that the era in which race was thought of as a southern dilemma is long dead and gone. The issues are American, not southern. Schools in the most defiantly resistant Black Belt counties in Mississippi and Alabama have desegregated, while Boston is in turmoil. People are especially sensitive to hypocrisy in times of defeated ideals, and the symbolism in Boston's present resistance has not escaped many observers. Massachusetts has a liberal and progressive reputation, which in many ways it deserves. Senator Brooke is the first black to sit in the US Senate since 1881, and recent Massachusetts leaders have by and large presented a decent set of faces to the world. Much Massachusetts liberalism has taken on an abstract, ceremonial, and symbolic cast of late, however. There are signs that the progressive promises of recent years are about to be reneged on. Budget problems have mounted. There are pickets at the state house protesting slashing cuts in all the social services. The governor and the legislature are dumping people off the welfare rolls and cutting off money for medical care; long lines of unemployed stand outside the state offices. The temptation to opt for a reactionary populism is enormous. In hard times, it is much easier to hold the line on taxes, to attack "bureaucracy," and to cut social services than to speak of compassion or economic justice.

Too, Boston has a reputation as a civilized city. Visitors think of it as a repository—perhaps museum would be a better word—for a good many ideals about American life, education, and culture. Some of the Bicentennial visitors may picture it as the home of the abolitionists, which is accurate so long as you remember that Garrison preached an end to slavery here, at the clear risk of his neck. The fact that mobs spat on Senator Edward Kennedy because of his stand on busing is difficult to square with an ideal of Boston and its past, or, for that matter, with the legendary love affair between the Kennedys and the Boston Irish. Yet it was in Boston that someone firebombed the old Kennedy home, birthplace of JFK, scrawling "Bus Teddy" on the sidewalk outside. The desegregation issue has done a lot to wedge apart liberal elites and the constituency for egalitarian change. Busing may yet inaugurate a new national era of fake, reactionary populism of the sort symbolized by the contrast between Governor Wallace's popular appeal and his tax program for the state of Alabama, which enriches the corporations.

The desegregation issue has become badly tangled. The attack on the legally mandated Jim Crow dual systems of the South is now almost complete. Southern desegregation has worked well in some places, and badly in others. Some systems in the South are turning into models of race relations that pose a shameful contrast to a good deal of what is happening in the North. Others got rid of dual schools by firing all black teachers. Extending the law to the North proved to be difficult. For a long time, the lawyers were bogged down in the distinctions between de jure and de facto segregation. Old-fashioned southern segregation was a matter of law and official policy, whereas northern-style segregation was the product of extralegal forces, the housing market and so on, and therefore beyond legal remedies involving the schools. Or so thinking ran. By 1970, however, civil rights lawyers began persuading the lower federal courts to give much more detailed scrutiny to the facts of urban segregation outside the South. The notion that a clear line separated de jure and de facto segregation has not in fact stood the test of evidence. Lawyers representing black plaintiffs in many cities outside the South have been able to show a good deal of segregation that is the result of action taken by school boards and school officials. Testimony in case after case shows similar patterns. Officials built schools in all-black neighborhoods, shifted school district lines to maintain segregation as blacks moved into neighborhoods, or worked the old scheme Linda Brown encountered in Topeka years ago, long-distance busing ("forced busing") of black children to faraway black schools instead of to nearby white schools.

It is this sort of evidence of official action, and not a hunger for radical social change, that compels sober and generally conservative

federal judges to conclude that a good deal of northern-style segregation throughout the country is a violation of black schoolchildren's
constitutional rights. This is what lies behind the wave of court
decisions in Pasadena, Denver, Baltimore, Detroit, Louisville, Boston, and many other cities. The question becomes what remedies the
courts can offer, for, as the old saying goes, rights without remedies
do not exist.

Here desegregation has run into some very big snags. While it is
often not hard to prove that school officials are contributing to
northern-style segregation, it is also clear that there are other, unoffi-
cial forces at work: zoning, patterns of housing discrimination, real-
tors, mortgage, insurance and loan policies of the banks, and so on.
Different levels of government are implicated, involving multiple
jurisdictions. Schools are often to blame, yet the sources of much
northern segregation also lie outside schools. The circle of remedies
is drawn far too narrowly if it only includes schools, yet there are no
precedents for widening it.

The other snag arises in cities with a majority black population.
There, what black plaintiffs seek in the courts is an end to discriminatory pupil placement policies. The Constitution entitles them to this.
In terms of the other, wider, goals of desegregation—moves toward
integration, better racial balance, or access to enriched resources for
education—there are clear limits to what schools can accomplish
with a majority black student population. For those still eager to
pursue these wider goals, the remedy would seem to lie in metropolitan schemes linking city and suburban schools. In 1974, however, the
Supreme Court shaped by Richard Nixon's appointments seemed to
say in a Detroit case that the lower federal courts may not reach out
to the suburbs in the search for remedies. The Detroit decision left
open the possibility of metropolitan remedies, if plaintiffs can show
that suburban schools are implicated in segregation. It is not clear
what the ruling really means or how final it is; a number of suburban-
city desegregation cases are still pending.

The Supreme Court decision did not stop the legal drive for
desegregation within the cities. To blacks mainly concerned with
ending discriminatory placement policies, the goal is not necessarily
any kind of racial balance, and discussions of suburbs and metropolitan schemes are beside the point. For those, black and white, who
still think that better racial balances of some sort are desirable and

educationally productive, the Supreme Court ruling has for the moment added a special air of futility to the desegregation battle in cities like Detroit and Washington, where most school kids are black. The ruling offered whites and blacks in the cities an unusually clear illustration of the fundamental and growing injustice of our whole network of urban boundaries. The legal units of our urban geography have always operated as fences for privilege; but the isolation of the poor and the dark-skinned has never been as great. In effect the Supreme Court suggested that the suburbs may be left alone. Shifts in both black and white thinking on desegregation also cloud the issue. As a tactical matter, desegregation is still widely supported by most blacks. Many oppose busing, however (especially to hostile neighborhoods), and many do not hold with the court decisions on racial balances, even though these seem the simplest remedy to enforce. Many insist that the issue is not racial balance at all, but putting an end to discrimination and giving black students equal access to the best education a school system has to offer. From this point of view, mainly black schools and all-black classes are fine. (There always was something inherently racist about the notion that black students need to sit near whites in order to learn.) Some are outright separatists. Still, even separatists are mindful of the tactical point that black children would have greater access to a full range of educational offerings in classrooms where white children are present as hostages, so to speak, of the system's good intentions.

The whole question of racial balance is obscure, and the confusion does not exist only in the mind of the public, which imagines that the courts in each case are insisting on a fixed racial balance. Contrary to what most people think, federal judges have by and large been studiedly ambiguous in the way they have talked about the demography of desegregation. Often the decisions imply some form of balance, but it is left vague. There is a wide spectrum of opinion, too, among black observers. Some focus mainly on an end to discriminatory pupil placement policies, which can still produce mainly black schools. Others insist on racial balances of some sort, either because they are intrinsically desirable, or because they may help guarantee black students' access to better education. In cities with a majority of black students, this second position extends into an argument for metropolitan schooling. These two quite different, not to say contradictory, emphases are seldom openly discussed in national debates on desegregation. In part this is because many blacks and civil rights lawyers are profoundly ambivalent on the question. And, in part, it is because people's positions are based on their local situation, which may be unique. Metropolitan solutions may be good in some places, but not others. This is not the only part of the desegregation issue where the necessity to frame policy in national terms generates new problems of its own.

The black dialogue over nationalism and universalism is old and tortured. It shifts over time, and there have been further developments since the separatist and community-control impulses of the late 1960s. The demand for community control in New York City arose primarily from the failure of school desegregation, and the seeming futility of desegregation as a policy in huge urban ghettos. The community control movement also reflected the very real breakdown of lay democratic control over unresponsive, chaotic, and indifferent school bureaucracies. Desegregation still remains an enormous puzzle in large city ghettos where blacks are not a majority, and the question of democratic control over the schools is far from being solved. Yet the tragic and ultimately futile contest for community control in New York City convinced many that the fight in that form on that turf was not worth while. Community control today is much less of a despairing ideological battlecry, because it has shifted to places like Newark, Detroit, Atlanta, and Gary, with their black majorities. It is now a pragmatic affair, conforming to some of the older patterns of American ethnic politics. The advent of black mayors, school boards, and—perhaps—political machines means a great deal. Like the electoral gains in the South, it gives a historically outcast group chances far more political power than it had before. At the very least, some old racist ghosts have been laid to rest: majority black school boards can make competent decisions and black mayors can govern, just as all-black schools can teach.

The rise of blacks to political power in all these places has prompted, predictably, a rash of proposals for metropolitan government. Blacks are suspicious of these schemes, and will rightly resist giving up the influence and political power they are winning, although they may be willing to make certain special services, such as schools, metropolitan. (Many current metropolitan schemes recall earlier Yankee attempts to shift power to the state level, as immigrants captured the cities.)

These pragmatic forms of community control are, however, no more of a panacea than the earlier ideological demands. The old joke that community control meant black ownership of Harlem in exchange for white ownership of General Motors was never very funny; it no longer seems funny at all in Detroit. Cities like Detroit, Newark, and Gary are not exactly brimming over with resources; they are ailing badly, and suggest new and gloomy variations on the old misleading theme of separate and equal. Separate in America never has been equal, and never will be.

It is clear that the pursuit of political power in cities with black majorities and near-majorities is in many respects at odds with the pursuit of school desegregation. If we were less of a national society this would matter less. Unfortunately policy gets framed nationally; there is a national politics of education, as well as a profoundly local politics. It is very hard to understand that and to understand that the situation in Detroit is very different from that in Boston, even though what happens in majority-black Detroit now helps shape the political climate in Boston, where blacks are a distinct minority.

There remains a pressing need for minorities to join with whites to work for egalitarian and majoritarian conditions that do not presently exist. Many blacks and whites still think of school desegregation as a step toward a truly integrated society, but the civil rights movement is in political tatters, a victim of its successes and also its failure to translate its demands into a broad program of economic justice. For a long moment in history, as these things go, an immensely creative national movement fused traditional and novel modes of lower- and working-class protest with traditional and novel middle-class styles of action and reform and created unprecedented changes. The French writer Charles Peguy said that: everything begins in mysticism and ends in politics. In America, the aphorism needs rewording: Everything begins in mysticism and ends in the federal courtrooms. Legal professionals have finally built a solid structure of precedents for attacking northern desegregation, but black support for it is weakening, and white pressure against it has risen. The mysticism has evaporated—"Did you think to gain unity through lawyers?" Walt Whitman asked—and this has left (integration-minded) blacks and whites speaking in subdued, practical, and tactical tones. Schools are important, but no substitute for jobs or political power, where power is accessible. Desegregation is right but it isn't likely to lead to a multiracial society terribly soon. The evangelism that made so many martyrs and produced so much change couldn't last forever. In Boston, where the parents and children are showing so much courage, where the grievances are extraordinarily clear-cut, where racial balance is still possible to achieve, and where the alternative of political power for blacks is not an option—even in Boston, supporters of desegregation wonder whether it is worth the political consequences. The plans the courts have seized upon seem the most enforceable schemes, yet in some places they are self-defeating, and probably do accelerate the flight of the middle class out of the city. The busing issue is building up extraordinary political countercurrents.

It is this political climate that fuels the efforts of groups like ROAR (Restore Our Alienated Rights). No federal desegregation order has been reversed by any court, yet the opponents of busing believe they can win, that "Never" is not just a slogan. They believe this because local leaders have assured them, and so, in veiled ways, have our nation's leaders. Richard Nixon signaled clear retreat on desegregation, and so has President Gerald Ford. The government speaks with a babble of tongues on the issue, and federal civil rights enforcement has slowed to a crawl.

"Busing" and "neighborhood schools" are slogans, although many parents do dislike busing and neighborhood feeling does run strong. Over 40 percent of the nation's children ride to school in altogether uncontroversial buses. If you add in other kinds of public transportation, the figure is over 65 percent. Busing is scarcely new in Boston. In the days before court orders, the Boston school system bused more children than it is now doing. (Admittedly, it had a larger school population then.) "Neighborhood schools" drawing on cohesive neighborhoods have for some time been the exception rather than the rule, even in Boston, where the sense of turf of many urban villagers is unusually strong. Yet there are many real grievances lurking beneath the slogans. In nineteenth-century Boston, Thernstrom shows, the working class and the poor were the most geographically mobile people. Elites were local and stayed put; it was the working class that had to hit the road. This may be one reason why we have an erroneous impression that the past was more stable than the present. If so, it is not the only instance where our collective memory has been refracted through the lenses of privilege. Since the Depression, however, the working class has moved less; the most mobile Americans tend to be the middle class and the very poor. The fight in Boston involves a clash between the values of some of the most mobile groups and some of the most geographically stable groups. Besides being racial, it is a cultural and class battle between cosmopolitan professionals and locals, between people who identify with national institutions and those who identify with neighborhood and local values. This feeds the neighborhoods' resentment of the professionals, the courts, the lawyers, and the media.

Desegregation would not be such a divisive issue if those supporting it could point to a host of gains for the working class in other realms. One of the tragedies of the political era we've lived through is that the most dramatically oppressed groups got much more attention and sympathy than those whose oppression was less well publicized. The recession and inflation have hit the Boston working class very hard; and now desegregation is reminding them how little the society has attended to their concerns in recent years. This makes white workers terribly vulnerable to fake populists who wave the bloody shirt of past ethnic grievances and promise that busing can be stopped. At the same time, many national leaders nurse the more current grudges, and dangle slogans of busing and popular property rights in front of the electorate without doing a single positive thing for any working man or woman. The failure of politics to cast people's grievances and aspirations in universal and democratic terms haunts the period of reaction we are living through.

Our traditions of school reform tend to be elitist. Often in the past democracy at the local school level has meant thwarting elitist versions of school reform. In the Progressive Era, for example, reactionaries in New York City tried to rework schooling into an outright caste system. This was stopped, although tracking and other policies favoring the children of the middle class remained. Common people have been able to veto elite plans for education, on occasion; this, in part, accounts for the continuing legitimacy of the schools. They have not, however, been able to do much in a positive way for the education of their children. The elites and the reformers have often promoted excellent ideas about good teaching, but in practice the reform style has rarely aimed at winning over teachers, let alone parents. This has been one of the minor tragedies of American education. Desegregation fits the old reform mold. It is meant to help blacks, a group historically cut off from opportunities in Boston's schools. It is initiated by black plaintiffs. And yet the whole way it is being done rehearses the old elitist patterns of reform. It sometimes looks as if we are getting an updated northern version of the old southern alliance of planters and blacks against poor whites, which seldom really benefitted anyone except the elites. Once again, the egalitarian promises of public schooling are being overwhelmed by the realities of inequality.

The fact that the residents of Charlestown and South Boston are resisting elite social planners, that they are defending community and neighborhood and even, in their prayer marches and American flags, the symbols of patriotic and religious nationalism, gives them a more respectable hearing now than they might have had five or ten years ago. The contrast between the country's universal ideals and the actual diversity of its peoples, races, and cultures has made for a history that swings between periods of universalism and tribalism. The universal ideals of the republic often serve as a mask for nativist and racist definitions of America; this is why, periodically, they fall into disrepute. Periods of tribalism are often healthy responses to the failure of the American consensus to acknowledge the genuine pluralism of the culture. The line between legitimate ethnic pride, nationalism and self-respect, and tribalism is not easy to draw, however. And it is never altogether clear whether the angry tribes are really spurning universal values, or whether they are simply protesting their abuse by successive groups of hypocritical elites. The distinction is important. You can share a sense of rage over the narrow definitions of America that have prevailed in the past and still feel that the elements of the common culture that have emerged are very much worth preserving and defending. I'm thinking of the political tradition that has fitfully offered levers to outsiders; of the language of rights; of the law, which seems so fragile in Boston today; of urban pluralism that accepts a diversity of peoples; and of the terrible failure of the protest movements of recent years to translate their aspirations for minorities into the universal language of rights.

Changes in intellectual fashions also altered the contours of the desegregation issue. In the aftermath of an era of liberal reform, there was a retreat among some intellectuals from universalism, as indeed there has been a retreat from rationality itself. The protest against uniformity and cultural oppression, which was valid, turned into a denial of our need for common ideals, which was not. (Just as the protest against a dessicated and "value-free" science that serves General Jack Ripper as cheerfully as anyone else, turned into an assault on the ideal of science itself.)

More directly, in both law and social science, influential voices called for a retreat from desegregation. In 1970, the late Alexander Bickel wrote in *The New Republic:* "Massive school integration is not going to be attained in this country very soon, in good part because no one is certain that it is worth the cost. Let us, therefore, try to proceed with education." Bickel elaborated arguments that have since become well worn. He cited the divisions of opinion among blacks, and the shifting political climate. He was especially worried about the possibility that the racial balances ordered by the courts would lead to resegregation, as whites fled the cities. Bickel hoped that compensatory education might substitute for desegregation.

More recently the sociologist James Coleman, who is something of an academic bellwether on these sorts of issues, has also raised doubts about desegregation. In 1966 Coleman's massive report, *Equality of Educational Opportunity,* made an influential case for integration, arguing that black children can benefit from going to school with middle-class whites without jeopardizing the achievement of the whites. Scholars, journalists, and others quoted the report as a brief for racial integration, although in fact its real emphasis was on the benefits of integration by social class, an idea whose time has yet to come. Coleman's 1966 report has been buffeted by some strange political winds. His findings that American schools for whites and blacks were not as radically unequal in terms of resources as many critics had thought undercut certain of the earlier arguments for integration. (Critics believe that his crude definitions of educational resources did not take into account many of the things that give some schools more promising atmospheres for learning than others.) And Coleman's emphasis on the decisive power of social class seemed, strangely enough, to discredit the rationale for compensatory education.

Now, to judge by an interview in *The New York Times Magazine,* Coleman has once again changed his mind. He still believes in the principle that the courts must protect black children when school officials violate their constitutional rights. However, he disagrees with the current legal remedies. Coleman would concede the courts' right to prevent deliberate segregation, but says they should permit circumstantial-de facto segregation. He especially disagrees with attempts to balance schools racially in proportion to the general school population of a city. This, he says, requires too much busing, which leads to resegregation as whites flee the cities. He would like to see desegregation proceeding along more restrained, voluntary lines.

Coleman's new crop of critics say that resegregation is more complicated than he allows. The middle class and others had, after all, been moving out of the cities decades before court-ordered desegregation and busing hit the North. Plainly people have been going out to the suburbs in search of better housing, jobs, safety from crime, cleaner air and green grass, human scale services, and a host of other reasons, besides an escape from busing and blacks. (To be sure, blacks stand as a handy symbol in many minds of all sorts of urban ills.)

Like many other opponents of what seem to be drastic remedies for desegregation, Coleman would like to expand choices for everyone involved, to create more situations in which voluntarism prevails. Actually this has happened in some desegregation efforts; Judge Garrity's plan gives Boston students options that would have been considered unprecedented a few short years ago. Choices are possible, but there is a point at which the current desegregation solutions do in fact have to impinge on the rights of white students to choose their schools. Otherwise there is no workable remedy. Coleman has little sense of the limits the courts face on possible remedies. They have hit upon the current schemes because it is not easy for them to administer more complicated ones. To some extent there is an inevitable contradiction between workable desegregation and voluntarism; this makes desegregation hard in a time when ordinary people have grown very tired of being pushed around. School desegregation has fallen heir to the accumulated rancor of the neighborhoods after several decades of profoundly undemocratic elite municipal planning. In many ways, Coleman's distinction between intentional and circumstantial segregation is altogether beside the point of most current desegregation cases. And his attack on racial balance is a blow aimed at a straw man. His focus on circumstantial-de facto segregation slurs over the main issue in cities like Boston, where lawyers for black plaintiffs have had little difficulty in proving that segregation has been official policy. Judge Garrity ended his long opinion this way:

. . . The court concludes that the defendants [the Boston School Committee and the administration] took many actions in their official capacities with the purpose and intent to segregate the Boston public schools. . . . Plaintiffs have proved that the defendants intentionally segregated schools at all levels, . . . built new schools for a decade with sizes and locations designed to promote segregation; maintained patterns of over-crowding and underutilization which promoted segregation at 26 schools; and expanded the capacity of approximately 40 schools by means of portables and additions when students could have been assigned to other schools with the effect of reducing racial imbalance. How many students were intentionally separated on a racial basis cannot be stated with any degree of precision; but the annual totals were certainly in the thousands. . . . For example, by using feeder patterns to channel black students to English (High School), defendants not only concentrated black students there, but also made high schools which the black students might otherwise attend more predominantly white.

The court concludes that the defendants have knowingly carried out a systematic program of segregation affecting all of the city's students, teachers, and school facilities, and have intentionally brought about and maintained a dual school system."

The fact that Boston and other cities have maintained what amount to dual school systems as a matter of official policy keeps getting ignored by experts like Coleman in all the recent academic debates, just as it has been totally obscured in the mind of the general public. Nor does Judge Garrity set any formula for racial balance; he has selected remedies that leave the question of balance ambiguous.

Nevertheless, Coleman's reversal is a straw in what looks to be a rising wind of retreat on the whole issue. Whether desegregation is the main cause of the white exodus to the suburbs or not, schools probably are a factor. Resegregation is not a happy prospect. However, Coleman errs in giving demographic balance in the cities equal standing with black children's rights. People have a Constitutional right to a remedy when they are sent to a segregated school on the basis of the color of their skins. Nobody has a Constitutional right to live in a city with a white majority.

Social scientists have played a curious role throughout the history of desegregation. Social science has influenced policy; it has also mirrored the changing politics of the issue. Studies of the effects of desegregation have been ambiguous, because people have seldom been precise about what it was intended to accomplish. Complexity of aim is not necessarily a bad thing; education itself usually reflects a variety of goals. But it makes research difficult. No one has been able to state exactly what the goal of desegregation was—higher achievement scores for blacks, racial harmony, shifts in racial attitudes, more political leverage for blacks, or simply a remedy for discrimination. The Brown decision quoted from the celebrated research of black social psychologist Kenneth Clark to the effect that segregation hurt the minds and hearts of black children. This was plausible in a broad sense; yet further research came to focus on lower achievement scores on tests. The idea developed that desegregation would in and of itself raise black children's test scores. Yet the evidence that desegregated schools would eliminate differences in achievement was very spotty. Some observers, seeing that desegregation does not automatically produce equality, have been led to argue that we must redefine our conception of educational equality to mean equality of outcomes. It is not clear how this could be done in education except by massive compensatory programs. Compensatory education has not always failed, as its critics say; it has in fact sometimes worked. Getting real gains in achievement, however, requires a great deal of money that is not apt to be forthcoming in a time when many cities are on the verge of bankruptcy.

Recent academic debates on equality have emphasized that improving schools is no substitute for more fundamental social change. That is an important point to keep in mind, particularly in following the elusive symbols in the desegregation issue. This is the sort of understanding that is useful if it provides perspective on the schools, and pernicious if it discredits educational reform without offering any real alternatives. It was perhaps never sound to rest the case for school desegregation on the shifting sands of social science research. The American public has yet to learn that social science is both faddish and profoundly political. Desegregation has always been a legal matter—a question of the redress of rights—and a political matter—a way of giving some of our society's strangers greater access to educational resources. For many, too, it has been and continues to be a moral issue.

It was also to be predicted that talk of desegregation would range over all the hurts and inadequacies of our national life without really focusing on the subject of education. Children in Boston are learning important lessons about the law, race, and other aspects of our society that were not exactly planned into their curriculum. And yet the instances of reasonably successful desegregation are now so many that in fact a good deal of practical educational knowledge is at hand. Knowledgeable people say that the number of nonwhites in a desegregated school should probably not go over 40 percent, if resegregation is to be avoided. (The numbers must not to token, however. David Riesman and others have long warned about the psychic costs paid by token minorities, including women, in newly desegregated institutions.) Desegregation of course seems a rather sad joke if children are bused to schools that are in fact inferior to the ones they originally attended. They should ideally be bused to schools near enough to their homes so their parents could remain involved in school affairs. Places like Denver—and increasingly Boston—are also showing how important it is to make use of citywide advisory groups of blacks and whites; such groups are even more important at the school level. (There seems no way in the 1970s to escape the need for participation, despite our confusion of ideas on the subject.) Special classes must not become dumping bins for minority children. Schools in some places have gone beyond desegregation—an end to discriminatory placement policies—and are actually working on integration, getting black and white students to know each other. Real integration has to take place in the classroom, and not at the school level. It means integrating such important symbolic realms as cheerleading squads and football teams. It means finding alternatives to the kind of across-the-board tracking that is becoming more and more common in our schools. There is nothing inherently wrong with ability grouping in individual subjects, like math and English. The problems for integration (and, I would argue, education in general) are posed by tracking systems that sort masses of students out in groups to second-rate curricula, on the premise that they will meet second-rate fates in life. Integration is more promising when it begins in the early years of school. It requires interracial staffing and planning. All these lessons have been learned in many places, at a great cost; yet one wonders if the unfolding politics of the desegregation issue will make them historical artifacts.

Numbers of our schools have desegregated; in some integration is going on. Numbers of schools are segregated and others are resegregating. Desegregating elementary and secondary schools is a different matter than attempting to preserve black colleges and universities. Nothing is gained by judicial fiats that eliminate workable black institutions without putting anything in their place. Dunbar High, a crack black high school in Washington D.C., was a victim of the inability of federal judges to frame policy in complex terms. It is very difficult to debate desegregation as a matter of national policy when there are so many local situations. Geography and demography make current desegregation remedies pointless in some places, and apt in others. Although this complexity has attended all our discussions of school reform and social policy in recent years, we have continued to speak the language of a strange one-eyed rationalism, an either-or language of national policy that bypasses the inconvenient muddle of American life. And it is not only the variety of the landscape that we have oversimplified. We debated desegregation versus compensatory education, for example, as though the two were mutually exclusive, when in fact many schools need both. In recent years we debated school reform versus other forms of social change as though we were master planners in the war room, and the Great Computer were offering us a clear choice between alternatives. There is no central war room or master planners, no Great Computer; our choices are far from clear. By any realistic political reckoning, it seems altogether probable in fact that school reform and other kinds of social change will operate in tandem, if they operate at all. Our thinking remains woefully apolitical.

Small elements of reform and change are occurring in some of Boston's schools today. There are many in the city who do not like what is happening, but who are working hard to keep the peace and do their jobs. There are many on the mainly Irish teaching staff and police force who sympathize with the antibusing protesters, but they are making the law work. Teachers and parents have shown more guts than anybody, except the schoolchildren. All are being asked to live up to ideals few in the city honor. When one considers Boston's current troubles, a despairing quote from St. Paul comes to mind: "Here we have no continuing city." However, Boston does continue. The schools are working, and seem in many ways healthier than other institutions in the city.

The desegregation issues are shadowy and symbolic; they are important, because we live by symbols, but a steady diet of such symbols hardens the heart. Some good and altogether ordinary things are taking place in Boston's desegregated schools, but the situation remains shameful. The law is so clearly the creature of the rich and the powerful, who are exempt from its consequences. Schemes of social engineering that confine desegregation to the deteriorating core cities and let the suburbs go free insult the intelligence of a democracy. Supporters of desegregation have not pointed this out enough. Those defending their neighborhoods and their children and protesting busing have not conceded that the issue is also race and the Constitutional rights of black children. Next to injustice, hypocrisy stings people hardest. People in South Boston are right to be outraged by the suburban liberals who call them bigots and racists, and wrong to think that black children's legal rights can be ignored merely because larger remedies involving the suburbs do not exist; they are mistaken, too, in thinking that their very real grievances, values, and sensibilities outweigh other people's Constitutional rights.

These things cannot be repeated too often. Nor can it be said too often that the depth of danger in the present situation is in large part the work of the old Boston School Committee and the other local and national politicians who are making such a good thing out of encouraging resistance to the law. The threat of violence has become so commonplace that we forget what a menace it is to democracy. Too many people in this country have begun to hope that somehow someone else's violence will advance their cause. The result has been a corrupting sense that violence is normal. In the long run of history, it has been, of course. That is a troubling thought. Bicentennial visitors wanting a taste of history should pause and test the air of Boston. Monuments, statues, embalmed artifacts, restored buildings, pictures of porcelain statesmen wearing powdered wigs do not give the real feeling of history. History feels like this: a city of frightened people making choices with divided minds, picking not right against wrong, but what they hope will be the lesser set of evils, and wondering what the consequences will be.